RETHINKING

LEARNING SUPPORT SERVICES

Please return on or before the last date stamped below

City College **NORWICH**

Sage Series on Violence Against Women

Series Editors

Claire M. Renzetti
St. Joseph's University

Jeffrey L. Edleson
University of Minnesota

In this series . . .

RETHINKING
VIOLENCE
AGAINST
WOMEN

Editors
R. Emerson Dobash
Russell P. Dobash

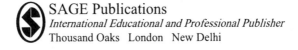

Sage Series on Violence Against Women

SAGE Publications
International Educational and Professional Publisher
Thousand Oaks   London   New Delhi

For information:

SAGE Publications, Inc.
2455 Teller Road
Thousand Oaks, California 91320
E-mail: order@sagepub.com

SAGE Publications Ltd.
6 Bonhill Street
London EC2A 4PU
United Kingdom

SAGE Publications India Pvt. Ltd.
M-32 Market
Greater Kailash I
New Delhi 110 048 India

Printed in the United States of America

Library of Congress Cataloging-in-Publication Data

Main entry under title:

Rethinking violence against women / edited by R. Emerson
Dobash and Russell P. Dobash.
  p. cm. -- (Sage series on violence against women; v. 9)
  Includes bibliographical references and index.
  ISBN 0-7619-1186-3 (cloth: acid free paper)
  ISBN 0-7619-1187-1 (pbk.: acid free paper)
  1. Women--Crimes against. 2. Sexual harassment of women.
3. Family violence. 4. Wife abuse. 5. Women--Social conditions. I.
Dobash, R. Emerson. II. Dobash, Russell. III. Series.
  HV6250.4.W65 R47 1998
  362.88'082--ddc21   98-9084

98 99 00 01 02 03 10 9 8 7 6 5 4 3 2 1

Acquiring Editor:	C. Terry Hendrix
Editorial Assistant:	Fiona Lyon
Production Editor:	Diana E. Axelsen
Editorial Assistant:	Denise Santoyo
Typesetter/Designer:	Rose Tylak
Indexer:	Trish Wittenstein

Contents

Acknowledgments

This anthology benefited from two conferences funded by the Harry Frank Guggenheim Foundation in 1993 and 1995, where scholars from diverse disciplines had an opportunity to discuss their work and current thinking about violence against women. For that early part of the project, we wish to thank Karen Colvard and Joel Wallman of the Harry Frank Guggenheim Foundation. We also wish to thank all the authors for their commitment to this project and willingness to continue as it grew and changed; Dorothy Anderson, who faithfully and professionally recorded the proceedings of the first conference in Carmona, Spain; and Lauren McAllister, who had more than her fair share of technological blips processing text and computer discs on the way to the final manuscript. We also wish to acknowledge support from the Scottish office, the Home Office, the Rockefeller Foundation, NATO, and the Carnegie Foundation. The final collection and the contents herein are the sole responsibility of the editors and authors.

1

Cross-Border Encounters

Challenges and Opportunities

Rebecca Emerson Dobash and Russell P. Dobash

The area of violence against women has become increasingly narrow and self-referential. Since the initial phase of development, when new theoretical ideas and methodological approaches were introduced and expanded, the field of study has become more rigid in scope and orientation. In many of the subareas or subdisciplines involved, an unwarranted confidence in theoretical ideas, empirical findings, and/or established ideologies has resulted in a circumscription of the field of study. Where this exists, it usually results in a reluctance to further develop new ideas or arenas of evidence within such subdisciplines or schools of thought. There is closure, often though not exclusively along disciplinary lines, against ideas and evidence from outside the circumscribed subdiscipline in a futile attempt to exclude "foreign" ideas and/or evidence from consideration or debate. In such a context, new ideas and evidence inevitably struggle to emerge in an ever-narrowing and unchanging circle of self-referential ideas and evidence.

The aim of this book is to resist this narrowing intellectual trend by opening for discussion and debate issues about the nature and causes of violence across a variety of disciplines that might not otherwise meet. The purpose is not to convert the exponents of one approach to that of another but to constructively introduce the ideas, evidence, and concerns of each to the other in the hope that such cross-fertilization will lead to innovations and enhance all of the respective approaches. At the outset, it is important to acknowledge that whereas much is now made of the notion of multidisciplinary work in terms of the prospects for intellectual innovation, there are, in fact, few opportunities to undertake such work, and the orientation toward circumscribed disciplines or subdisciplines remains strong. Without the opportunity to "practice" such thinking in an open intellectual environment, it is unlikely that intellectual innovation will overcome the "certainties" embedded within and sustained by rigid arenas of thought and research. The routes to opening intellectual thought through exposure across disciplinary lines are neither well worn nor easy to follow. Though opportunities may lie in cross-disciplinary exchanges, such encounters require an extra component of intellectual curiosity and flexibility, an element of good will, and a desire to risk discovering the new rather than remaining within the certainties of the old.

Cross-border clashes can be intense, and they sometimes get nasty. As with political struggles, intellectual territory may be defended with ferocious attacks on neighboring "camps," discussions in seminars may more closely resemble those in "war" rooms, and, of course, there is the intense training of "new recruits" in the art of instantly identifying the "enemy" and thereby dispensing with them with as little intellectual engagement as possible. Thus, the mind of new students is introduced with care to the subtle nuances of the "home" discipline but left in ignorance of the "foreign" and/or equipped with easy dismissals that are often misinformed. Reporting on academic boundary disputes, Aisling Irwin notes that some "protagonists have said extremely rude, naive, and ignorant things" (Irwin, 1994), such as "I hope you rot in hell" (scientist to theologian), "liar" (sociologist to biologist), and "poor record over the last 2,000 years" (biologist to philosophers). One result of hostile cross-border disputes is that academics fail to grasp the fundamental concepts of a "rival" discipline [and sometimes] borrow ideas that are tied to fundamental assumptions that are incompatible (Irwin, 1994). The purpose is not necessarily to reach consensus but to explore the potential and the limits of various disciplinary approaches to a given topic of study and to consider if and how the boundaries of knowledge and explanation might be expanded through intellectual cross-fertilization. Productive arguments are inevitable in struggling with new ideas but, "shouting matches do not lead to fertile thought if people are merely becoming entrenched in their positions" (Irwin, 1994).

The contents of this volume include contributions from the disciplines of sociology, anthropology, criminology, social policy, philosophy, and evolutionary psychology. They are intended to push the boundaries of current knowledge and thinking about the issue of violence against women. It is our belief that empirical knowledge and theoretical understanding must be joint rather than separate activities; theoretical ideas need to be empirically informed, and empirical knowledge needs to have theoretical underpinnings. Any undertaking of value must have both explanatory and empirical import. While the emphasis might vary from one project to the next, none escapes this dual mission.

Although some would claim otherwise, it is also our contention that many different methods can and must be employed in seeking to expand empirical knowledge and theoretical insights, and that there is no "perfect" method nor one that is always the "best." Instead, there is a wide array of methods that suit the different tasks necessary to make up the whole area of study. Accordingly, these chapters use an array of methods to examine different but related topics concerning violence against women. These topics include the following:

- a well-designed national survey meant to provide extensive empirical evidence about the prevalence and correlates of violence against women in a Western, industrial society;
- an intensive study of a relatively closed, kin-based society that lasted several years and is meant to reflect on the complex and intersecting net of specific cultural beliefs and practices associated with the "making" of a woman and wife, particularly through alteration of the body;
- a series of intensive interviews with couples from a small religious sect, particularly with one couple whose experiences are used to introduce a general theory about the construction of gender;
- an extensive set of data about homicide from official sources (police/courts), used to reflect on patterns of killing of women and children in intimate relationships, with the purpose of reflecting theoretically on the nature of human psychology;
- a comparative evaluation study used to examine the nature of violent events and violent relationships, particularly in relation to violence and the cultural concept of masculinity; and

- an examination of the use of violence against women in the home in the context of societies where other forms of violence, such as war and terrorism, are widespread.

The issue of "definitions," what counts as violence and to whom, is present throughout but is also addressed explicitly in the chapter on sexual violence. The notion of "context" is central to this overall project and is strongly woven into each chapter. For the most part, violence is deemed to be a cultural product enacted by individuals located in different cultural contexts.

Violence(s), Concepts, and Definitions

When focusing on definition(s) of violence against women, several issues arise. One concerns the breadth or narrowness of the term *violence*. The word/concept has been used in a broad, inclusive manner to encompass verbal abuse, intimidation, physical harassment, homicide, sexual assault, and rape; a long list of orientations, acts, and behaviors has been referred to as "violence against women." In some cases, survey analysis and/or archival research have used a very inclusive approach to produce national or group-specific rates of "violence." This may have political advantages (e.g., the issue appears very large and thus even more significant), but it may have implications for research and explanations that are not always beneficial. A more "narrow" or circumscribed definition of violence, with each type examined in its own right and statistics gathered accordingly, may sometimes have the advantage of increasing clarity about the nature and context of a specific form of violence but may simultaneously lose the prospect of generalizing across a much wider spectrum of violence(s). Whether the definition of violence is broad and more inclusive or more narrow and differentiated dictates very different starting points for researchers. The object here is not to arrive at an agreed-upon, single definition but to explore the advantages and disadvantages of different approaches in terms of theorizing and conducting research. Allied to this is the issue of terminology. Should we continue to use the word *violence* or *violences,* should we use *abusive behavior,* or should we adopt some other term(s)? What about the source of definitions: Do we use the perspectives of victims? Of those who perpetrate these acts? Of researchers? Of the law? Of policymakers? Should researchers attempt to develop distinct, abstract, and definitive conceptualizations of these acts?

This is clearly an area in need of more discussion and clarity because the current use of the term *violence* among researchers, policymakers, and activists includes both clearly specified domains of inquiry (e.g., physical attacks on women by a male partner/husband, marital rape, rape by a stranger, and the like) and broader referents that may include behaviors ranging from verbal harassment, flashing, and unwanted advances to date rape, attempted murder, or murder. This is explicitly addressed in the chapter by Kelly and Radford and used in the research of Johnson. While specificity in the concept is needed for a scientific agenda in order that the term not be misunderstood or devalued, there is concern about how narrow the definition can or should become and still reflect a close approximation to the reality of those who experience violence in its multiplicity of overlapping forms. There is also the issue of how public awareness and the concerns of social agencies and policymakers are affected by whether a problem is deemed to be one of greater or lesser magnitude, an issue inextricably tied to the definition of violence adopted for the purposes of gathering facts and figures. The intersection between social research and its political, cultural, and moral contexts forms much of the undercurrent of these deliberations.

Many positions are offered concerning whose definition should be advanced and why. They include the subjective definitions of women who experience violence, of men who perpetrate violence, of researchers who interpret information provided by concerned individuals or contained in official records, or some combination of these. There are dilemmas and limitations associated with each. What credibility and authority ought to be given to different types of accounts? What are the rights, responsibilities, and limits of the researcher when interpreting such accounts? While some see the task as seeking an agreed-on authoritative definition of violence, others seek a more nominal definition. In the end, whose definitions actually prevail and with what consequences? Is it the voice of the most powerful individuals, groups, institutions, or societies? The voice of the populace? The voice of activists? The voice of the victimized?

The dilemma of universal concepts and specific cultural forms is also addressed. Cultural relativity is raised in terms of moral, historical, and cultural issues, each demanding some form of attention. What is considered "acceptable" within different societies poses perplexing and ethical problems for others, such as Western researchers studying "violences" like infibulation and infanticide among groups whose personal beliefs and cultural practices differ from their own. Such issues confront the beliefs and taken-for-granted assumptions of many observers, as discussed in the chapter by Boddy. Somewhat similar (though not identical) problems confront the study of the orientations and behavior of men who may not view their abuse of women either as violent or as unacceptable (Dobash and Dobash, Chapter 6, this volume). A further fracturing of the definition of violence in various cultures or subgroups is noted in more recent thinking about differences among women who occupy positions based on class, ethnicity, or group. Here we struggle with notions of the universal and of the particular (Merry, 1996). Whether the task is one of definition, of scientific questions and research methods, of social policy, of social action, or of social change, the topic contains at once both the notions and the lived experience of that which is specific, local, particular, and relative and that which is universal and more general or encompassing. While there are those who attempt to remain clearly in one camp, at the same time denying the concerns and validity of the other, both clearly exist simultaneously and must somehow be addressed if advances are to be made in theoretical understandings, in empirical knowledge, and in relevant areas of policy development and social change. Both the universal and the particular must be questioned for the purposes of rethinking the causes and continuation of violence against women and the effective approaches to its elimination.

Working Across Disciplines

Although working across disciplines may be valuable because of the additional insights produced, the process is, nonetheless, exceedingly difficult, time-consuming, and not always successful. One of the major problems is language and terminology. Terms can be highly specialized and specific to a single discipline, and words can have different meanings across disciplines that may not be recognized, yet nonetheless hinder communication in a complex fashion. Although each discipline carries its own baggage of concepts and foci that may productively be put to work in innovative and creative ways, this cannot be done in the context of intellectual rigidity and territoriality. As most disciplines have a legacy of self-containment and of subject matter that is more or less "complete" in content and perspective(s), cross-disciplinary work of necessity disrupts this intellectual "tidiness." It is disquieting to individual scholars who must exercise a degree of intellectual adventure and flexibility if they are to be exposed to other disciplines, and even more disquieting because the outcome is unknown.

The outcome of cross-disciplinary encounters may prove to be desirable; however, because the process of dialogue and exchange is unfamiliar and time-consuming and has no prescribed or predetermined route to knowledge, many scholars simply choose to remain within their respective disciplines. Intellectual enclosure offers certainties, security, and order, and also provides clearer and more certain routes to productivity, whereas interdisciplinary sojourns are more risky and offer only the *possibility* of innovations in theoretical and methodological development. The discussions and debates among the authors presented here illustrate some of these contradictions and tensions. Similar observations were made by members of the United States Panel on the Understanding and Control of Violent Behavior reflecting their experience in compiling *Understanding and Preventing Violence:*

> Reflecting on its own experience, the panel believes that the difficulty of communication across disciplines and violence-control agencies is a major barrier to developing effective interventions. Interdisciplinary communication requires each researcher to invest substantial time and effort in learning one another's vocabularies, in learning how phenomena at different levels of description are measured and classified, and in learning about the related disciplines. It also requires forums for interdisciplinary exchanges of research findings—something that does not naturally occur in professional meetings. (National Research Council, 1993, pp. 321-322)

In this volume, we have begun the exploration across disciplinary lines by highlighting some issues for initial discussion. This can only illicit initial reactions. Further development may occur on subsequent reflection and expansion by others. The focus is primarily on the preeminence of cultural, political, and institutional factors and an examination of how they support and/or tolerate violent behavior— but the "biological" and the "psychological" are also included, particularly as they intersect with these cultural conditions. Sociologists and anthropologists have traditionally focused on the cultural and institutional, psychologists have focused on the individual and interpersonal, and evolutionary psychologists have emphasized biology. It seems clear that further advances in knowledge may be achieved through cross-fertilization and the productive use of the advances made in each of these and other disciplines in undertaking the complex study of violence between intimates.

Methods of Study

Although all researchers have learned the method(s) of their respective disciplines, some may also have been exposed to the techniques of other disciplines. Despite training and experience, or perhaps because of it, most scholars tend to use a single approach. As with theoretical perspectives, concentration on a single approach is less time-consuming, offers greater security and stability, and leads to more certain and predictable products. Again, although the outcome of developing the skills and approaches of other disciplines may offer the prospect of rewarding innovations, the process is demanding and time-consuming and must be weighed against the uncertainty of the outcome. Another deterrent to the use of new, different, or multiple methods resides in the strong and unshakable belief among many researchers in the inherent superiority of their chosen method. Curiously, this notion has been used to privilege both quantitative and qualitative methods and to pit one against the other.

Adopting methods that are relatively "new" to a discipline, even those well-established and highly regarded within another, may generate difficulties when attempting to publish outside the narrowly defined set of "approved" methods acknowledged within a given field. Despite such problems, a growing number of scholars are using multiple methods and introducing "new" or "foreign" methods within various subject areas in an attempt to best match research methods with the phenomena being studied in order to expand empirical knowledge and enhance theoretical understanding of a given subject. Each provides opportunities for advances and innovation and also presents dilemmas involving research methods, ethics, and other issues.

For example, intensive forms of study, such as ethnography, participant observation, and depth interviews, focus on process, motivations, meanings, and explanations of cultural beliefs and social practices and more easily capture the "whole." They also require enhanced levels of empathy and an ability to get close to those being studied. This can sometimes create problems, and the position of the researcher is sometimes unclear. There are also issues about the responsibility of the researcher in terms of representation: for whom? for what? against whom? against what? Issues of power differentials are not unique to such approaches, and there are lessons for all. By contrast, large surveys and epidemiological research focus on individual characteristics such as demographic characteristics of victims or perpetrators and general patterns of violence or risk factors associated with violence or homicide. They are used to establish prevalence and examine demographic correlates. Particular attention is given to methods and methodology and the pragmatic application of findings. Ethical issues also concern the possible exposure of respondents to further violence through the research process. Using official statistics or public records avoids the problems of possible distress and/or subsequent violence to respondents but presents the inevitable problem of data collected for one purpose that must be further developed and modified to serve another.

Until recently, many (although certainly not all) feminist scholars have stated a clear preference for qualitative methods, believing them to be more humane and more likely to produce valid results about sensitive issues. This orthodoxy has now been challenged (Reinharz, 1992), and examples of different methods, including the strongly quantitative and a combination of quantitative and qualitative, have now joined the once exclusive domain of qualitative research among such scholars. The combination of qualitative and quantitative methods is showing that both explanation and description may be enhanced and respondents can still be treated with sensitivity. Debates about methods are sterile if they begin with the assumption that only one approach is correct. It is more useful to begin by asking what is required to best describe and understand a given problem within its social, cultural, and/or personal contexts. The general point is that there is certainly no perfect method; all contain problems and present dilemmas, but some are better suited to certain tasks than others. Accordingly, a wide range of research methods is used herein.

The Importance of Context

It is clear from the work of all of the authors included here, and from the wider literature in this field, that violence directed at women occurs within a wider context composed of responses from social agencies and general beliefs and attitudes about the relationships between men and women, husbands and wives, and about the use of violence to achieve various aims. Throughout our own research, we have consistently stressed the importance of context in explaining the emergence and continuation of this violence and identified four general levels of importance: the individual, interpersonal, institutional, and ideological. In delineating the "context-specific approach" (Dobash & Dobash, 1979, pp. 27-30; 1983a, pp. 261-276; 1992, pp. 253, 267, 282), we specify that an understanding of the specific context(s) in which violence occurs is essential if we are to have some purchase on explaining the violence and on developing meaningful responses to victims and to perpetrators. For example, the work of Boddy approaches the question of infibulation with a clear focus on providing a detailed analysis of the context in which such acts occur and continue, revealing an understanding of context that is essential if the practice is to be addressed at the source. Similarly, Lundgren takes us into a world of religious fundamentalism where violence emerges and continues in a specific set of contexts, and McWilliams examines violence against women in the context of a wider society, where political unrest and violence in the streets overshadow public responses to violence between intimates.

The Extent of Violence Against Women

The Violence Against Women Survey undertaken by Statistics Canada, under the directorship of Holly Johnson and her colleagues, is a landmark in survey research on violence against women and represents a watershed in the comprehensive approach to the design and implementation of surveys in this field of study. It is a model of this type of research and has influenced subsequent studies in other countries. The approach represents a wholesale rethinking of every facet of the survey method and shortcomings previously identified in obtaining "reliable statistical data to estimate the extent and the dimensions of violence against women and to investigate its social and economic correlates." From design to implementation, nothing was left unexamined or unaltered in the careful attention brought to every detail of the entire research process.

In Chapter 2, Johnson outlines the problems and shortcomings of traditional crime-victims surveys and the Conflict Tactics Scale (CTS) and delineates the innovations and improvements built into the Violence Against Women Survey, including an extended consultation process at the first stage of research design. Across the country, various stakeholders were consulted, including academics, government, various agencies, shelter groups, and victims. Using focus groups and an intensive qualitative approach, they were asked to examine the general aims, content, approach, wording of questions, respondent safety, and ways of improving statistical reliability. The process of consultation continued from development to presentation of findings. Interviewers were trained, monitored, and given feedback throughout the research. A toll-free telephone number was given to respondents should they need to return calls to interviewers. The issue of stress for respondents and interviews was addressed, and computerized lists of local services were compiled should women need such assistance. To our knowledge, no national survey even begins to approach this level of attention to detail and consultation, and Johnson notes that these innovations yielded enormous benefits in the type and quality of data obtained as well as in the care and attention given to respondents and interviewers. Great care was also given to constructing the definitions of violence used in the research as well as the nature and ordering of questions and the stated purpose of the research. Another innovation includes the addition of information about the context and consequences of violent events. All were found to make important improvements on previous survey research concerning violence against women.

By telephone, a stratified probability sample of 12,300 women 18 years and older was questioned about experiences of sexual and physical assault by past and present male partners and by strangers. "The results were intended to help understand how violent marriages differ from nonviolent ones; which personal and interpersonal characteristics of offenders and marital relationships predict violence; which risk factors predict very serious, potentially life-threatening assaults; and other more general issues surrounding violence and women's personal security." In addition to delineating the innovations in method, Johnson uses the findings to examine the social control theory of wife assault and concludes with a brief discussion of the "limits to what a statistical survey can accomplish," the necessary and complementary knowledge that can be obtained using ethnographic and qualitative studies and the utility of a combination of methods.

Physical and Sexual Attacks on the Body: Definitions of "What Counts," "Marking" the Body, and "Making" the Person

Kelly and Radford's detailed work on the definition of sexual abuse, with its ever-expanding contexts and configurations, challenges the use of more narrow definitions in research, policy making, and social activism. In Chapter 3, they explore the "range of forms, locations, and contexts in which sexual violence occurs" and identify some unresolved problems. While maintaining that "definitions are critical," they do not view their task as proposing a single definition of sexual violence. Instead, they move through the many elements that compose both the reality and the definition of several forms of sexual violence: sexual harassment, particularly in the context of employment; sexual assault of women and girls; and rape within a wide range of relationships and social locations. They consider how the victimized are defined, as "victim," "survivor," or neither, and draw attention to hidden and neglected consequences of these and other definitions and "the struggles about meaning and conceptualization." They note that "if sexual violence is defined narrowly and is therefore relatively rare, it is the exceptional that requires explanation. If, on the other hand, it is defined more broadly and is a common experience in the lives of women and girls, then the opposite prevails (and rests squarely in the middle of what our culture defines as 'normal' interaction between men and women)." In their exploration, they examine power, male domination, and male sexual aggression, as well as individual and institutional responses to sexual violence. Particular attention is given to the twin concepts of "normalization" and "resistance," and they challenge the presumption that sexual violence is rare and/or outside "normalized" behavior. Kelly and Radford have made a major contribution to thinking about the nature and consequences of the definitions used to study and respond to sexual violence.

"Remaking" the Body in Order to Make the "Perfect" Woman

Kinship and the institution of the family remain the most important forces in many cultures and are fundamental to understanding social life and the nature and extent of violence within it. The focus on kinship and the family also serves as a reminder, or a corrective, to the almost exclusive concentration on political or economic institutions sometimes adopted by policymakers and researchers. Within kinship-based societies, the self must be conceived of differently, often as a corporate sense of identity within an ideal of extreme cohesiveness and less-articulated conflict. Hierarchies of the family radiate through kin, community, state, and political ideology, all emphasizing the importance of conformity. Gender is an important aspect of identity, social membership, and divisions of labor. Violence may vary considerably across cultures, depending on belief systems, forms of organization, and patterns of residence, and traditional patterns articulate with new forms, destabilizing the one and creating uncertain outcomes in the other (Counts, Brown, & Campbell, 1992). Immigration, colonization, and migration all serve to create social change, and violence and women's autonomy are often transformed, for better and for worse.

In Chapter 4, the discussion of infibulation in the Sudan provides considerable insight into how such a practice is viewed within the context of a society in which it is normative, and it highlights the contradictory aspects of the social integration of women and, depending on one's view, of body mutilation, alteration, or "formation." In the Sudan, the physical transformation of the body, the infliction of pain, conceptions of self, and limited forms of female power and autonomy are all intertwined in a complex and multilayered social system now in a state of flux. Again, this discussion provides important insights regarding women's support for such practices and the complexities facing those who might seek to alter them.

With sensitivity and informed insight, Boddy takes us into the world of women for whom infibulation is central to the lived experience of their individual lives and to the cultures in which those lives are embedded. We embark on an intellectual and, of necessity, political journey whose mission is understanding that which to many in Western industrial societies seems beyond comprehension. This is not a simple journey to the land of "cultural relativity" where, as tourists, we watch exotic others engage in acts that on the surface may be deemed to be bizarre or barbaric but that, after all, are of little interest or concern, as they are simply an example of another way of life. Nor is this a romantic journey in which a cultural practice that on the face of it may seem to be painful or harmful to health is sanitized, neutralized, and elevated to the level of a sacred cultural icon beyond scrutiny of its everyday consequences. It is also not a search-and-rescue mission where the enlightened save the uninformed, the oppressed, the enslaved. Instead, it is a challenging, nuanced, and thoroughgoing engagement with the culturally embedded practice of infibulation. The purpose of the journey is to increase understanding based on knowledge of what this practice means to those who support its use and continuation. This, in turn, may have a more subversive intent. No practice that is deeply woven into the life of a society can be completely and simply stopped by order of kings, declarations of the United Nations, or the will of radical activists. Those who would think of social change must engage sensitively and knowledgeably with the individuals and cultural practices that sustain this activity.

Intimate Violence in the Context
of Violence in the Wider Society

When the wider society is in the throes of war, terrorism, or genocide, what then for women in terms of interpersonal relationship with violent husbands at home or soldiers in the streets? Does it matter in terms of the type, level, and responses to woman abuse that the wider society is itself engaged in more or different types of violence than usually experienced? Who better to reflect on this question than Monica McWilliams, an academic and activist who has studied violence against women in the home and sought changes in public policy and institutional responses? She currently represents The Women's Coalition at the peace negotiations in Northern Ireland, which is charged with formulating proposals for peace and for considering new arrangements in public and private life following peace.

With this combination of knowledge and experience, McWilliams considers, in Chapter 5, the additional violence to women, additional problems in seeking assistance, and additional problems of finding meaningful and sustainable solutions to such violence at the same time the wider society is itself experiencing increased levels of violence through terrorism or war. Using examples from several societies, McWilliams identifies how personal forms of violence are amplified and problematic when the wider society is itself engaged in violence and identifies issues that are unique to such conditions. These insights can also be applied to specific communities where the "volume of violence" has been turned up to a higher level than that of the society as a whole. For example, particular communities within a city, or cities within a nation, may experience conditions more akin to those identified by McWilliams, even though the wider society in which they exist is not at war or experiencing terrorism.

McWilliams opens new areas of thinking and provides enormous insights for others seeking solutions to public violence in ways that do not ignore or minimize private forms of violence that can so easily be forgotten or deemed less important in such a context. During the American Revolution, Abigail Adams declared that the makers of the new nation should "remember the ladies" in the making of the new land. She referred explicitly to the abuses of women in marriage and the home, lest those making the brave new world of America transform public life while leaving untouched the abuses of women in private life (Grant De Pauw, 1976, p. 1). Both intellectually and politically, McWilliams is engaged in no less a task.

The Violent Event, Masculinity,
and the Context of Male Culture

Despite the fact that the topic of violence against women has been studied in myriad ways during recent years, there has been less attention to a close examination of the violent event, per se, as a process with a beginning, middle, and end in which men, women, and children are differentially involved. Contexts, motivations, intentions, and outcomes are all vitally important, although research on these issues remains underdeveloped. More careful, detailed, and thoughtful examination is necessary if we are to more accurately describe the nature of the phenomenon and to understand why it occurs and persists. In Chapter 6, Dobash and Dobash examine violent acts and violent actors in the context of a marital relationship delineating the conflicts of interest between intimate partners that focus on issues such as domestic work, money, children, alcohol, possessiveness and jealousy, restrictions of social life, sex, and male power and authority. We identify a "constellation of violence" made up of the physical acts of violence, injuries, and various forms of controlling behaviors. Based on a depth study of violent men and women partners, we use data from the Violence Assessment Index (VAI), the Injuries Assessment Index (IAI), and the Controlling Behaviour Index (CBI) to compare the accounts of men and women and reflect on the similarities and differences between them.

We theorize about masculinity and male power in relation to the differences between acts of violence perpetrated by men against other men and those perpetrated against women. For boys, messages about motives and violent repertories are socially organized, structured within institutions, practiced in schools and sport, and used as expressions of friendship, authority, and masculine identity. In some cultures, the male body is normatively linked with physique and violence (Bourgois, 1996). The ideal of heroic masculinity is often associated with aggressive bodily display where the objective is not to employ the body in actual violence but to use it as a means of intimidation. Yet the perpetration of and participation in violent encounters are equated with masculinity, regardless of the outcome; even the scars and wounds of "the loser" may be useful for display and status conferring among some young males. This differs when men use violence against women. The consideration of masculinity may have implications for long-term prevention and for addressing issues of social change relative to the abuse of women. Such changes will require innovative thinking about the object of change, the forces resisting change, the beliefs and conditions that might facilitate change, and the strategies that might be pursued.

While accumulating evidence does suggest the existence of "male" violence against women in all societies and across time, which might in turn suggest an inherent, universal male characteristic, research also shows variation in both the nature and level of this violence between men and women across different societies and/or cultures. This variation suggests cultural specificity and the importance of different contexts rather than an unvaried, universal behavior. This theme is examined differently in the chapters by Lundgren in her consideration of the construction of gender, and by Wilson and Daly in their examination of the concept of an evolved male psychology, particularly in relation to possessiveness and the killing of wives. Many agree that masculinity is shaped and lived within a cultural context and that it is not static but at the same time has commonly recognized features.

Constructing Gender Through Violence, Enacting Gender Through Violence

Punishing the Body to Make the Model Woman

In Chapter 7, Lundgren undertakes three tasks at once. At one level, she uses information from a series of interviews with a small number of couples who are members of an extreme religious sect to illustrate the use by husbands of both violent punishment and loving affection to shape the woman into the idealized notion of a wife. The interviews, particularly with one couple, are used to present the complex and vacillating reality experienced by abused women who live with men who are not simply violent and abusive but can also be loving. This provides insight into some of the dilemmas faced by abused women when deciding to leave or stay in such a relationship and helps explain why offers to help her leave are not always or easily taken. This duality of abuse and affection may also serve to illustrate why abused women are often more reluctant than others to simply define men as solely abusive and/or unworthy of intervention. The language of the interviews is closely examined in terms of the differing channels of communication (visual, auditory, or kinesthetic) used by the man/husband engaged in the process of "making" the ideal wife through the use of education, guidance, affection, and physical punishment and by the woman who is at once the object of this undertaking and also a subject in her own right with a will and ideas of her own that must be "reshaped" if she is to meet *his* ideal of a good wife and woman.

For Lundgren, abuse involves a combination of sex and violence undertaken in ways that are laden with patterns, acts, symbols, and roles. Within this context, masculinity is constituted through a link between sexual violence and physical attacks on the body. Here it is important to distinguish between what has become known as "ritual" abuse (satanic abuse is sometimes falsely referred to as ritual abuse) and the routines or rituals sometimes associated with abuse. The ritualized aspects of sexual abuse may include the use of props and contain acts with symbolic meaning for those involved but do not necessarily involve the "devil" worship of satanic abuse. Rape and sexual abuse may also involve elements of ritual, such as preselected music or symbolic dress or routines. This is an area in which terminology has become very confused, and there is a need for careful articulation of concepts, descriptions of phenomena, and evidence.

At another level, Lundgren uses her empirical data as a touchstone for a much broader theoretical and philosophical project, as "a basis for more abstract reflections on gender theory." She "interweaves biological and symbolic gender" to contribute to a more dynamic, "open theory of gender," focusing on "fundamental rules (constitutive) and applied rules (regulative)." She details her conception of the constitutive level (internalized and hard-coded within individuals) and the regulative level (more changeable, such as masculinity and femininity) whereby "regulative rules are applied rules that can somehow be derived from basic rules. *Constitutive* rules are stable but not static, whereas *regulative* rules are more flexible and in constant flux." As such, both "stability" and "change" form vital parts of the dynamic process of gender construction and practices. For Lundgren, "the use of symbols and bodily (violent) behavior" are intimately related and tightly intertwined, and this highlights the fruitless nature of distinguishing between biological and symbolic gender in the context of her thesis. In this philosophical project, Lundgren uses the work of the French feminist philosopher Luce Irigaray as a "sparring partner" and examines the language of gender, whether phallocentric or gynocentric in nature.

While maintaining that the body must be reintegrated along with the social in a theory of gender, Lundgren notes that much of feminist thinking and research first ignored the body in favor of the social in the project of attempting to achieve social change and then introduced it in ways that separated rather than integrated the bodily and the social. It also defined it as a "static basic constitutive category," albeit in a positive light, stressing women's unique biological nature. "Thus the body became relevant, but hardly for change." When feminist research focused so unilaterally on social change, it was damaged by this implicit confirmation of the static nature of the biological. This "static" biological gender, along with notions of a hierarchy of the "fixed biological" over the more "fluid social," meant that the project of social change became either impossible or undesirable. Lundgren posits an interrelationship between the "biological," the "social," and the "symbolic," without a hierarchy of status among them. She also envisages both flexibility and change as well as stability, claiming that "one of the overall aims of feminist research must be to reclaim the body as a category of change."

We are taken to yet another frontier in Chapter 8 by Wilson and Daly, who use evolutionary psychology to examine male sexual proprietaries in the use of lethal and nonlethal violence against women partners. The social science reader who knows the critiques of the sociobiology of the 1970s might at this stage be inclined to close their mind or ignore this chapter. For those who feel "intolerant" of this approach or elevate themselves to the level of expressing a condescending "impatience" with ideas not their own, we quote from a knowledgeable critic of the approach, Stephen Jay Gould: "Humans are animals and the mind evolved; therefore, all curious people must support the quest for an evolutionary psychology" (1997, p. 50). Even an observer as stern as Gould maintains that the thinking person cannot ignore and should not dismiss out of hand the notions that evolution now brings to our understanding of the human and its social environment. It is not our intention to enter the debate about evolutionary psychology nor to pronounce a verdict about the outcome, but rather to engage intellectually with the new and sometimes challenging ideas presented by this model.

With respect to the killing of wives (uxoricide) and children, the overall work of Wilson and Daly has revolutionized thinking about these intimate forms of homicide and provided empirical evidence about issues not hitherto examined by others. They consider the "functions" of violence. While not accepting the inevitability of lethal and nonlethal violence, they examine how it might at one level reflect a "functional" approach to ensuring "ownership" of a woman partner for the purposes of reproduction, which, when taken to the extreme of homicide, becomes a dysfunctional manifestation of the "normal" notions of male sexual propriety.

Although many social scientists and feminists might altogether dismiss what they fear to be the biological determinism of elements of this approach, there are nonetheless many similarities in some basic notions and empirical evidence used by each. For example, there is likely to be considerable agreement about the evidence showing that in intimate relationships, men are far more likely than women to be violent and aggressive; that it is men who beat wives rather than the reverse; that men are more likely to act with violence, even homicide, in response to jealousy and possessiveness; and that this seems to occur in virtually all societies and has done so over time. While the quest to document, understand, and explain this phenomenon is common to all, it is at the point of explanation that challenges and divisions occur and involve each tradition differently. One of the challenging intellectual questions involves the relative place and importance of the "biological" as broadly defined and the "cultural," as the respective disciplines vie for preeminence of explanation.

For many social scientists, the fact of the "biological" has now been acknowledged and is now included in some topics of study—especially among those studying the body. The disputed terrain may lie in theoretical terms and concern the relative importance of "social" explanations versus "biological" ones or of some creative combination of the two. While many in the "cultural" camp may have difficulty even thinking about how the biological might enter the world of their perspective, some of those in the "biological" camp face a similar challenge. For those able to include both within their perspective, the questions differ and become those of the respective positioning and explanatory value of each. In this volume, Lundgren explicitly discusses the inclusion of these different domains within a single perspective and posits that there should be no hierarchy between them in terms of the ordering of their explanatory power or place. The verdict is still out with respect to this issue.

To the extent that this perspective takes the form of "biological determinism," cultural factors may be included but will do so as one of the many consequences of that which is "biologically" determined. The structure of such "first" and "second" order explanatory factors resembles the structure of the economic determinism of popular Marxist thinking so familiar in many social and political writings of the 1960s and 1970s with the economy (the infrastructure) in the explanatory driving seat and culture/beliefs/ideologies (the superstructure) as an essential but secondary factor. Should this format be repeated in the structure of argument shaping the theoretical thinking about evolution, a "biological determinism," it would follow that the first order of explanatory factors, "biology" in its widest sense, would take the explanatory driver's seat, whereas the second order of explanatory factors, the "social" or "cultural," would be an essential yet dependent set of factors. It may be here that the greatest areas of defense and dispute are yet to occur and here also that the greatest opportunity for creative thinking about this relationship remains to be addressed.

In that respect, one challenging question concerns not the fact of the existence of male violence against intimate partners in every and all societies throughout time but the patterning or variation in the amount, type, and contexts of male violence and, perhaps more important, the patterning of "nonviolence" among males. That is, although it seems indisputable that in every society there is evidence that men have used violence against women with whom they have intimate relations (evidence in support of a universal male psychology despite local cultural variations), there is also evidence of considerable variation across cultures in the type and amount of violence and the proportion of the population that actually engages in its use (evidence in support of the effect of specific cultural conditions on the "universal" of male violence).

Wilson and Daly's discussion of lethal and nonlethal violence is interesting here. It has been argued that specific cultural conditions are themselves evolved, making such differences more superficial than real and thus subordinated to the primary "biological" principles driving the evolutionary train—in this case, reproduction. Here, the two camps might argue hotly, both armed with evidence or anecdotes in support of their theory, but as yet it seems difficult to resolve. However, the more difficult problem both for a theory positing the universality of an evolved male psychology that leads to the use of violence against women partners and for the feminist who would argue in a similar vein that "all men are potential rapists" or that "all men have the potential to beat their wives" is, quite simply, that *not all* men do either. In fact, within most modern, industrial societies, *most* men do neither. Whether describing patriarchal culture or an evolved psychology, both perspectives are confronted with a conundrum as yet unresolved. There can be little doubt that the work of Wilson and Daly will help advance this thinking and this debate whatever its outcome.

Wilson and Daly present their findings about the risk of uxoricide (wife killing) and consider whether similar risks occur with respect to nonlethal violence against wives (woman abuse). They posit two important assumptions relating to their hypotheses about risk patterns: (a) "violence against wives is a product of motives whose adaptive function is coercive control," which might be shared by acts of nonlethal and lethal violence; and (b) men's sense of "ownership" or "possessiveness" (male sexual propriety) is related to cues about potential challenges or threats to her fidelity and his ability to manage those threats either by coercing her through isolation and/or violence or by seeing off rival men. They call for examinations of cross-cultural variations in risk patterns, some of which are addressed in other chapters herein.

This collection is meant to stretch boundaries as far as conceivable; to open rather than to close issues; and to seek new ideas and possible ways forward rather than to make definitive statements and seek rigid and untimely closure. It is hoped that by crossing disciplines, being exposed to different areas and giving a voice to all participants, this mixture of ideas and information might stimulate new thinking about violence against women. We are, of course, more accustomed to closure and the definitive. While "cross-border talk" might be stimulating and constitute a condition for thinking in new and different ways, it is uncomfortable for academics and activists alike. Developing new thoughts and new methods is important and necessary, but it takes both time and reflection for new ideas to germinate.

2

Rethinking Survey Research on Violence Against Women

Holly Johnson

In the global context, Canada, the United States, and Great Britain are in the enviable position of having acquired a rich store of knowledge about the multidimensional aspects of sexual assault and violence against women. Interest and activism around these issues were initiated in all three countries by the modern-day women's movement, whose grassroots members long ago undertook to provide shelter, counseling, and support for women victims and their children, thereby opening up for public discourse discussions about violence and power in intimate relationships.

Research has gone hand in hand with these undertakings, focusing in the early stages on studies of female victims and their contacts with rape crisis centers, hospitals, and shelters for battered women or with men who had been tried and convicted of such offenses. From this research came a rich body of information—powerful, vivid accounts of sexual violence and battering relationships and initial explanations of the phenomena—which helped galvanize public attention as well as action in the academic arena, in communities, and at various levels of government. Public consciousness around these issues has gradually

AUTHOR'S NOTE: Research supported by a grant from the Social Sciences and Humanities Research Council of Canada.

evolved, and services and support for victims have proliferated, originally with volunteer labor and later with the help of public donations and government funding.

Over this period of time, violence against women has become a mainstream issue for research and study. Both governments and activists now recognize the need for good quality research to help influence policy making and to examine the effectiveness of innovative responses. Some seek reliable statistical data to estimate the extent and the dimensions of violence against women and to investigate its social and economic correlates. Still others seek information to inform the development of prevention strategies, policies, and programs for victims and offenders. No single research method is best suited to all of these tasks. Evaluation research techniques are best suited to examine new interventions—small, intensive studies to gain maximum insight into the phenomenon of violence and its complex complement of contexts, motivations, and intentions, and national surveys using probability samples to gather information about the extent of the problem and its correlation with other social, economic, and individual factors. Policymakers, activists, and academics in various countries have been informed through evaluations of experimental interventions, qualitative studies focusing on the actual experience of violence, and surveys of entire nations or strategic sites across different geographic areas. The various approaches to research often serve different, albeit sometimes overlapping, purposes, and all have continued to develop and improve their techniques. However, all have delimitations, that is, boundaries of the type of contributions to knowledge that can be made using a particular technique as well as limitations in the quality or scope of any specific study or approach.

Whereas evaluation research and the uses of intensive studies are discussed in other chapters, the purpose here is to concentrate on the national survey, meant to measure the dimensions and the nature of violence against women. An overview is presented of the efforts undertaken in Canada to address many of the shortcomings of the use of this approach and to rethink it from the initial stages of the development of the study to the final presentation of findings. In order to place these innovations in the wider context of this type of research, some of the critiques of traditional crime-victim surveys and targeted family-violence surveys shall be presented, followed by a description of the methodology of the national survey, an overview of some of the results, and a test of a popular theory.

Traditional Crime-Victim Surveys

Crime-victimization surveys, such as the National Crime Victimization Survey (NCVS) in the United States, the British Crime Survey (BCS), and the victimization component of Statistics Canada's General Social Survey (GSS), were originally designed to complement police statistics by capturing both incidents that were reported to the police and those that victims kept private. By so doing, these surveys helped cast light on the volume and types of offenses not brought to police attention and the reasons for not reporting. Because they interview a random sample of households, victim surveys are also useful tools for assessing citizens' perceptions of crime, neighborhood safety, and their use of the criminal justice system.

But crime-victim surveys are essentially omnibus surveys with a wide-ranging focus on a variety of crimes and issues; they were not designed to measure the very sensitive experiences of violence that primarily affect women and have been severely criticized for failing to do so (Koss, 1992; Stanko, 1988). As a result of the methodology used in crime-victim surveys, they have consistently portrayed sexual assault and violence against wives as far less prevalent than rates reported by specially focused surveys on these topics (Koss, 1989, 1992; Smith, 1987, 1990).

The undercounting of these events on traditional crime-victim surveys is a consequence of a number of features of this approach (Johnson, 1996):

1. Many women are not comfortable relating their experiences to interviewers, perhaps because of the lack of sensitive question wording, lack of special training for interviewers, and the use, in some cases, of male interviewers. Very few considerations were made for the enormous sensitivity of the information being sought.

2. In their attempt to measure a wide variety of both personal and property crimes, victim surveys have been unable to adequately measure these events or provide meaningful context. Questions about assault tend to be unidimensional and lack detail.

3. These surveys orient respondents in the early part of the interview to think about the level of crime in their neighborhoods. Women who are unsure whether to consider physical abuse by husbands or boyfriends or sexual assaults by dates or family members as crimes very likely will not offer these experiences to interviewers when asked whether they have been assaulted.

4. As part of the orientation toward "crime," these surveys also restrict their questioning to criminal acts. Noncriminal acts of sexual harassment are a routine part of women's lives, but because these acts are not "criminal" in the legal sense, they typically are not considered appropriate for inclusion in victim surveys or analyses of women's fear. These experiences are reminders to women that they are targets for sexual violence and serve to undermine their feelings of security. Although they are not technically crimes, such incidents may have profound implications for women's safety and well-being, which are untapped by the usual approach.

5. This relates to the one-year reference that most crime-victim surveys use to estimate the incidence of criminal victimization. If respondents do consider their experiences appropriate to report but they happened outside the one-year reference period, they will not be counted. This practice draws an artificial boundary around certain experiences and confounds discussions about violence and feelings of vulnerability. The arbitrary assignment of "victim" status to women who have been sexually or physically assaulted in the previous year and "nonvictim" status to those not victimized very recently misclassifies many women. Some of those classified as nonvictims in reality have been victims of very serious violence that fundamentally alters both their vulnerability to further violence and their *perceptions* of their vulnerability.

Recent efforts to enhance the capacity of these surveys to address sexual assault and assaults on wives in Canada and the United States have yielded positive results. With improved question wording, the Canadian GSS in 1993 produced rates of wife assault 27% higher than the previous cycle, from 15 to 19 per 1,000 women aged 15 and over. Rates of sexual assault increased from a statistically negligible rate to 29 per 1,000 women (Johnson, 1996). Following a redesign of the NCS in the United States, rates of sexual assault in that country rose fourfold from 1 to 5 per 1,000 for females aged 12 and over. Rates of wife assault doubled from 5 to 9 per 1,000 (Bachman, 1994; Bachman & Saltzman, 1995). The improved question wording in both surveys entailed more specific questions about sexual assault and specifically advised respondents to consider acts by family members when responding to questions about assault. This illustrates how critical question wording is to the results obtained in population surveys and what a difference it can make in surveys that were essentially unchanged in other ways.

The Conflict Tactics Approach

A concerted program of survey research around the issue of family violence had been under way in the United States for some time when

Canada entered the field. The approach to survey research undertaken in the United States has been dominated by the Conflict Tactics Scales (CTS) methodology developed by Murray Straus and his colleagues at the University of New Hampshire (Straus, 1990). From the perspective of the CTS, spousal violence is a form of family violence similar in its condition and genesis to other forms, such as child abuse or sibling violence. Assaults on wives are treated in the same way as assaults by wives on husbands as ways of handling interpersonal conflict. Because the conditions and circumstances of these various forms of family violence are thought to be similar, explanations also tended to be all-encompassing.

The CTS consists of 18 items intended to measure ways of handling interpersonal conflict in family relationships. The items range from "verbal reasoning" (from calmly discussing the issue to bringing in someone to mediate) to "verbal aggression" (from insults and swearing to throwing, smashing, hitting, or kicking something) to "physical aggression" (from throwing something at the other person to using a knife or gun). Male and female respondents are asked how frequently they had perpetrated each act in the course of settling a disagreement with a spouse, a child, or a sibling and how frequently they had been the victim of these acts. Sexual assault is absent from the scale.

The way the CTS has traditionally been applied has been criticized by many researchers on the grounds that it ignores the gendered power imbalances that exist within marriage and excludes crucial details about motives, intentions, and consequences (Browning & Dutton, 1986; Brush, 1990; DeKeseredy & MacLean, 1990; Dobash & Dobash, 1992; Dobash, Dobash, Wilson, & Daly, 1992; Saunders, 1988). The fact that males and females report symmetry in the incidence of violence inflicted on them by spouses has been accepted uncritically by some researchers, leading them to conclude that spousal violence is not primarily wife battering but is one of "mutual combat" (Steinmetz, 1977-1978; Straus, 1980). Although some users of the CTS have subsequently taken into consideration social and cultural factors when interpreting the data, such as the economic and physical disparity between men and women within marriage (Gelles & Straus, 1988), the scale itself treats a slap, a push, or a shove by a man as equivalent to the same acts by a woman and fails to measure the damage or consequences of those acts. It also fails to consider victims' ability to repel or restrain assailants and their ability to retaliate, and it fails to take into account empirical evidence of men's tendency to minimize and deflect responsibility for their violence (Browning & Dutton, 1986; Dobash & Dobash, 1992; Dobash, Dobash, Wilson, & Daly, 1992; Makepeace, 1986).

Some of these criticisms have been addressed through a revised version of the scales in which the list of items was altered and greatly expanded (CTS2), including the addition of a battery of questions designed to measure sexual coercion and injuries resulting from violence (Straus, Hamby, Boney-McCoy, & Sugarman, 1996). Still missing are important contextual items related to male partner's attempts to maintain dominance and authority, which are often associated with physical and sexual violence toward wives, and that might help clarify the results (Dobash, Dobash, Cavanagh, & Lewis, 1996; Johnson, 1996).

Straus acknowledges the need to give primary attention to wife battering as the more pressing social policy issue on the basis that men tend to underreport their own violence, are more likely to use very dangerous and injurious forms of violence and more repetitive violence, because of the economic and social constraints women face in terminating the marriage, and because much of women's violence is committed in defense of assaults by husbands (Gelles & Straus, 1988; Straus, 1990). Straus concedes that it is "advisable to base analyses of violence by men on data provided by women" (Stets & Straus, 1990, p. 162).

Even if it were just applied to women's accounts of male violence, significant methodological problems remain with the CTS. For example, the introduction is problematic. Introductions are crucial components of sample surveys in that they establish the context of the survey at the outset and ensure that respondents have a common understanding of the focus of the questions to follow. Reliability will be badly affected if there is ambiguity in the wording of the questions or if respondents are likely to attach significantly different meaning to the same questions. Validity is affected by questions that poorly represent what the researcher is attempting to measure. Respondents to the CTS are introduced to the items on the scales as a list of ways of "settling differences." While some respondents may think about experiences of violence as ways of settling differences, a great many others may not. There can be little doubt that violent relationships are conflict-ridden; however, there is substantial evidence that many acts of aggression by men against their wives are not precipitated by an argument or disagreement between them, and many respondents may not consider these acts appropriate to include (Browne, 1987; Dobash & Dobash, 1984).

The Violence Against Women Survey

In the early 1990s, Statistics Canada embarked on the design of a national population survey to assess the nature and dimensions of violence against women in Canada in order to provide statistical information relevant to the detection, prevention, and treatment of sexual violence and assaults on wives. In full consideration of the shortcomings previously listed, the crime-victim survey approach of interviewing randomly selected samples of respondents was considered to hold the greatest promise for this task. Decades of effort had gone into refining techniques of interviewing, data capture and editing, complex weighting procedures, and questionnaire design. It was reasoned that, if conducted carefully and ethically, a random sample survey dedicated entirely to women's experiences of violence could be developed to meet rigorous standards of reliability and validity, at the same time overcoming many of the limitations of traditional crime-victim surveys and the CTS. The results were intended to help understand how violent marriages differ from nonviolent ones; which personal and interpersonal characteristics of offenders and marital relationships predict violence; which risk factors predict very serious, potentially life-threatening assaults; and other more general issues surrounding violence and women's personal security.

A stratified probability sample of 12,300 women, 18 years of age and over, was interviewed by telephone for this survey in 1993 (1% of this population live in household without telephones). They were questioned about their experiences of sexual and physical assault by husbands and common-law partners (past and present), dates and boyfriends, other men known to them, and male strangers.

The definitions of sexual and physical assault were designed to conform to the Canadian *Criminal Code*. The survey included contextual information about controlling physically and emotionally abusive acts by spouses; the level of seriousness of physical and sexual assaults; the effects of violence on women in terms of physical injury and emotional effects; and decisions that women made to tell others, to leave and then to return to violent partners, to get medical help, to use shelters and other social services, and to report incidents to the police.

It was recognized in the early stages of planning and development that, due to many considerations entailed in interviewing women over the telephone about these issues, procedures of survey design and implementation would need to be constantly scrutinized as the project progressed. The essential principles that guided the development of this survey were:

- A survey of this nature asks respondents to disclose the most intimate and perhaps the most troubling details of their lives to a stranger over the telephone.
- Questions asking respondents to relive very troubling memories have the potential to raise serious emotional trauma.
- With every telephone call is the possibility that the respondent is living with an abusive man and her safety could be threatened should he learn of the focus of the survey.
- Measures of sexual and physical violence and sexual harassment needed to be developed that were valid and reliable, that conformed to Canadian law, and at the same time were sensitive and respectful of the women responding.

These issues were raised and discussed with a wide variety of stakeholders during an extensive consultation process that continued throughout all phases of the project. Each issue gave rise to unique methodological challenges that enriched our understanding of the impact of violence on women's lives and, in many respects, challenged traditional views on victimization survey research.

The various stakeholders included academics and other researchers, government policymakers, a police advisory group, shelter workers, crisis counselors, and other grassroots women's groups, as well as victims of violence seeking support from these agencies. The broadest range of groups was selected with the intent of eliciting diverse perceptions, opinions, and concerns around the proposed research. An evolutionary process was undertaken whereby concerns raised by these groups were incorporated into discussions with other groups so that everyone involved had an opportunity to consider every aspect of the project. Discussions were qualitative in nature and took the form of intensive focus groups that discussed the general aims and content of the questionnaire, specific wording of questions, feedback about drafts of the questionnaire, as well as face-to-face interviews with battered women on drafts of the questionnaire. (See MacLeod [1992] for more detail about the reactions of community groups to the survey.) In addition, two large-scale field tests were undertaken with random samples of women. Overall, the groups offered valuable suggestions about how to address issues of respondent safety and trauma, ways to improve the utility of the survey, and its statistical reliability.

The Selection and Training of Interviewers

Many of the issues raised throughout discussions with community groups relating to respondents' willingness to participate and to disclose experiences of violence, respondents' safety, and emotional trauma were addressed through the careful selection and training of interviewers.

It is a common concern among survey researchers that results will be biased if a large proportion of respondents refuses to participate in the survey or refuses to answer specific questions. A number of reasons why a woman may not wish to reveal experiences of violence to an interviewer over the telephone have been articulated by Smith (1994); she may feel it is too personal or painful to discuss; she may be embarrassed or ashamed about it; she may fear further violence from her abuser should he find out; or she may have forgotten about it if she considered it to be minor or it happened a long time ago.

It was reasoned that through careful selection and training, interviewers would be able to develop a relationship of trust with respondents and a climate in which women would feel comfortable responding to such questions, and this would enhance participation and response rates. Recruitment of interviewers was done through temporary employment agencies and Statistics Canada interviewing staff. A screening interview was conducted to assess interviewing experience and skills and suitability for the job. A second interview, conducted with a clinical psychologist, was aimed at assessing emotional stability, ability to handle stress, and sensitivity to the issue of violence against women. Although community groups strongly endorsed the idea of hiring only shelter workers and others who had training and experience helping abused women, priority was given to recruiting those with good interviewing skills who also had some sensitivity to the survey content. It was argued that, with good training, women with these skills might be more objective and less likely to hold preconceived notions about the rate of violence that women should be reporting. Not surprisingly, however, the subject matter attracted many women who had specialized training or experience in the subject area. A cursory review of the background characteristics of interviewers and their job performance, measured by response rates and disclosures of violence, indicates that specialized education or experience had very little effect on either measure (see Norris & Hatcher, 1994).

Only women were considered for the job of interviewing because of the concern that many women would not feel comfortable responding to these questions with male interviewers, which would have a negative effect on participation rates. Forty interviewers were initially hired and given 8 days of training. Additional, shorter training sessions were held to bring on extra staff as some interviewers left, for reasons mostly related to the temporary nature of the job. Interviewers were monitored and given feedback throughout the training, field testing, and interviewing periods to ensure consistency of the data collected and maintaining professionalism on the part of interviewers.

The safety of the women responding to the survey was of paramount importance. Through training, role playing, and direct experience, interviewers became skilled at detecting whether respondents had privacy and were able to speak freely. Every opportunity was given respondents to reschedule interviews if they did not feel comfortable proceeding at the appointed time. At the outset of the interview, and at additional points when appropriate, respondents were provided a toll-free telephone number they could use to call back to resume the interview in the event that they had to hang up suddenly. No callbacks were made into respondents' households, which gave them ultimate control over their participation.

A great many women took advantage of the callback option. A total of 1,000 calls were received on the toll-free line over the 5-month interviewing period; 150 calls were from women who wanted to continue an uncompleted interview that they had to interrupt or who wanted to add additional information to a completed interview. This kind of interest and commitment to the interview process signals the level of emotional engagement that this line of questioning can provoke and to which survey researchers must be prepared to respond. Over one half of all calls were from women wanting to verify the legitimacy of the survey, many at the point of sensitive questions about violence in their lives. One quarter wanted additional information or had questions about the sponsorship of the survey or how they could obtain the results.

Responding to Trauma

As a general principle, researchers have an ethical responsibility, at the very least, to do no harm to the subjects under study. In a survey of this sensitivity, survey managers have an added responsibility to offer support in the event that the process in any way elicits emotional trauma. This applies to respondents, but it applies equally to interviewers who may be distressed by the personal stories they hear. Even experienced interviewers can become distressed as a result of a particular interview or cumulatively over the course of many weeks or months of interviewing on this topic.

One important component of the training that interviewers received was information about the effects of sexual violence and spousal violence on female victims and the trauma that can occur when these events are triggered in the victim's mind after the fact. A great deal of care was taken by the survey designers to develop question wording that was sensitive and respectful, and through role playing, interviewers learned how to conduct the interviews in a sensitive manner.

To enable them to respond to a respondent in distress, interviewers had available to them a computerized list of shelters and other services across the country for abused and sexually assaulted women. When the interviewer activated a special computer key, services in the respondent's geographic area appeared on the screen, linked to the area code and prefix of her telephone number. (This was facilitated by the Computer Assisted Telephone Interviewing system.) This way, interviewers were able to make concrete offers of assistance and were left feeling less helpless than if no such tool had been available. It was stressed throughout the training program that interviewers were not to view their role as one of counselor, no matter how distressed a respondent may appear and no matter what kind of training or counseling experience they may have had previously. Referring women to support services in the community addressed the need to respond to participants' distress without compromising the role of the interviewer or the objective of collecting statistical data.

The psychologist hired to help in the selection of interviewers also took part in training sessions and conducted regular debriefing sessions to help interviewers manage any stress they were feeling as a result of their work on the survey.

The success of this survey was due in large measure to the care taken at every stage of the process to respect the position of the women responding, to be sensitive to the difficulty many women have relating these experiences, and to anticipate and respond to difficulties that interviewers may have as a result of hearing personal stories about violence. The measures taken to address these issues are important not only from an ethical point of view, but from the point of view of collecting reliable information about the prevalence and dimensions of women's experiences of male violence.

Constructing Definitions of Violence

Definitions of violence against women in the research literature vary widely. Some include psychological and emotional abuse, financial abuse, sexual coercion, as well as physical and sexual assault as legally defined (e.g., DeKeseredy & Kelly, 1993; Koss & Gidycz, 1985). The prevalence of "violence" was estimated by this survey using questions designed from legal definitions of physical and sexual assault as contained in the Canadian *Criminal Code*. Five additional items describing husbands' controlling behaviors were conceptualized as "emotional abuse" and will be discussed in the final section of this chapter.

Violence Outside Marriage

The behaviors considered sexual assaults under Canadian law include acts ranging from unwanted sexual touching to violent sexual attacks with severe injury to the victim. Rape (i.e., penetration) is included but is not essential to this definition. The following two questions were devised for this survey to measure women's experiences of sexual assault. Each of these questions about sexual and physical assault was asked first of strangers, then of dates and boyfriends, and, lastly, of other known men apart from spouses.

1. *Sexual attack:* Has a male stranger (date, boyfriend, or other man known to you) ever forced you or attempted to force you into any sexual activity by threatening you, holding you down, or hurting you in some way?

2. *Unwanted sexual touching:* Has a male stranger (date, boyfriend, or other man known to you) ever touched you against your will in any sexual way, such as unwanted touching, grabbing, kissing, or fondling?

It is important to note that in questioning women about sexual violence involving intimate partners (both dating and marital relationships), they were asked about violent sexual attacks but not about unwanted sexual touching (more about spousal violence later on). While technically these latter behaviors do fall under the legal definition of sexual assault, when the questionnaire was tested in focus groups and in random samples of women, a majority of respondents found this concept to be ambiguous and confusing when applied to boyfriends and husbands. These questions were excluded because of a concern about the reliability and validity of the results.

Physical assaults under the *Criminal Code* range from face-to-face threats of imminent attack up to and including attacks with serious injury. Physical violence outside marriage was measured through responses to the following two questions:

1. *Physical attack:* Now I'm going to ask you some questions about physical attacks you may have had since the age of 16. By this I mean any use of force, such as being hit, slapped, kicked, or grabbed, to being beaten, knifed, or shot. Has a male stranger (date, boyfriend, or other man known to you) ever physically attacked you?
2. *Threats of attack:* The next few questions are about face-to-face threats you may have experienced. By threats I mean any time you have been threatened with physical harm since you were 16. Has a male stranger (date, boyfriend, or other man known to you) ever threatened to harm you? Did you believe he would do it?

Incidents that had both a sexual and a physical component were counted only once as sexual assaults.

Violence by Spouses

The method used to derive estimates of wife assault differs substantially from the single-question methods typically used in crime-victim surveys. Ten specific questions were used to measure violence by a common-law partner or spouse, ranging from threats of physical harm to use of a gun or knife, including violent sexual assault. This method is intended to take into account the advice of Smith (1994) and others: to offer many opportunities for disclosure in order to counteract a reluctance to disclose painful or embarrassing experiences. Obtaining details about specific types of violent acts also adds important information about the dimensions and the range of seriousness of assaults on wives.

These 10 items, in the order in which they were asked, are as follows:

1. Has your husband ever threatened to hit you with his fist or anything else that could hurt you?
2. Has he ever thrown anything at you that could hurt you?
3. Has he ever pushed, grabbed, or shoved you?

4. Has he ever slapped you?

5. Kicked, bit, or hit you with his fist?

6. Hit you with something that could hurt you?

7. Beat you up?

8. Choked you?

9. Threatened to or used a gun or knife on you?

10. Forced you into any sexual activity when you did not want to by threatening you, holding you down, or hurting you in some way?

The Violence Against Women Survey (VAWS) departs in a number of ways from the conflict tactics approach and from the crime-victim survey approach. For example, it uses an extensive lead-up to questions about spousal violence, through detailed sections about fear of violence in public places and safety precautions, sexual harassment, sexual and physical violence by nonspouses, and attempts by husbands to control or limit the woman's autonomy (see Statistics Canada, 1993). Moreover, the introduction to the section inquiring about wife assault did not attempt to normalize physical aggression by reference to "verbal reasoning" or "verbal aggression" tactics but instead stated very directly that "we are particularly interested in learning more about women's experiences of *violence* in their homes. I'd like to ask you to tell me if your husband/partner has ever done any of the following to you."

This survey was concerned not with ways of settling disagreements but with violence against women, and this context would have been established at this point. The inclusion of an item concerning sexual attacks was an important addition, both empirically and theoretically within the context of violence, which does not fit theoretically in the context of family conflict or settling differences.

This is a complex survey, which was designed to test theories about the instrumentality of husbands' use of violence against wives and about the etiology of wife battering through details about witnessing battering in childhood, partners' alcohol abuse, type of marital union (common-law and registered marriages), as well as demographic characteristics of women and their partners. There is a focus in this survey on contextual information about the seriousness and consequences of assaults and the actions women take as a result of violence. Questions about outcome include the level of physical and emotional injury, whether medical attention was received, women's use of alcohol or drugs as a reaction to the violence, the presence of a weapon during the event, the frequency of violent episodes, and the woman's perception that her life was in danger. Intervention and help-seeking on the part of the woman include talking about the violence to friends, neighbors, family members, doctors, clergy, social service agencies, and the police, as well as physically leaving the situation, either temporarily or permanently.

Response Rate

The response rate to this survey, based on 19,300 eligible households contacted, was 63.7%. Nonresponse occurred for a variety of reasons, including refusals, language difficulties, and unavailability of the woman selected for the interview. Most nonresponses occurred before a respondent was selected. In households in which a respondent was contacted (13,500), 91% agreed to be interviewed.

Random selection helps ensure that those who respond are statistically representative and that the results can be generalized to the population at large. Responses were weighted to reflect the sex and age structure of the sampling areas based on census projections. National estimates are expected to be within 1.2% of the true population at the 95% confidence interval. Estimates of subgroups of the population will have wider confidence intervals.

The Prevalence of Violence Against Women

An advantage of random sample surveys, such as the VAWS, is that by interviewing a relatively small sample, the responses can be weighted to represent all women in the general population, within a measurable range of reliability. The responses of the 12,300 women who participated in this survey were each given a weighting factor that represents other women in that geographic region who were not interviewed. The survey findings presented in this section represent the approximately 10.5 million women 18 years of age and over living in Canada in 1993 and the 9.06 million women who had ever been married or lived with a man in a common-law relationship.

Both one-year and adult lifetime rates of violence (since age 16) can be estimated from this survey. The decision to expand the focus of the survey to include all experiences in adulthood was based in part on the problematic "victim/nonvictim" distinction utilized in most surveys of this nature and in part on the need to learn more about the long-range decisions women make to use shelters and other services, to report to the police, to leave and to return to violent partners, to

Table 2.1. Type of Violence Reported by Canadian Women 18 Years of Age and Over

	Number in Millions	*Percentage*
Total Canadian women	10.5	100
Total women victimized	5.38	51
Total sexual assault	4.09	39
Unwanted sexual touching	2.62	25
Violent sexual attack (nonspousal)	2.13	20
Sexual attack by spouses	.73	8[a]
Total physical assault	3.58	34
Nonspousal assault	1.77	17
Assaults by spouses	2.65	29[a]

SOURCE: Violence Against Women Survey, Statistics Canada, 1993. Used with permission of the Minister of Industry.
NOTE: Figures may not add to totals because of multiple response.
a. Based on the number of women who have ever been married or lived with a man in a common-law relationship.

terminate the marriage, as well as their satisfaction with the criminal justice system and other services. These important issues cannot be addressed within the scope of a one-year snapshot. On the other hand, one-year rates are necessary for risk analysis and for an assessment of the number of women affected by violence within a current time period.

Table 2.1 shows the estimated number and the percentage of Canadian women who have experienced various types of violence since the age of 16. Half of all women have had one of these experiences, and 10% have had one experience during the year prior to the survey. Sexual violence is more common than physical assault in situations outside marriage. Within marital relationships, physical assaults are more common.

Consistent with previous research, this survey shows that women are more vulnerable to attack by men they know than by strangers. It should be noted that the terms *marital relationships* and *ever-married women* throughout this text refer to both common-law and legally registered marriages. Accordingly, 29% of ever-married women have been assaulted by a spouse, 16% of all women by a date or boyfriend, and 23% by other men known to them (Table 2.2). Taken together, this amounts to 45% of women who have been victimized by men they know compared to 23% by a stranger.

As illustrated in Table 2.3, the most common forms of violence inflicted on women by marital partners were pushing, grabbing, and shoving, followed by threats, slapping, throwing something that could

Table 2.2. Relationship of Perpetrator in Acts of Violence Against Women

Relationship	Number in Millions	Percentage
Total Canadian women	10.5	100
Total women victimized	5.38	51
Date/boyfriend	1.72	16
Spouse or ex-spouse	2.65	29[a]
Other known man	2.46	23
Stranger	2.46	23

SOURCE: Violence Against Women Survey, Statistics Canada, 1993. Used with permission of the Minister of Industry.
NOTE: Figures may not add to totals because of multiple response.
a. Based on the number of women who have ever been married or lived with a man in a common-law relationship.

hurt her, kicking, biting, and hitting with fists. Although the percentage of women who have been beaten up, choked, sexually assaulted, or had a gun or knife used against them is less than 10% in each of these categories, between 400,000 and 800,000 Canadian women have been affected.

Overall, rates of violence in previous unions were significantly higher than in intact unions: 48% in past unions compared to 15% in marriages that were current at the time of the interview. This emphasizes the importance of including all of women's experiences, not just those that happened in the previous year or the current marriage, to be able to understand the range of events, the impact on victims, and the decisions they make to respond to the situation, including terminating the relationship. Some of the most serious battering relationships eventually end, but the consequences for the women involved are no less important for contributing to our knowledge about the dynamics of these events and the choices that women make.

Figures 2.1 and 2.2 graphically illustrate the important contribution of specialized victimization surveys to research in this area. These graphs show the differences in the number of women who reported these experiences to the Violence Against Women Survey, Statistics Canada's General Social Survey, and the police in 1993. Over the 12-month period preceding the interview, an estimated 572,000 women experienced at least one incident of sexual assault, and 201,000 women experienced violence by a spouse. The specialized survey of violence against women captures almost twice as many incidents as the traditional crime-victim survey, four times as many cases of wife assault as are reported to the police, and about *38 times*

Table 2.3. Number and Percentage of Ever-Married Women 18 Years and Over Who Reported Violence by a Marital Partner[a] by Type of Assault

Type of Assault	Number in Millions	All Marital Partners (%)	Current Partner (%)	Previous Partner (%)
Total ever-married women[a]	9.06	100	100	100
Total victims of wife assault[a]	2.65	29	15	48
1. Threatened to hit her with his fist or anything else that could hurt her	1.69	19	7	35
2. Threw something at her that could hurt her	1.02	11	4	21
3. Pushed, grabbed, or shoved her	2.22	25	12	40
4. Slapped her	1.36	15	4	30
5. Kicked, bit, or hit her with his fist	.96	11	2	22
6. Hit her with something that could hurt her	.51	6	1	12
7. Beat her up	.79	9	1	19
8. Choked her	.61	7	1	14
9. Threatened to or used a gun or knife on her	.42	5	1	10
10. Forced her into any sexual activity when she did not want to by threatening her, holding her down, or hurting her in some way	.73	8	2	17

SOURCE: Violence Against Women Survey, Statistics Canada, 1993. Used with permission of the Minister of Industry.
NOTE: Figures do not add to totals because of multiple response.
a. Includes common-law partners.

as many cases of sexual assault as police statistics. These GSS figures are the result of improved question wording modeled on the Violence Against Women Survey, but still embedded in the traditional format of asking about a wide variety of crimes and conducted without special training for interviewers or support for respondents. This graphically illustrates the extent to which victim-type surveys more completely represent the population of assaulted women than police records do and how a dedicated survey can be even more comprehensive.

The divergent approaches used by the Canadian survey and those of the CTS reflect differences in theory, definition, context, and research paradigm. In the Violence Against Women Survey, the social meanings of sexual assault and violence against wives are placed within the larger social context of relatively minor forms of abuse,

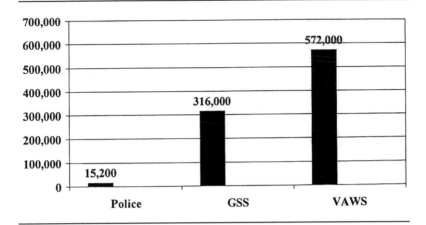

Figure 2.1. Number of Sexual Assaults Against Women in 1993 Recorded by Police, the General Social Survey, and the Violence Against Women Survey
SOURCE: *Violence Against Women Survey: Public-Use Microdata File Documentation and User's Guide.* (1993). Ottawa, Ontario: Statistics Canada, Ministry of Supply and Services. Used with permission.

such as sexual harassment and controlling behavior by spouses. It is important to include these noncriminal acts in order to address as far as possible the full range of acts that women find frightening and offensive, up to and including those that cause psychic distress and physical injury. This structuring of the survey instrument is founded on the assumptions that this range of acts is similar in form and consequence, that the cultural and societal preconditions for these events are similar, and that assaults on wives by their husbands are more similar, theoretically and in form and substance, to sexual assault and sexual harassment than to other forms of violence in the family. Sexual assault and assaults on wives cannot be understood outside the broader social context in which they occur, and the approach used in the Violence Against Women Survey aims to provide some context.

Test of a Theory of Assaults on Wives

Random sample surveys are advantageous tools for social science researchers because they allow comparisons to be drawn from the life situations and personal characteristics of people who have experienced certain events and those who have not. This allows researchers to test the applicability of certain theories and to identify segments of the population at highest risk of these events. The results can help

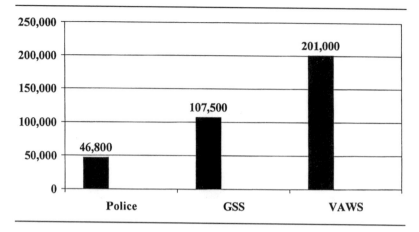

Figure 2.2. Number of Assaults on Wives in 1993 Recorded by Police, the General Social Survey, and the Violence Against Women Survey
SOURCE: *Violence Against Women Survey: Public-Use Microdata File Documentation and User's Guide.* (1993). Ottawa, Ontario: Statistics Canada, Ministry of Supply and Services. Used with permission.

suggest interventions that might reduce rates of violence for particular groups and determine important warning signs or points of intervention that might help prevent violence or help avert an escalation. One-year rates of violence are useful here to draw an accurate depiction of current life circumstances for those personal characteristics and variables that change over time (such as respondents' age, education, income, and type and duration of the union).

One type of theory gaining prominence in the study of wife assault is that of social control (Fagan, 1993b). (For a test of this and other theories, see the special edition of the *Canadian Journal of Criminology, 37,* 1995.) Traditional social control theory emphasizes the strength of the offender's bond to society, predicting that integrated individuals with strong social ties to conventional others and conventional pursuits will be less inclined to break the rules than those whose ties are weak (Hirschi, 1969). Police, courts, and other authorities represent formal social control, but informal mechanisms, such as family and friends, schools, and communities, play a more salient role in monitoring crime and deviance because of their prevalence and their relevance to the lives of individuals (Horwitz, 1990).

Recent work by anthropologists has broadened notions of social control to consider social embeddedness and isolation by female victims as well as by offenders. Those who have studied domestic violence have observed that in primitive and developing cultures around the world, the level of wife battering varies according to the level of support that victims and batterers are able to generate within their social networks (Counts, Brown, & Campbell, 1992; Levinson, 1989). The most vulnerable wife is one who stands alone against a husband who has extensive support from others in the social network. Least vulnerable is the woman who manages to generate sufficient support from people in her network who are willing and able to come to her defense and censure her husband's actions (Baumgartner, 1993).

The results of the Violence Against Women Survey add support to this theory. The occurrence of wife assault is linked very strongly to factors associated with weak levels of social control and embeddedness. These include differential levels of isolation from community and potential avenues of support and intervention, attachment, and commitment to conventional others and conventional pursuits (stake in conformity), and norms and beliefs supportive of violence against wives. This survey finds very robust relationships between the occurrence of violence against wives and many of the variables tested (Johnson, 1998).

Isolation

Isolation is a function of weak social bonding that reduces the extent to which both victims of assault and violent partners are able to sustain attachments to friendship and community networks and receive social support to end the violence. Social and physical isolation is a characteristic of many violent marriages. One way for a batterer to assert dominance and control over all aspects of the woman's life is to keep her isolated and dependent on his demands. Violent men often isolate their victims from family and friends and prevent them from working outside the home (at the same time becoming extremely demanding and critical about his expectations concerning domestic work), going to school, or associating with anyone outside the immediate family. In some cases, fear and shame of detection lead battered women to voluntarily withdraw from social and family interactions as their injuries become progressively worse.

Questions relating to isolation are the following: How isolated or removed are the woman and the man from other people who might challenge his behavior and provide support for her? How many interventions (formal or informal) can the woman rally to her defense?

The following isolation variables were assessed for their significance in predicting violence against wives:

- Employment status of the man
- Employment status of the woman
- Living in a common-law relationship
- Children in the household
- Other adults living in the household
- Intentional efforts on the part of the man to isolate the woman
- Attempts to limit her autonomy by prohibiting access to the family income

Among these predictors (based on zero = order odds ratios and a significance level of $p < .01$, unless otherwise stated), all were significant predictors of assaults on wives, with the exception of children living in the household. Although the presence of other adults is assumed to deter violence (Gelles & Straus, 1988), this variable was associated with increased odds of violence ($p < .1$). On closer examination of the data, most women who reported other adults living in the household were disproportionately cohabiting women under 25 years of age. A household of young adults living together is unlikely to be extended family members. Rather, they are just as likely to be young friends and supporters of the violent male who perceive little personal gain, and perhaps much personal risk, in intervening on the woman's behalf.

In the sense of isolation and connections to community and family, the presence of children would tend to predict increased community participation and strengthened social networks. Children tend to connect parents to schools, teachers, and neighbors and to expose the family to broader social networks, which increases the potential for support. But the presence of children also complicates the woman's ability to leave a violent marriage or threaten divorce, particularly if she is economically dependent on the abuser or if she places a priority on keeping the family together.

Among the remaining isolation variables, those with the strongest predictive power were living in a common-law relationship and intentional efforts on the part of the man to isolate the woman and limit her autonomy. The latter were assessed through three statements against which respondents rated their spouse with a "yes/no" response:

"He tries to limit your contacts with family and friends."

"He prevents you from knowing about or having access to the family income, even if you ask."

"He insists on knowing who you are with and where you are at all times."

The first statement was a stronger predictor of violence than any of the other isolation variables, followed by the second statement, then the third.

Next in predictive power were periods of male unemployment and unemployment by the female victim. Unemployment was measured by Statistics Canada's standard unemployment question: "During the past 12 months, were you ever without a job *and* looking for work?" Long-term unemployment on the part of male partners was the most important of all the employment variables.

Theoretically, working outside the home can have both positive and negative effects for women. Paid employment serves an important function because it decreases isolation and may expose the woman to opinions and norms about wife assault that conflict with the dominant norms in her home (Eckberg, 1995). Employment also provides a certain degree of economic independence that can help break down isolation and present the possibility of escape. But employment and earned income are sources of power for women, and this can be threatening to a domineering and controlling man, especially if he is periodically unemployed or feels himself to be underemployed relative to his training or aspirations. Refusing to allow the woman to work is one tactic in restoring the power balance in his favor; violence is another.

Employment for men may have a similar effect of exposing them to people who may challenge their perceived right to assault their wives. On the other hand, paid employment may expose these men to like-minded peers who support and encourage male domination and violence against wives. Unemployment can have a more profound effect on men because their status and identity are more closely tied to the breadwinner role. Lack of paid work can cause financial insecurity as well as insecurity about his ability to fulfill the dominant role of the head of the household. If status is at stake in one arena of the man's life, there may be attempts to reinstate it at home through physically abusing his wife. Unemployment cuts women off from potential attachments to colleagues and diverse opinions and may also contribute to stress in low-income families.

If isolation is low and the family is well connected to the community through work, family, and community networks, a potentially violent man is under surveillance. There will be guardians and supporters of the couple and their children who are available to provide sanctions for him and sanctuaries for her (Counts et al., 1992). A feature of modern Western society that mitigates against connections to community and other informal controls and enhances isolation is common-law marriage. This was found to be a strong predictor of violence against wives.

Cohabitants differ from registered married couples in ways that are important for predicting assaults on wives. Both men and women in cohabiting couples are much younger, on the average, and men are more likely than married men to experience periods of unemployment and more likely to experience the stresses associated with low or unstable family income. Young men, and especially young men with poor employment prospects, may have less of a "stake in conformity" and less to lose in terms of a tarnished reputation if they abuse their partners, because they will not feel the effects of social disapproval (DeKeseredy, 1989). Married men have a greater stake in conformity and more to lose in terms of reputation and therefore may be more likely to be deterred from abusing their partners by the threat of social disapproval and legal action. Cohabitants are also more likely to be childless and therefore have fewer connections to schools and the community.

Because of the relative youth of the partners, available leisure time, and the temporary or insecure nature of some common-law relationships, the attentions of other young males toward the woman may be more likely to be perceived as a threat. In fact, one or both partners may be more likely than married partners to be on the lookout for alternatives (Daly & Wilson, 1988b). This can lead to feelings of jealousy and conflict over how free time will be spent, resulting in intentional isolation on the part of the male partner (Daly & Wilson, 1988b; Ellis, 1989).

In the eyes of many common-law couples (and others), they are not bound to the norms that govern marriage to the same degree as are married couples. In the absence of a formal wedding ceremony, in-laws and extended family members of cohabiting couples may not feel they have the same right to be involved or to legitimately influence the couple. The couple also may not feel compelled to live up to the expectations of in-laws and extended family. If the young couple is living together despite disapproval from parents and other family members, they may be quite isolated from potential sources of family support in times of trouble. A state-sanctioned union brings two families, and the extensions of these families, together. In common-law unions, the families are not brought together, either symbolically or in reality.

The couple's isolation may be exemplified by the response of others to the woman when she calls on them for help. If a woman living in a common-law relationship calls the police for protection, they may regard the woman as amoral for living with a man outside marriage and may be less inclined to provide her with assistance. Low income, combined with common-law marital status, may cause others to perceive her as unworthy of protection. When the woman finds no support available from the police or other people to whom she turns, there is little to dissuade the abusive man of the moral rightness of his position (DeKeseredy, 1989).

Attachment and Commitment

The element of attachment assumes that people who have valued attachments to significant others in their lives, such as friends, parents, and other family members, and are sensitive to the opinions of these people will try to avoid incurring disapproval by abiding by the law. Similarly, the greater the commitment to conventional goals and pursuits, such as higher education, building a career, and raising a family, the greater is the man's concern with status and reputation, which might be spoiled by assaulting his wife. The following attachment and commitment variables were assessed for their significance in predicting violence against wives:

- Man's age
- Woman's age
- Man's employment status
- Man's education
- Woman's education
- Family income
- Duration of the relationship

Social control theory predicts that bonds to conventional society and concern about reputation are strengthened throughout adulthood, which brings with it job stability and commitment to work, higher education, and higher income (Sampson & Laub, 1990). The duration of the relationship signifies attachment and commitment to the marriage and is also strongly related to age. It was predicted that the incidence of assaults on wives would be affected by these attachment and commitment variables.

The majority of these predictions were true. The odds of assaults on wives were highest for men and women 18-24 years of age and declined with age and were highest for marriages of less than 3 years' duration. Age and duration of the union are also highly correlated with living in a common-law relationship, which was previously shown to be an important predictor of wife assault. The man's education is inversely related to the use of violence as is household income. (As education and income increase, the odds of assault decrease.) As discussed above, periods of male unemployment also increase the odds of assault on wives. The woman's education was the only one of the attachment and commitment variables that was not a significant predictor of spousal assault.

Norms and Beliefs Supportive of Violence Against Wives

Social control theory assumes the existence of a common value system in society to which most members subscribe and that is eventually internalized into a belief system by the majority of societal members. This can be assumed to be true for most forms of crime and deviance, but the existence of a common belief system regarding violence against women is questionable. As Williams and his colleagues point out, there is sufficient normative ambiguity about assaults on wives that a clear moral consensus does not, in fact, exist (Lackey & Williams, 1995; Williams & Hawkins, 1989). This ambiguity arises because striking a family member is seen by many people as acceptable under certain conditions. This normative ambiguity permits people to suspend the moral belief that violence is wrong and neutralizes the harm of the act.

In society, there is a diversity of objects available for forming attachments and commitment, and some may not be effective for reducing deviance. In fact, some may have the opposite effect if attachment, involvement, and commitment are strengthened in a network that endorses male dominance values. Societal values have not consistently denounced assaults on wives but, in fact, throughout history, have upheld men's rights to subjugate their wives by force. Groups and individuals that uphold the right of men to assault their wives with impunity are available in a wide variety of male social networks. A strong social bond in these circumstances can serve to increase, not reduce, the likelihood of violence.

The following variables related to norms and beliefs were assessed for their significance in predicting violence against wives:

- The man witnessed wife assault as a child
- The woman witnessed wife assault as a child
- Sexual jealousy on the part of the man
- Degrading name-calling on the part of the man

There is considerable evidence that witnessing assaults on one's mother in childhood puts boys at risk of adopting similar techniques as an adult and increases the risk of victimization for girls; this relationship is stronger for boys than for girls (Fagan, Stewart, & Hansen, 1983; Hotaling & Sugarman, 1986; Johnson, 1996). This is typically interpreted thus: Boys who witness battering are learning a powerful message about the rights of husbands to demand conformity and obedience from their wives and to use violence to achieve it. These boys also learn that violence is the basis of power and control in families and that women have fewer rights and less value than men. Girls see that their mothers are powerless to stop the violence and may transfer these perceptions to their adult relationships.

Sexual jealousy stems from the belief that men have rights of exclusive ownership over their intimate partners and the right to expect complete obedience. This was measured in this survey by "yes/no" responses on the part of the female respondent to the statement: "He is jealous and doesn't want you to talk to other men." Degrading treatment against female partners is another tactic that often accompanies violence, which serves to undermine the woman's perceptions of her rights and value and her capabilities as a person, increasing her dependence on him and his assessment of the situation. This was measured by responses to the statement: "He calls you names to put you down or make you feel bad."

These variables related to norms and beliefs supportive of violence against wives were highly correlated with assaultive behavior. Exposure to wife assault in childhood was an important predictor for both men and women but was stronger for men than for women. The odds of committing an assault on their wives were highest for men who degrade their wives through name-calling and jealously guarding her contacts with other men. In fact, put-downs and name-calling were the strongest predictors of all of the social control variables tested and remained so when the effects of all of the others were held constant.

Summary

This chapter has presented alternative ways of thinking about survey research in the sensitive areas of sexual violence and assaults on wives and described one innovative survey that addresses male violence against women in Canada. The utility of the results for broadening our understanding of violence in marital relationships was demonstrated through a test of a popular criminological theory. The results show that sexual violence and assaults on wives affect large numbers of Canadian women and that wife assault is linked in many ways to social embeddedness and isolation of female victims and abusers.

The experience of Statistics Canada illustrates that creative thinking, together with broad-based community involvement, results in greater confidence and participation of respondents, improved reliability of results, and a wealth of statistical information to enhance policy and programming for women and abusers. Naturally, there are limits to what a statistical survey can accomplish. For example, statistics cannot capture the nuances and subtleties of human interactions and cannot describe complex social processes. Surveys like these cannot describe the wider historical, cultural, or institutional context in which these events occur. Statistics cannot be understood outside the actual experience of individuals and their perceptions of events. Ethnographic and qualitative studies are needed for real-life accounts of violent events. Qualitative data are essential for understanding decisions to leave and return to violent spouses; motives, intentions, processes, and interpretations of events; how the violence and the relationship changes over time; and what are men's motives for stopping their violence when they do (Dobash & Dobash, 1979, 1990a).

These two forms of acquiring knowledge—statistical surveys and qualitative studies—are complementary, and both are necessary for our understanding of these events. Women's accounts of their own experiences add richness and texture to purely statistical descriptions of prevalence and incidence, and detailed statistical information adds complexity in other ways. When combined, they can have enormous benefits to battered women and those at risk of violence. Researchers, both qualitative and quantitative, must continue to strive for improvements to the question wording, content, and approach of their work, always mindful of the sensitivity of what they are doing and the potential for danger and trauma to respondents if handled carelessly or inappropriately.

3

Sexual Violence Against Women and Girls

An Approach to an International Overview

Liz Kelly and Jill Radford

Most contemporary feminist movements internationally have focused on rape for three reasons. First, sexual assault is one of the ugliest and most brutal expressions of masculine violence toward women. Second, rape and the historical "discourse" around it reveal a great deal about the social relations of reproduction. Third, rape reveals a great deal about the way in which the woman's body is seen as representing the community (Kumar, 1993, p. 128).

In the late 1960s and early 1970s, rape was one of the earliest organizing focuses for women's liberation movements in the United States, the United Kingdom, India, and many other countries. Sexual violence and sexuality have subsequently become central concepts in feminist theory, and women throughout the world have organized in a variety of ways to highlight, respond to, and campaign against the sexual victimization of women and girls. Within this global concern, reflected in successful attempts to have violence against women formally recognized by the United Nations as a violation of human rights, are issues of similarity and difference—similarity in some of the forms of sexual violence and in the fact that women and girls are disproportionately its targets and men overwhelmingly its perpetrators; difference in the geographical distribution of some forms and whether and how they are legitimized through law and culture; similarity in the ways that women and girls are accorded responsibility for the behavior of men and boys; difference in the precise ways in which this is articulated and the social and personal consequences of sexual victimization; similarity in the ways in which social responses through law, rules, and institutions construct some women and girls as "deserving victims"; difference in whether and how this has been challenged. The similarities and differences become even more complex when variations between women within and between societies are acknowledged. No single paper can do justice to this complexity.

Our twin goals are to draw attention to the burgeoning literature (there are now seven specialist journals and two regular abstract listings addressing these issues) and to explore some critical tensions and debates. We attempt to integrate discussion of various forms of sexual violence, rather than reproduce artificial analytic separations, within eight thematic headings: the emergence of issues; definitions; explanation; offenders; impacts and consequences; institutional and social responses; and finally, from normalization to resistance.

Emergence and Development of Issues

Much of the research, commentary, intervention, and reform strategies to date have emerged in relation to specific forms of sexual violence and separations rather than connections that have been the order of the day. Thus, methodological and conceptual innovation in research, insights developed through practice, and attempts to create change seldom cross over from one field to another. There are many international, national, and local "histories" for each form of sexual violence, yet only a few have been documented (see Matthews [1994] on rape crisis centers in Los Angeles; Breckenridge & Carmody [1992] on Australian responses to rape and child sexual assault; Kapur [1994] on Indian feminist legal strategies against sexual violence). Does it matter whether a particular issue is the "first" form of violence against women to be raised within a society, if it is raised by women's groups or professionals, and/or if it has high-profile funding for services and/or research? These and many other questions can only be answered through wide-ranging comparative studies.

Alongside these local histories is the fact that the conditions that enable the creation of particular forms of knowledge and support vary in different societies. Where basic subsistence is fragile, national and regional conflict is extensive, and/or the government is authoritarian, fundamentalist, or militaristic, research programs and forms of intervention deemed essential elsewhere are unlikely to exist. Therefore, knowledge is skewed toward Western countries, particularly the United States. Even here, however, some groups have been disproportionately excluded from most research and services (especially disabled women and girls and those who do not speak or write in English). Currently, the only way to include countries that do not have a tradition of research on sexual violence is to use available sources such as interviews, journalistic reports, and discussion papers. Small entries often tell large stories, such as: Enloe (1994) notes in passing that women textile workers in Guatemala began to unionize in 1991 in response to sexual harassment, and some of the troubles in South African townships in the late 1980s concerned the extent of rape of women and girls by local gangs of young men (Mabaso, 1992).

In Western societies, there is considerable variation in how various forms of sexual violence emerged onto the public agenda. Rape was first addressed through feminist activism, it tended to be understood as a single event, and crisis intervention responses and campaigns for legal reform predominated. Sexual abuse of girls was linked with activist work about rape and concerns of professionals and child welfare organizations (Finkelhor, 1979); the focus has been on repeated events within family contexts, and responses in terms of protection, investigation, and treatment have become increasingly contested (see Campbell, 1988; Myers, 1994). Sexual harassment emerged out of activist concerns and/or trade union work on women's equality and tends to be defined in terms of repeated and cumulative incidents located in the workplace. Responses have been primarily through institutional policy and antidiscrimination provisions. It has become increasingly separated from other forms of woman abuse through its location in personnel and employment frameworks. Female genital mutilation was raised as an issue in the mid-1970s by white Western feminists but was previously and continues to be addressed by African women; its naming and definition (as child/woman abuse, a cultural practice, and/or a health/human rights issue) along with appropriate responses are still contested. It embodies debates about neocolonialism, racism, and cultural relativism, as can be seen in the chapter by Boddy in this volume.

These broader histories are accompanied by varying research focuses and methodologies. The variations are both issue- and country-specific, with North American research giving a much higher significance to quantitative methods than European studies, where the importance of context and meaning remains a core interest (for examples, see chapters by Johnson and by Dobash and Dobash in this volume). The global predominance of the English language means that much significant and innovative research, legal and policy reforms, and support work fail to inform international debate.

Definitions

In exploring the range of forms, locations, and contexts in which sexual violence occurs, we do not propose a single definition of sexual violence, but identify some unresolved problems. Definitions are critical. In general, they affect individual perceptions and the overall view of the issue as well as inform research questions and legal and social responses (see Dobash & Dobash, 1990a, 1990b). Specific definitions of sexual violence constitute arenas of political struggle and underpin much professional and public debate (Kelly, 1988). A number of core issues are involved: (a) what counts as violence—whether definitions should be broad and inclusive or limited and exclusive; (b) who/what is offended against or violated—the woman, the family, group, national honor, and/or men who have proprietary claims over women or girls; and (c) the meaning and consequences of events for those who experience them.

The term *sexual violence* and the similar Scandinavian concept of *sexualized violence* (see Lundgren, 1995b, and Chapter 7, this volume) are contested. "Sexual violence" has been used as a broad conceptualization of male violence or, more narrowly, to refer to assaults and intrusions that have an explicit sexual content. Both approaches have been defended in the literature, the former to highlight both the sexual abusive components of domestic violence and the gendered distribution of offending and victimization and the latter to enable more detailed and accurate documentation of the many forms of woman and child abuse. Where distinctions are made, the fact that these are analytical rather than experiential boundaries needs to be acknowledged; for example, rape is frequently an element in domestic violence and may also occur in the contexts of sexual harassment and trafficking. The danger of emphasizing distinctions is that connections between forms of violence—such as woman and child abuse in families—

as well as the accumulation of individual, lifelong experiences and consequences may be neglected. Concentration on distinctions also tends to reinforce hierarchies of seriousness embodied in legal and other discourses. The concept of a "continuum" of sexual violence was developed to enable differences and connections to be addressed at both experiential and theoretical levels. One definition stresses two meanings of continuum:

> First "a basic common character that underlies many different events"; and second, "a continuous series of elements or events that pass into one another and which cannot readily be distinguished." The first meaning enables us to discuss sexual violence in a generic sense. The basic common character underlying the many different forms of violence is the abuse, intimidation, coercion, intrusion, threat and force men use to control women. The second meaning enables us to document and name the range of abuse, intimidation, coercion, intrusion, threat and force whilst acknowledging that there are no clearly defined and discrete analytic categories into which men's behavior can be placed. (Kelly, 1988, p. 76)

The "more or less" aspect of this continuum relates *only* to prevalence: There are forms of sexual violence that the majority of women experience, often on more than one occasion (sexual harassment broadly defined), other forms that many women experience (sexual assault, rape, domestic violence), and some that a minority of women experience (sexual murder). With the possible exception of murder (femicide), "seriousness" was not imputed to either forms of violence or their location within the continuum; the impacts of victimization were conceptualized as the outcome of a complex amalgam of factors at the time and over time. There are, however, other definitions of continuum and, indeed, different interpretations of this conceptualization. For example, Leidig (1992) proposes a range from "brief annoying contact" to "brutal incidents," with sexual assault of children being defined as the most serious. It remains a matter of contention whether prostitution and pornography should be included as forms of woman abuse, although more consensus exists in relation to trafficking and sex tourism, and all are considered forms of abuse where children are involved. That women working in the sex industry, especially when this involves "street work," are extraordinarily vulnerable to sexual and physical assault has been increasingly documented (Hatty, 1989; Hoigard & Finstad, 1992).

The central problem in defining sexual violence is that with the exception of female genital mutilation (and even here there are three different variations—see Boddy this volume), each form includes a range of acts/behaviors that are not mutually exclusive. Sexual harassment encompasses visual, verbal, and physical forms of assault and, in some instances, rape. Rape has a variety of forms and contexts, and sexual abuse of girls combines what is covered in rape, sexual assault, and sexual harassment. One potential route out of this confusion is to specify boundaries in terms of age and context. Thus, child sexual abuse is what occurs before adulthood; but this in turn requires a consensus about the boundary between child and adult. Various ages from 15 onward have been used. The United Nations has defined it as 18, but this counters ages of heterosexual consent and legal codes in many countries, and child marriage represents a particular conceptual dilemma. Of course, the age selected has consequences for estimates of prevalence. Similarly, limiting sexual harassment to employment contexts means that many acts occurring in the public sphere—what Germaine Greer (1971) termed *little rapes* and what is legislated against in India as "eve-teasing"—that is, words, signs, gestures, and molestation prohibited in public places and defined as nonbailable crimes—disappear from view. Finally, the location of flashing and obscene phone calls—in our view best conceptualized as forms of sexual harassment—also becomes perplexing.

Rape, sexual assault, and harassment of women and girls can be committed in a wide range of relationships and locations. Abuse can be perpetrated by family members, current and former sexual partners, other relatives and friends, acquaintances (including colleagues and clients), those in a variety of authority relations (including bosses, doctors, therapists, caregivers, religious leaders, teachers, police, military, institutional staff), and strangers. Sexual assaults most commonly involve one assailant, although multiple offenders are not uncommon. The ages of offenders and victims may be similar or vastly different, and many combinations of race, ethnicity, class, status, and sexual orientation may also occur. Whereas virtually any space can be a site for abuse, some represent risk based on potent combinations of gender power and other power/authority relations, such as prison/police cells and residential facilities for women/girls. The many possible combinations of location and relationship mean that sexual violence can be in private or public locations and may be opportunistic or organized and, in some instances, "ritualized" (see Lundgren, this volume). These varying settings and the combinations of relationships that form the context of sexual violence could be usefully studied in greater detail. The forms/categories of rape we have discovered so far illustrate the way that contextual elements are used in definitions, with most drawing on relationship variables, including marital rape, familial/ incestuous rape, acquaintance/date rape, stranger rape, gang rape, rape by an authority figure, landlord rape, caste rape, custodial rape, rape of prostitutes, rape of minors, and war rape.

Context could also be fruitfully explored in terms of the female life cycle. Sexual violence is possible at each stage, but changing relationships and everyday locations produce different probabilities. For example, in childhood, the contexts of family, peer relationships, education, play and recreation, and religion are central. (In some societies, child labor and living on the streets are also significant.) In adolescence, heterosexual courtship, paid employment, and public space exploration are added, and in adulthood, marriage and paid work become more salient, along with migration and travel. For elderly women in developed counties, relationships with caregivers and institutions are an important context, and this is an issue throughout for disabled girls and women and girls who are not living with parents/kin. This range and variation are seldom reflected in the definitions and meanings that are encoded in dominant discourses, including religion/cultural belief systems, the law, literature (including myths and legends), medicine, and media reporting and representation.

Feminist challenges to limited definitions have involved two potentially contradictory approaches to naming: to create collective nouns describing a wide range of experiences, most commonly "rape" and "incest" and to develop and create terms and descriptive typologies that focus on elements of difference. There is currently no consensus about an overall definition or how to build an inclusive typology.

Sexual harassment is a useful example. It tends to be discussed primarily in terms of employment contexts and authority relations. There are a number of problems with this definition: (a) a high proportion of harassment is by men who are women's peers or when the woman occupies a position of authority (women doctors and nurses harassed by male patients, women teachers harassed by male students); (b) for some women, their workplace is their (and more important, their employer's) home (e.g., domestic service); and (c) forms of harassment that occur outside employment are generally excluded in terms of redress.

The location of sexual harassment as an employment issue was cemented by MacKinnon's groundbreaking work (1979), which defined it as a form of sex discrimination. Even when a broader definition exists, growth of concern about sexual harassment is nonetheless attributed to the increased entry of women into paid employment. Even within studies on sexual harassment in employment, few have addressed the ways in which constructions of gender, heterosexuality, and paid work create contexts in which women are routinely sexualized, an exception being Adkins' (1995) study of women in the British tourist industry. Thus, the way of responding to an issue has a major influence on how it is defined. Although it may be the case that the increased entry of women into paid work creates a context in which men use sexual behavior as a form of gendered power, studies focusing on other contexts have revealed that terms other than sexual harassment also exist: for example, "bundles" in British schools, "eve-teasing" for street harassment in India, and "punch" in Tanzanian universities. It is, of course, possible that a particular construction of sexual harassment can create a legitimacy of complaint that enables naming and resistance. Overall, this uncertainty of definition has theoretical consequences, resulting in confusion as to whether sexual harassment is an issue concerning women's access to public space, employment rights, or control over one's own body and personal integrity. Each of these infers slightly different approaches to sexual harassment.

Explicit and unresolved debates about definitions of sexual harassment reflect three current concerns: how sexual harassment is conceptualized, the lack of correspondence between women's reports of actual behavior and the attribution of sexual harassment, and how to handle differences of definition between women (see Chapter 4, this volume, for an illustration of differing definitions between women). The construction of typologies of sexual harassment is debated in the literature, with distinctions drawn between forms of behavior and levels of intrusiveness. Gruber (1992) points to inadequacy in defining research categories, which are often neither mutually exclusive nor exhaustive, and some forms that have legal and policy relevance are frequently excluded. He is also critical of the reliance on survey methods and research instruments that exclude context, particularly the overall workplace environment. Many of the U.S. surveys use instruments that have much in common with the Conflict Tactics Scale used frequently in domestic violence research, listing forms of behavior abstracted from context and meaning (for a critique, see Dobash & Dobash, 1992, and their chapter in this volume). Fitzgerald and Hesson-McInnis (1989) also note the limited amount of conceptualization in many studies using checklists of behaviors that are not theorized. She proposes three areas: gender harassment, sexual coercion, and sexual harassment, arguing that the issue is not of one of severity but of the nature of interaction and type of behavior.

Consistently, in studies, far more women report experiencing specific behaviors than define themselves as having been sexually harassed (see Ellis, Barak, & Pinto, 1991). This has also been evident in some research on rape and sexual abuse (Kelly, Regan, & Burton, 1991; Koss & Oros, 1982), but it has not been as consistent a focus, and the meaning and consequences of this apparent paradox have not been broadly addressed. This puzzle about sexual harassment may reflect the notion that there are some contexts in which sexual harassment is normalized and also that naming oneself as someone who has been victimized may encompass significant costs that women attempt to limit or escape by avoiding the label. Several studies have noted that naming and reporting sexual harassment were seen by most women as worsening the situation (see later section on normalization and resistance). Similar findings have been noted in research on rape, particularly the work of Koss (1988a) in a U.S. study of 6,159 U.S. college students—when an analytic definition of rape was based on a composite of legal codes, only 27% of women whose experiences fitted the research definition named their own experience as rape. The study was replicated on a smaller scale by Gavey (1991) in New Zealand with very similar findings with regard to victimization and self-definition.

Another unresolved issue is how to define those who are victimized: as victims, survivors, or neither. Kelly, Burton, and Regan (1996) question the separation between victimization and survival. It results in the neglect of coping and survival strategies at the time of assaults and immediately afterward; it fails to recognize survival as a minimal goal; and it suggests a necessary complete resolution in order to "qualify" as a survivor, which fails to address the variation in the impacts and consequences of sexual violence for individuals. They argue that, over the long term, neither "victim" nor "survivor" is helpful as a core identity.

Definitions are not static, with changes reflecting levels of social awareness and action. The purpose of naming sexual violence was to give it social recognition, and some of the strategies used to dramatize and draw attention to a hidden and neglected issue have had a series of unintended and unanticipated consequences. Debates about definitions are struggles about meaning and conceptualization. They are ongoing and not resolvable either through forms of words or experiential knowledge. Kitzinger (1994) notes that new social problems are always contested because they constitute an opportunity to challenge taken-for-granted meanings and definitions. She also outlines the most common strategies that are marshaled to resist challenges to accepted obligations: "the frequency game"—if it is rare, then it is not a serious problem and if it is common, then it is normal rather than problematic; victim blaming; reference to unwarranted incursions of the state into private life; reversals—such as an overemphasis on abuse by women; and boundary disputes. All of these occur in response to attempts to extend definitions of what constitutes sexual violence. Indeed, as discussed in the introduction to this volume, boundary disputes also occur among academics engaged in rethinking the general area of violence against women.

Debates about definitions have influenced the design of research methodology, and prevalence studies are increasingly sophisticated (see Johnson, this volume), but there are still a number of areas that bear further reflection and study.

A significant proportion of reported rape cases involve more than one assailant—Gidycz and Koss (1990) report as much as one third in some U.S. police rape statistics—yet few studies address this directly. There is a similar lack of research regarding sexual abuse rings (exceptions being Burgess, Groth, & McCausland [1981]; Gallagher, Hughes, & Parker [1994]; and Wild [1989]). Gidycz and Koss compare group and individual assaults from within a larger survey (44 of each). Group assaults were more violent, involved more resistance by the woman, and were more likely to result in a formal report and/or the seeking of support. Interestingly, group assaults were more likely to be committed by both strangers *and* relations. Reeves Sanday's (1990) study of fraternity gang rape focuses on a particularly American phenomena.

There are some attempts to examine how gender, class, and race interact (see Neibuhr & Boyles [1991] on sexual harassment; Wyatt & Powell [1988] on sexual abuse and sexual assault), and some larger-scale studies challenge the presumption that black women do not report sexual victimization. Russell (1984) and Wyatt and Powell (1988) show higher reporting rates among African American women than white women, but we still lack studies that elucidate the legacies of colonialism and attempt to unpick the sexual organization of racism. In another context, Vogelman and Eagle (1991) argue that statistics for reported rape and sexual assault in South Africa are some of the highest in the world (19,368 recorded rapes in 1988, currently 20 to 30 cases are reported each weekend in Soweto). The explanation they propose involves interacting power imbalances, leading black men to focus on the one arena where they can assert power: over women and girls. A culture emerges in which violence against women becomes deeply entrenched and is accepted rather than challenged.

The one study on harassment of lesbians is based on a volunteer sample of 400 U.S. lesbians, using questionnaires and some follow-up interviews (84% reported harassment at some point, and two thirds reported an incident in the past year). Few formal reports were made. White women reported more verbal harassment; women of color reported more threatened actual violence and rape (Von Schulthess, 1992). There are also unresolved difficulties in research and practice regarding disabled women and girls. Elvik et al. (1990) report on a study of 35 women with disabilities in which none was able to provide a "sexual history" and abuse was suspected for over one third (see also McCarthy, 1996). Whether disabled women and girls are differentially targeted by abusers remains a critical question.

Power and Male Domination

Both definitions and prevalence estimates influence what requires explanation. If sexual violence is defined narrowly and is therefore relatively rare, it is the exceptional that requires explanation. If, on the other hand, it is defined more broadly and is a common experience in the lives of women and girls, then the opposite prevails:

> That sexual violence is so pervasive supports the view that the locus of violence rests squarely in the middle of what our culture defines as "normal" interaction between men and women. (Johnson, 1988, p. 146)

There are different explanations for particular forms of sexual violence at particular points in time, but we shall focus on power and male domination. Although this framework holds in common several key concepts, there are nonetheless a number of linked but different variations. The common thread is an explicit emphasis on gender and an understanding of power as socially produced. We have identified the following variations:

- Sexual violence as the outcome of women's inferior status (Reeves Sanday, 1981; West, 1987).

- Sex and sexuality as an arena of power that is used to create and maintain male dominance (MacKinnon, 1989).
- Heterosexuality: A number of theorists have located sexual violence within a critical analysis of heterosexuality; here, heterosexuality is defined as an institution that requires reinforcement and at times is enforced (Adkins, 1995; Rich, 1980).
- Construction of masculinity, particularly exploring the individual and social determinants that support aggressive masculinity (Enloe, 1994; Reeves Sanday, 1990).

A number of issues remain undertheorized and underresearched, in particular, how differences between women themselves articulate with gender relations. One example is the concept of racial sexual assault (Hall, 1985), developed to encompass assaults in which gender and race elements are combined. Another is whether there is a cross-cultural valuation of younger women/girls and privileged sexual access to them for high-status men (fathers, religious leaders, chiefs, employers of servants, slave owners, rich Western tourists) (for a discussion, see Wilson and Daly in this volume). Here the relations of gender, age, status, and wealth may produce potent constellations of power. Recent revelations about "war rape" have raised questions about how relationships between men (in terms of race, class, caste, nation) are played out through sexual violence. The sexualization of culture in Eastern Europe in the 1990s also begs critical attention. A potentially fruitful area for exploration is why and how particular contexts encourage or limit sexual aggression. The precise connections between power, sex, violence, and pleasure also need further elaboration.

Offenders and Male Sexual Aggression

Who is defined as an offender is an implicit issue in the literature on sexual violence. The initial focus was restricted to those convicted of a sexual offense (a much narrower range than reported cases) and has been extended to encompass "undetected" offenders. Clinical research on offenders predominates, although there are some sociological studies (Scully, 1991, on rapists; Conte, Wolf, & Smith, 1989, and Waterhouse, Dobash, & Carnie, 1994, on child sexual abusers; O'Connell Davidson, 1995, on sex tourists). Most samples still comprise convicted offenders, although Lisak and Roth (1990) include a small sample of "undetected" rapists. This body of work has been augmented by studies of male sexual aggression, predominately done in North America with samples of college and university students. Rapists and child abusers are unproblematically labeled offenders or perpetrators, whereas equivocation abounds in relation to such naming for sexual harassers, flashers, and men who assault their wives. Thus, criminalization involves both statements about the seriousness of behavior and a challenge to its normalization.

The majority of studies have informed the two preoccupations in the literature: developing typologies of offenders and elucidating the components of particular forms of "sexual deviance." There is no consensus on typologies, with Knight and Prentky (1987) recording nine subtypes for rapists alone. Grubin (1992) maintains that most typologies have not been clinically tested and are based on arbitrary decisions with respect to poorly differentiated motivational factors, such as Groth's (1979) distinction between power and anger rapists. Grubin develops this analysis, drawing on interviews with 142 convicted rapists, demonstrating that meaningful distinctions can be made using a range of offense variables (e.g., solo or group rapes, single or serial offenses, targeting specific groups of women or girls), offender characteristics (e.g., adolescent or adult, ethnic origin), and contextual variables (e.g., substance abuse, relationship to victim/s). Serious reflection on the variables used in typologies is needed in order that the selection of meaningful differences can be both justified and theorized.

In experimental studies, the most common method involves testing sexual arousal to depictions of consensual and aggressive heterosexual sex and to sexualized depictions of children and adult women. Many use penile tumescence measures. Barbaree and Marshall (1991) review the literature to date and isolate two approaches: response and stimulus control models. Both rely on a presumption of "sexual deviance" and that there are definable and detectable differences in sexual arousal between offenders and other men. Studies using control groups and those exploring the connections between pornography, sexual arousal, and sexual aggression have raised serious doubts about this presumption of, and search for, difference.

Psychodynamic frameworks are also common and frequently suggest that relationships with hostile or absent mothers distinguish sex offenders from other men. However, Lisak and Roth's (1990) in-depth study of 15 unconvicted rapists and a control group found that hostility to fathers was the most significant family background variable distinguishing the two groups. Craig (1990) takes a somewhat different approach, defining rapists as men who have a particular disposition to sexual aggression, who seek out particular women, act to decrease women's resistance, and at the same time limit their own responsibility. Scully's (1991) study of convicted U.S. rapists investigated "vocabularies of motive" that enable men to deny, minimize, or justify their actions. The emphasis on how child sex abuse can be understood as deliberate action has been explored in terms of the planning and "grooming" process (Conte et al., 1989; Waterhouse et al., 1994) (for a discussion of how perpetrators understand and use physical violence against women partners, see Dobash and Dobash, this volume).

Because women represent an extremely small proportion of convicted and "undetected" sex offenders, it is not surprising that the literature on them is sparse and that there is minimal reference to women as "rapists." Research on women as perpetrators is limited to sexual abuse of children. Two published studies from the United States (Faller, 1987; Mathews et al., 1989) rely on samples of women convicted for offenses. While not concurring on all issues, both suggest significant gender differences in the contexts in which women abuse. There is hardly any evidence of women abusing in stranger situations or of the development of a "career" of abuse. Mathews et al. (1989) argue that the gendered differences in motivational factors between women and men are so pronounced that they require entirely different treatment approaches.

Sampson (1994) maintains that most treatment programs for men now use integrated explanatory models to inform their work (most commonly those of Marshall & Barbaree [1990] or Finkelhor [1986]), which combine behavioral and cognitive methods. Although some evaluations of treatment programs with sex offenders have been conducted (see Morrison, Erooga, & Beckett, 1994), few have tracked participants for extended periods of time, and most have been primarily concerned with whether the content of particular programs demonstrates changes in perception, thinking, and, in limited ways, behavior. Comprehensive reviews are uncommon, because the range and variation in content, length, and location of programs are many. A number have attempted to develop risk assessment indicators, and the practice of "offender profiling" (now used as an adjunct to police investigation) has emerged. Chesney (1991) argues that the study of sex offenders has on one level been a search for the difference between them and other men. None of the studies to date includes men who have raped their wives, which research suggests is the most common form of rape.

The studies of sexual aggression in one sense mirror those on offenders, because they focus on exploring its "normality" rather than pathology. For example, Koss (1988b) reports that one quarter of the male students confessed to using sexually coercive behavior, and a further 35% reported that under certain circumstances they would use it. One in 12 of these young, educated men reported acts that could legally be defined as rape, although 84% did not label their own behavior as such (see also Briere & Malamuth, 1983; Malamuth & Check, 1983). Petty Jnr, McLeod, and Dawson (1989) report similar findings and argue that the use of force in heterosexual interaction was deemed acceptable by a large enough proportion to suggest that it is not outside the range of "normal" male behavior (p. 355); they also echo some of the work on constructions of masculinity stressing the role of peer pressure and masculine bravado (p. 360). Although not as extensive, sexual attraction to children among "normal men" has been also been explored (Briere & Runtz, 1989). In many of these studies, the self-reported likelihood of using coercion and force increases when assurances of nondetection are included in the questions. The male students in the Petty Jnr et al. (1989) study rated the likelihood of detection or conviction for acquaintance rape as very small, and Smithyman's (1978) study of undetected rapists revealed that these men regarded rape as having low risk and high benefit. A smaller study (Tang, Critelli, & Porter, 1993) in Hong Kong explored differences between U.S. and Chinese male students with U.S. men reporting much higher levels of use of, and willingness to use, sexual aggression. Malamuth (1981) postulates a continuum of likelihood, for men, of using sexual aggression, which is significantly connected to attitudes of women and belief in rape myths, which, in turn, are affected by consumption of pornography. What remains underresearched and largely untheorized is why some men eschew violence and coercion.

Impacts and Consequences

The dominant approach to the aftermath of sexual victimization in research has emphasized "effects," using medical and psychological frameworks, with minimal account taken of the social and cultural context in which sexual violence occurs. The term *effects* is therefore a more limited one than our heading for this section—Impacts and Consequences—referring to emotional and behavioral outcomes at an individual level. Even within this delimited focus, psychological reactions, such as fear and anxiety, have been emphasized, to the detriment of physical injury, social and economic costs, and broader health implications. Heise (1994) has begun to map out the health costs and consequences of violence against women, drawing on material from industrial and developing countries, and concludes that victimization is a major cause of health problems among girls and women.

We use impacts and consequences to encompass a wider frame, within which it is possible to explore the impact of individual assaults and repeated violation of individuals as well as the cultural meaning of victimization for women and girls within and between cultures. There appears to be a level of commonality, in that women and girls are frequently held responsible for male sexuality, but there is considerable variation in the exact content and mechanisms whereby this is constructed and contested. One potential for future research would be tracking continuities in these ideas, how they are resisted, and the reworkings ("new mythologies") that emerge to take the place of those that have become unacceptable. For example, the challenge to the denial of child sexual abuse has undermined the frequency with which children are not believed, but in the wake of this shift, the concept of "false memory syndrome" has emerged alongside widespread accusations that overzealous practitioners pressure and coach children into "disclosures" (Myers, 1994).

There is considerable agreement about the immediate reactions to assaults, with the following physical and psychological responses being reported: intrusive memories, anxiety, mistrust, depression, distrust of one's own reality, self-blame, self-harm, chronic pain, sleep disorders, eating disorders, unwanted pregnancy, venereal disease, and HIV infection. However, a number of researchers and commentators agree that there is no simple correspondence between the type of assault and specific impacts. Impacts are connected to the meaning of victimization for the woman or girl and are mediated by coping strategies and the possibilities for recognition and support. In some cultures, "telling" can have very negative consequences, thus silence becomes a survival strategy. But silence is still commonplace in societies in which it is more possible to speak about sexual assault. Choosing to forget or minimize events may transcend culture as a response to the trauma of victimization.

Koss and Burkhart (1989) argue that the trauma involves several elements: experience of the world as not safe, that one has been targeted for intentional harm, and an awareness of a pervasive and malevolent social context. The responses of others can often confound these issues. When there are few resources for resolution of these conflicts, individuals may either internalize blame or minimize the event and even attempt to forget it. Women frequently report that the conflict between their subjective experience and the response of their external and internal social environments leads to a sort of cognitive-emotional paralysis, wherein their only recourse is to simply deny that the experience really happened (Koss & Burkhart, 1989, p. 32). This response to traumatic events (Herman, 1992) has, in the case of sexual abuse in childhood, become an arena of intense dispute through the creation of a so-called syndrome—false memory syndrome. We use the term "so-called" quite deliberately, because there is no professional recognition of the condition; it is a concept coined by an organization established to defend "accused parents"—the False Memory Foundation, based in the United States. The extensive debate and legal contests have led researchers to conduct studies that confirm that events can indeed be "forgotten" (see Family Violence Sexual Assault Institute, 1995; Williams, 1993).

Research on the impact of sexual victimization has begun to challenge taken-for-granted assumptions that have long informed legal discourse. For example, although the letter, and particularly the practice, of law continues to define rape by known men as less serious (Estrich, 1987), research suggests otherwise. Several U.S. studies have found that women raped by known men reported higher levels of distress 3 years after the assault than women who were raped by strangers (see, e.g., Koss & Oros, 1982). Other differences have also been noted—the closer the relationship, the less likely women are to report assaults, and the more likely they are to blame themselves.

Much of the work on the effects of victimization has been directed toward developing more appropriate and effective forms of intervention for those experiencing sexual violence. The limited, and frequently behavioral, focus has led to conceptualization of such responses as "dysfunctions," which intervention is designed to correct. A framework that begins from a recognition of coping and survival strategies makes a considerable difference to methodology, findings, and interventions. Coping responses are defensive and self-protective actions taken in contexts of threat and distress. They serve important physical and psychological survival functions for individuals and are resistant to simplistic behavioral, medical, and crisis intervention approaches (these have been especially common in responses to rape). Koss and Burkhart (1989) distinguish between two outcomes of different coping styles: accommodation and resolution. Accommodation involves taking responsibility for or denying the event; it requires defensive coping strategies that can become rigid and nonadaptive. Resolution relies on addressing the assault(s) and a process of reinterpretation and integration as an aspect of personal history. This model suggests that some form of resolution is dependent on redefining the event, particularly who was responsible for it, finding meaning, changing defensive coping strategies, and seeking support. There is, however, no easy route to resolution; Silver, Boon, and Stones (1983) report that 80% of a sample of women who had been incestuously abused were still searching for meaning up to 20 years afterward. This is just one of the reasons why support needs to be available at the point at which women and girls need it, which may be many years after the assault(s).

As awareness of the extent of sexual violence has developed, so have professional responses to it. In many Western societies, this response has become increasingly therapeutic and individual, displacing feminist frameworks that stressed collective support and response through self-help groups and political activism. The past decade could be described as a "decade of disorders" in relation to the impacts of sexual violence. A range of syndromes and disorders has been proposed, researched, and debated, with some being formally recognized as "diagnoses" in the *Diagnostic and Statistical Manual of Mental Disorders* (*DSM*). All have, however, proved inadequate in encompassing the range of victimization and its consequences (see, e.g., Finkelhor, 1986). Herman (1992) has proposed an integrated traumatic response model that includes single events, repeated assaults, and the potential for cumulative impacts. While undoubtedly a more inclusive framework, the emphasis on damage and personal healing has eclipsed an earlier stress on social justice and collective action. (See L. Armstrong, 1994, for an analysis of this transformation in relation to incest.)

Institutional and Social Responses

Historically and cross culturally, some women and girls have attempted to use the avenues that existed to resist violation and attain justice. Collective and concerted attempts to create appropriate responses emerge where the self-organization of women develops. The basic elements in these challenges involve recognition of sexual violence (issues of definition and prevalence); challenging victim-blame and allocating responsibility to perpetrators; support for, rather than stigmatization and silencing of, women and girls; and some form of access to justice. The forms such responses take vary between state and nonstate societies, but key institutions in both include kinship networks, communities (especially women's networks), and religious institutions. In state societies, government, professional bodies, and justice systems become increasingly significant.

All attempts to create change involve questioning who decides "what counts" as victimization and who defines its meaning and seriousness. At issue here is the creation of a climate in which testimony and experience of women and girls are accorded credibility and importance. This cultural shift in Western countries has been attempted in broadly similar ways—through establishing new organizations and forms in which "speaking out" was possible. These ranged from the actual "speak out," at which courageous women spoke publicly and gave "testimony" about their experiences, to consciousness-raising, self-help groups, and anonymous telephone help lines. In the 1970s, most of these forms were elements of community organizing within the women's movement; state funding was eschewed and groups were frequently involved in visible and creative campaigns at local levels. The innovative community-based services developed two methods of support—anonymous phone lines and mutual support groups. From these activist beginnings, locally based support services have mushroomed (with one estimate of 1,000 rape crisis groups in the United States in 1979), and many now draw on frameworks from more traditional therapeutic services (L. Armstrong, 1994; Matthews, 1994). Finding ways to ensure access for groups of women traditionally excluded from many forms of service provision (black women, women whose first language is not that of the dominant group, disabled women, young and elderly women, lesbians, women who work in the sex industry, and women in refugee camps) continues to be a key issue in the 1990s. Debates persist as to whether the appropriate feminist response to sexual violence is to develop effective support services or to concentrate on politicizing the issues at stake (L. Armstrong, 1994).

Some suggest that there has been a universal process of reform whereby sexual violence is more likely to be recognized and responded to as a crime, whereas other international examples suggest the opposite. One example is the Islamic law on rape introduced in Pakistan in 1979 (Mehdi, 1990). To bring a charge, a woman has to have three male witnesses to support her story, and she can be punished for anything found to be a false complaint. Mehdi argues that it makes conviction virtually impossible, and none has occurred in which the complainant is an adult. Bueno (1994) documents a recent campaign to reform law in Bolivia, where charges of rape are not made unless the victim is a minor or a virgin. There is still substantial variation in the context and content of laws, with the most radical law reform to date in Canada and parts of Australia where the responsibility for explicitly seeking consent is placed on the accused.

Significant changes in policy and practice among health practitioners and pediatricians have also occurred, both in their role as forensic examiners and as long-term supporters of women and girls. The most-developed examples are the sexual assault centers attached to many U.S., Canadian, and Australian hospitals. An unintended consequence of these processes has been the "medicalization of rape" (Breckenridge & Carmody, 1992; Kelly, 1989) and the "professionalizing" of responses that, in some areas, has eclipsed or even replaced earlier rape crisis centers (Foley, 1996; Matthews, 1994). While debate continues as to whether, and how far, responses to rape have been professionalized, this is indisputable in the case of sexual abuse in childhood. The proliferation of literature focused on appropriate methods of investigation, assessment, and treatment responses is but one demonstration of this fact. Indeed, debates in the field are increasingly limited to matters related to investigation (see, e.g., Department of Health, 1995; Myers, 1994) rather than the wider social implications that raise complex questions about masculinity, childhood, and the family (Driver & Droisen, 1989; MacLeod & Saraga, 1988).

Concern about sexual assault limiting women's use of the public sphere was initially addressed through actions such as "Reclaim the Night" marches and community self-defense classes. The formal response to this issue has been a proliferation in "safety advice" to women (Stanko, 1996), and assertiveness training has become the predominant organizational response to sexual harassment. Both implicitly reassert women's responsibility for policing men's behavior and suggest that it is the content of individual interactions that is the issue rather than gender inequality. Similar arguments can be made in relation to child sexual abuse prevention programs, which are almost entirely focused on teaching children strategies to escape/avoid assaults—strategies that many have already used (Kelly, Burton, & Regan, 1993; Reppucci & Hauggard, 1989). Few efforts have taken up the challenge of "primary prevention," interventions intended to stop men and boys from using sexual aggression. Without a radical goal of eliminating rather than simply responding to sexual violence, prevention tends to be directed toward victims or potential victims. One recent example of a radical approach to public education and prevention is the Zero Tolerance Campaign, based in Edinburgh,

Scotland, which aims to simultaneously empower women and challenge men.

The contradiction of making demands on the state, at the same time implicating the state in the problem, is a central one in contemporary movements for social change (for a discussion, see Dobash & Dobash, 1992, pp. 99-145). Here, again, national contrasts in approach can be observed. The Australian concept of "femocrat" and the Scandinavian concept of "state feminism" reflect the intentional employment by state agencies of feminists to address women's inequality. Heated debates about co-option and institutionalization continue and in some instances have been extended to encompass the emergence of hierarchies of position within women's organizations (see, e.g., Matthews, 1994). One consequence of the targeting of the state and state agencies as sites for social change has been an increasing neglect of the importance of informal networks and communities as sources of both potential support and challenge and locations in which climates of toleration persist. Work developing among indigenous peoples and in some developing countries offers illuminating contrasts to strategies in most Western countries (Atkinson, 1990; Kelly, 1996; Kumar, 1993).

Normalization and Resistance

The twin concepts of normalization and resistance have relevance at both the micro and macro levels, from individual responses to the threat and reality of assaults to local climates of tolerance and intolerance, institutional responses, and national policy. Feminist perspectives on sexual violence have encompassed both a challenge to the presumption that sexual violence is rare—demonstrating that on some levels it is "normalized"—and a statement of, and call to, resistance. Recent debates about so-called "victimhood feminism" have emphasized the former while ignoring the latter (Kelly et al., 1996). In fact, resistance to sexual violence has been, in the late 20th century, a major organizing focus for women, not only in Western counties but also in Brazil (Rafino, 1994), the Caribbean (Mohammed, 1991), India (Kapur, 1994), and South Africa (Mabaso, 1992).

Data on resistance have most commonly been collected in rape research, is seldom addressed in studies of sexual abuse, and is defined as coping strategies in sexual harassment research. This difference may be due to the tendency to conceptualize rape as a single event and sexual harassment and sexual abuse as repeat experiences. Including questions on coping and resistance is important in challenging constructions of victim's responses as "passive." Unfortunately, the main focus in rape research has been on demonstrating that resistance can prevent assaults (Kleck & Sayles, 1990). These studies have been based on women's actions and cannot address the motivation and intention of perpetrators. No strategy or combination of strategies has been found that is always effective, and all strategies are less effective when the attacker is known.

When the threat and reality of sexual violence are routinized in individual lives, both normalization and resistance may coexist, with one being more salient at particular points in time. Women routinely adapt their behavior with reference to the potential for sexual violence (Stanko, 1990) and, at times, resist in personal and, to a lesser extent, collective ways. Furby, Fischhoff, and Morgan (1991) compiled a list of 1,140 different strategies that individuals and societies might use to decrease the potential of sexual assault. At the individual level, they explore the decision-making process of making split-second judgments about whether and how to resist and evaluating trade-offs between the potential costs and benefits of various actions. Similar, albeit less pressurized and personally dangerous, thought processes inform the decision making of activists with respect to campaigns for social change.

Whether forms of sexual violence are normalized affects the meaning of such assaults for individuals. The predominant response by women to harassment is that "nothing really happened" (Kelly & Radford, 1996), this coping response—minimizing—has the unintended consequence of reproducing normalization. Individual attempts to create personal safety have the unintended additional consequence of a level of "acceptance" of the reality of sexual violence, although many may alternate at different times between accommodation and resistance. What enables women and girls to resist at both personal and collective levels is underresearched, but basic questions here include whether a sense of violation, which is the prerequisite of resistance, depends on a sense of self and value as a woman/girl; how shifts from individual to collective responses occur; and how individual and social forms of normalization and resistance may be connected.

Certain forms of sexual violence, or particular elements of it, have been legitimized by the state; the exclusion of rape in marriage from legal codes is an obvious example. Rape in war is another; and the presumption that military men need sexualized rest and recreation has only recently been challenged (Enloe, 1994; Sturdevant & Stolzfus, 1992). The tolerance, and even explicit promotion, of sexual violence on "enemy women" by military men needs to be linked, as Enloe has begun to do, with high levels of abuse of female partners and children, sexual harassment of female colleagues (Neibuhr & Boyles, 1991), and women living in towns where the military is stationed. The infamous "Tailhook" incident in the United States revealed the extent to which sexual harassment and assault is routinely tolerated, and even organized, within the military; "the silencing of women to preserve the honor not just of individual men but of a nation turns out to be an integral part of the processes of war and post war order" (Enloe, 1994, p. 188). Exploring how such cultures of toleration develop and are maintained is a potentially fruitful area of research, which would extend current knowledge. The concept of normalization raises additional questions about the risk of sexual assault relative to the "value" of different groups or categories of women (e.g., elderly women, poor women, disabled women, ethnic women).

Feminist challenges to the many and varied ways in which sexual violence has been normalized has, in turn, resulted in resistance from those who wish to preserve the status quo. The extensive public debates about "date rape" and whether children and adults' accounts and memories of abuse in childhood are "believable" attest to both the impact of feminist research and activism and the profound threat that questioning normalization involves for substantial sections of the population. Rather than representing these responses as a "backlash," they should be understood as evidence of the success, albeit limited, of attempts to imbue women's and children's voices with authority and credibility and an affirmation that attempting to wrest from men the authority to define reality remains a key arena of political struggle.

A persistent theme in academic and activist debate is whether change should focus on services, agencies, the state, or more deep-rooted social transformation, whether improving services leads to normalization rather than resistance. It ought to be possible, at least in principle, to move beyond this either/or dichotomy, to seek to create social justice in the longer term, at the same time as addressing individual justice in the shorter term. Two recent attempts (in Canada and Scotland[1]) to link short-term responses to a longer-term strategy use the concept of "zero tolerance." These visionary, comprehensive attempts to confront the implications of taking violence against women seriously offer us alternatives to the services and reform versus social justice and social change conundrum, encapsulated in the Canadian Panel on Violence Against Women (1993) report title: *Changing the Landscape: Ending Violence, Achieving Equality.*

Note

1. The Scottish campaign began in Edinburgh, drew inspiration from Canada, and has since been adopted by most local government areas in Scotland. It has also run in a number of cities and regions in England.

4

Violence Embodied?

Circumcision, Gender Politics, and Cultural Aesthetics

Janice Boddy

It is evident that female genital mutilation can be abolished and wiped out in our lifetime. We are able to teach those who cling to distorted beliefs and damaging practices some better ways to cope with themselves, their lives, reproduction, and sexuality. We know that everyone on earth has the capacity to learn. . . .

"Why am I pursuing this?" I feel that my own personal sense of dignity and worth as a woman and human being is under attack by these mutilations, inflicted on helpless children for no other reason than that they are female. I cannot tolerate this. I find it impossible, indeed absurd, to work for feminist goals, for human rights, for justice

AUTHOR'S NOTE: My thanks to participants in the H. F. Guggenheim Foundation conferences on violence against women for their comments and suggestions on this piece, but especially to Russell and Rebecca Dobash, Karen Colvard, Liz Kelly, and Monica McWilliams. I am grateful to Claudie Gosselin and Ronald Wright for help in sharpening the argument. The Canada Council, Social Sciences and Humanities Research Council of Canada, and Connaught Fellowship Fund of the University of Toronto have funded my research—I acknowledge their support with gratitude. But my deepest debt is owed to the women of Hofriyat; our dialogue, I hope, continues.

and equality, while ignoring senseless attacks on the essence of the
female personality, which these operations represent. . . .

These operations have continued for 2,000 years to the present
time only because they are demanded by men.

—Hosken, *The Hosken Report:*
Genital and Sexual Mutilation
of Females, 1982, pp. 2, 14, 15

[My aunts] . . . asked me if I wanted to be circumcised as well. I told
them yes, I wanted to—all the girls my age wanted to because it's
shame not to. . . .

They do the circumcisions outside, with a lot of clapping and
singing so people won't hear you cry. They were going, "Lululululu-
lulu" and singing my father's name and my lineage's name, saying
that they were the best. I was so proud when I heard all this. I said,
Yes, why not? to myself. They put gold on me everywhere, and money
everywhere, and they took me outside under one of the tall trees in
the yard. . . .

I was shaking all over my whole body when my mother came
back. . . . I was proud, so I told her to be happy for me. I said, "They
did it because they love me." . . .

You know, Rahima, I've heard many Europeans, many white
people no matter where they come from, they're trying to educate
Africans about circumcision. But would they accept it if I educated
them to circumcise? . . . If Somali women change, it will be a change
done by us, among us. When they order us to stop, tell us what we
must do, it is offensive to the black person or the Muslim person who
believes in circumcision. To advise is good, but not to order.

—Barnes & Boddy, *Aman:*
The Story of a Somali Girl,
1994, pp. 52-57, 280

No other "exotic" practice that harms and refigures human bodies
attracts such opprobrium from Western observers as female circumcision,[1] found in various forms throughout Africa, parts of the Middle
East, and among immigrants from these areas now residing abroad.
As an anthropologist, I have explored the custom's meanings with
both Sudanese and Somali women who have undergone the most
radical procedure: excision and infibulation. Despite vigorous international debate and official condemnations, these and similar damaging practices persist, albeit with attenuating severity, among urban and
educated groups (El Hassan, 1990).

I began with two biographical statements, which speak past each
other, indeed mock each other, because they provide a frame for

discussing both the insidiousness of power and the complexity of women's subordination. Circumcision is less the object of my argument than the lens through which it is focused. Consideration of discourses surrounding the issue reveals it to be far less transparent than some Western feminists (e.g., Daly, 1978; Hosken, 1982) would concede. Rather than adopt an oppressor/oppressed model to "explain" this as "violence against women," I want to examine the subtle authorization of harm in the cultural orders of those whom we count as its victims. In fact, I want to challenge commonsense understandings of the phrase "victims of violence" by interrogating its terms and destabilizing their semantic fields. We often speak as though violence were separable from everyday life: abnormal, socially aberrant. But, I will argue, distinguishing violent from nonviolent acts can obfuscate matters, rendering unproblematic the finely nuanced quotidian formulations of body and self through which subjects endlessly produce and reproduce themselves, and existing power relations are recuperated even as they are transformed. Indeed, this seemingly rational distinction may be a technique of power in itself.

Moreover, conceptualizing women as "the dominated" and men as "the dominators" encourages us to view men as agents, as "having" and wielding power, and women as passive recipients of men's acts, violent or otherwise. In addition to effacing the intricacies of power noted above, this bipolar model replicates profoundly embedded Euro-American gender constructs by failing to examine them as such. It is hardly surprising that when analysts transport such assumptions abroad, they find their own templates confirmed. But the apparent universality is illusory, its foundations specious. More, it is dangerous, for "universal" too readily yields to "natural" and "inevitable," playing into whatever regime of truth one is trying to explore and perhaps undermine. I do not rule out the possibility that universality at some level exists, as discussed within. My point is that we cannot assume it to be the case upon generalizing from one culturally specific model to an unmediated universal "truth."

I am not suggesting that we recalibrate an elusive Archimedean point to achieve greater "objectivity." One can never be truly outside of one's culture; there is no such "non"-place to be, no "view from nowhere" (Nagel, 1986). To say that one's cultural positioning mystifies realities is incontestable; but taken to its logical conclusion, this observation applies equally to the culture of the analyst, granting Hosken, for example, no unmediated purchase on the practice she decries. Even in the most sophisticated and critical of models, the analyst's localized, commonsense world obtrudes. I am also not suggesting that meaning is utterly open, interpretation unbounded, or social life free of the limitations of embodied existence, a popular postmodern epistemology that Bordo (1993, p. 218) describes as the "dream of everywhere." I do, however, believe it is crucial to cultivate awareness of the temporal, local, and gendered specificity of one's conceptual currency, to recognize that our epistemological ground is always *somewhere,* to be continuously self-aware when traveling in alien realms. Admitting her position clarifies the analyst's responsibility to take seriously what people "elsewhere" (and indeed, at home) have to say for themselves, to credit the contexts of their lives. Understanding, whatever its limitations, does not come by Olympian fiat or therapeutic empathy.

In their article "Nothing Really Happened," Kelly and Radford (1996) analyze reports of sexual harassment that were deeply frightening to the women involved but legally uncategorizable and therefore dismissed because they had not resulted in physical harm. The dearth of publicly recognized categories for such events reflects the subordinate positioning of women in general: An existing power structure reveals itself as much through silence as through speech, and feminists have long recognized the importance of *naming* one's otherwise inchoate experiences to avoid trivializing or negating them, to render them actual "events." Equally, however, we know that terms become reified and thus appear given; periodically, we need to remind ourselves of their preconstructedness and examine them for what they embrace and what they exclude. This is as true of the categories "violence" and "victim" as it is of "woman" or "man." It is also true of the term *female genital mutilation,* which, though seemingly descriptive, forges a single decontextualized fact out of diverse practices and meanings and imbues it with specific moral and ideological significance. In the rarified domain of scholarly debate, we might venture to "un-name" such terms, heuristically subvert their givenness and loosen their hold on perception, so that otherwise obscured continuities and differences among culturally disparate phenomena can emerge. A continuum of intelligibility linking "violent" or "mutilating" and "normal" acts might then be discerned. By decentering accepted meanings, our own experiences become less familiar and others' less exotic. Such radical uncertainty is required if we are to do meaningful cross-cultural research, research that does not itself perpetuate violence or stultify humanitarian change.

Practices and the Literature

"Female circumcision" of some type is found in over 20 African countries as well as in Oman, Yemen, the United Arab Emirates, among Muslim populations in Malaysia and Indonesia, and Bohra Muslims in India, Pakistan, and East Africa (Dorkenoo & Elworthy, 1992; Hosken, 1982; Toubia, 1995). It is increasingly met with in Western countries to which people from these areas have moved. While it is frequently described as having spiritual significance, its practitioners include followers of Islam, Christianity, Judaism, and indigenous African religions, though African Muslims account for a sizeable number of those affected, and the practice supports the preservation of premarital chastity that is strongly associated with Islam. The operations are usually considered to purify the body and are performed, for the most part, on children, including some infants but mostly those between 4 and 10 years old. In a few areas, excision takes place shortly before marriage and in at least one society just before the birth of the first child (Dareer, 1982; Dorkenoo & Elworthy, 1992, p. 7; Hosken, 1982; Myers et al., 1985). Age preference generally coincides with that for the circumcision of boys.

The World Health Organization (WHO) (1979, 1986; Cook, 1979), adapting a classification system first devised by Shandall (1967; also Verzin, 1975) and used by most writers on the topic, identifies three forms of the practice:

1. *Excision or clitoridectomy:* amputation of the clitoris (in some societies ablation by cauterization) and all or part of the labia minora. This is the most prevalent and geographically widespread of the practices.

2. *Infibulation or pharaonic circumcision:* removal of the clitoris (sometimes not in its entirety) plus all of the labia minora. The labia majora are then pared or incised in order to create raw surfaces that are stitched together with silk, suture, or thorns, leaving a sheath of skin that covers the urethra and occludes the vaginal opening (see Toubia, 1994). In some areas, all external parts are scraped away by razor and the remaining skin stretched and likewise fastened over the wound (Boddy, 1982; Boddy, 1989, p. 51; Lightfoot-Klein, 1989a, p. 87). In both cases, a narrow implement such as a reed or matchstick is inserted posteriorly to allow for the passage of urine and menstrual

blood. The girl's legs are bound together from ankle to hip, and she remains relatively immobile for up to 40 days to promote healing. The formation of a thick, resilient layer of scar tissue results. Upon marriage, she may require the services of a midwife to widen her vaginal orifice; this may be done surreptitiously, for her husband is expected to perform the task either with his penis alone (a virility test in southern Somalia [Abdalla, 1982; Barnes & Boddy, 1994; Talle, 1993]) or aided by a sharp and rarely hygienic utensil. Moreover, in labor, a birth attendant must be present to cut through her scar and release the child. Infibulation is the most severe female genital operation and accounts for some 15% of cases (Toubia, 1995, p. 10). It is the principal form in Somalia, Djibouti, Eritrea, and Sudan; it is also practiced to some extent in Mali and southern Egypt.

3. *Sunna circumcision*, which WHO calls "circumcision proper": removal or incision of the clitoral "hood" or prepuce. This is the rarest type, despite being labeled *sunna,* meaning (in Arabic) "the way of the Prophet" but often mistranslated as "traditional." However, because all Muslims follow *sunna,* the term may be applied to whatever form is normal in a given Islamic society; in practice, it is often confused with excision and sometimes a modified pharaonic operation (Dareer, 1982; Gruenbaum, 1982). Toubia (1994) questions calling the *sunna* operation "circumcision proper," as in her medical practice in Sudan she has "not found a single case of female circumcision in which only the skin surrounding the clitoris is removed, without damage to the clitoris itself" (p. 712).

These types are approximations only. The techniques of operators (who may or may not have medical training) vary tremendously, groups have distinct preferences, and practices evolve. Excision, for example, is sometimes accompanied by a cut in the perineum (introcision) to enlarge the vagina for easier childbirth (Mohamud, 1991, p. 204). In Sudan during the 1920s and 1930s, British medical personnel, encouraging eradication of the practice, introduced a modified and somewhat medicalized form of pharaonic circumcision. Over the years, this has gained considerable ground. On the strength of my informants' contrasts between their own and their daughters' operations, it involves less cutting of the labia than before (Boddy, 1982, 1989); moreover, only anterior parts of the outer lips are joined, resulting in a larger genital opening (cf. Toubia, 1994, p. 712). A compromise between *sunna* and infibulation now practiced in urban Sudan is called *sunna magatia*—[likely] "*sunna* with amputation."

Following clitoridectomy, the labia minora are roughened and lightly stitched to provoke adhesion; this is also known as a "sandwich" (Lightfoot-Klein, 1989a, p. 35). Gruenbaum (1991, p. 642) reports a newer operation, apparently tempering the above, in which the clitoris remains uncut but is sewn beneath a small flap of tissue. It resembles a procedure I was told of in the late 1970s, wherein the labia majora were (reversibly) joined so as to enable the otherwise intact daughters of educated parents to save face before their radically circumcised playmates at school (Boddy, 1982). According to one of Gruenbaum's midwife informants, the increasing demand for (actual) *sunna* operations that followed the 1989 Islamist coup in Sudan was nonetheless accompanied by a request for some covering of the urethra "in order to avoid the sound of urination, which is considered unfeminine" (1991, p. 642). Such meliorations of pharaonic procedure have been possible not only because the operation is un-Islamic, but also because men's ignorance of women's natural bodies and what the operations entail (Boddy, 1989; Dareer, 1982) provides women space in which to maneuver and still behave appropriately. That said, many Sudanese and Somali women request reinfibulation after each birth because they "feel naked," impure, or ashamed when no longer "closed." The remedial practice is said also to please the husband, to whom the reinfibulated wife is presented as a bride, with her socially constructed virginity renewed (Abdalla, 1982, p. 21; Boddy, 1989; Dareer, 1982; Hayes, 1975; Lightfoot-Klein, 1989a, 1989b; Mohamud, 1991, p. 208; Toubia, 1994, p. 715; Van der Kwaak, 1992, p. 781).[2]

It is important to clarify that those who perform the operations and those who most vociferously defend them are women, despite the strengthening cadre of indigenous educated women who oppose circumcision and work for change. My central concern is to cast light on why and how that should be so. To do this, it is necessary to consider what is at stake for women in being, or not being, circumcised. It is more usual to ask about the procedures' consequences—physical, psychological, and social—and why they are performed. Answers may well suggest themselves to readers disturbed by foregoing descriptions, but their "obviousness" must not be allowed to render them impervious to analysis. Such answers have their own material and ideological effects. As early as the 1920s, they led Western feminists to speak out on behalf of their African sisters; since then, they have fueled admonitions and efforts at eradication that by and large have failed (e.g., the 1946 law against infibulation in Sudan; cf. Pedersen, 1991). The practices continue, and the international women's movement remains divided on their relevance. Many non-

Western women are rightly indignant when "female genital mutilation" is placed center stage in international forums meant to draw attention to women's subordination, whereas their wider economic and political oppression goes undenounced. They resent Western feminists for presuming to define their oppression and for arrogating circumcision as the quintessential form of woman abuse under patriarchy (see Mohanty, 1991). The 1980 Non-Governmental Organizations Forum in Copenhagen was especially split on this issue (see Boulware-Miller, 1985; Gilliam, 1991; Gosselin, 1996; Kirby, 1987; Thiam, 1983; Winter, 1994). We must therefore be prepared to consider the stakes for Western women who publicly decry the operations. What are their understandings, on what are these based, and how are they phrased? How is it that Aman and Hosken speak past each other?

The terrain becomes increasingly muddy here, traversed by incommensurable discourses and political interests. Much Western writing on the subject, especially that intended for a mass audience, is rhetorical and self-referential, building on itself within a closed universe of meaning. Classifications and "facts" are endlessly recycled, decontextualized "reasons" for the practice are hyperbolized and dismissed as "irrational," the same studies summarized repeatedly (Van der Kwaak, 1992). It becomes clear from this literature that it has seized on a "truth"—one that bears repeating, that hits, as we shall see, on some serious investments of Western society and its gendered/feminist selves.

The majority of articles and books on the topic, medically oriented or not, provide details of the operations' medical sequelae (e.g., Koso-Thomas, 1987; Toubia, 1994). Yet information about proportions of the infibulated population who suffer complications are notoriously rare and, when available, not particularly reliable. Given the illegality of the operation in some quarters and its association with sexuality and shame, figures from hospitalizations are bound to be underrepresentative. At the same time, gynecologists whose experience is derived from women reporting problems may overstate their prevalence (Badri, 1984). Writers who suggest that the operations are "frequently fatal" (Pugh, 1983, p. 9) or use phrases such as "if she survives" (Lightfoot-Klein, 1989b, p. 378) but do not provide a basis for their claims betray intent more polemical than scientific. Importantly, circumcision can continue precisely because, although it condemns women to lives of suffering, it is seldom immediately lethal—in fact, WHO (1986, p. 31) identifies several more pernicious practices, for example, precocious childbearing and grand multiparity (having numerous children in rapid succession (see Boddy, 1998b; Gruen-baum, 1996). But before tackling discursive problems in greater depth, and in order to appreciate why such problems exist, I outline some of the medical consequences of the operation, concentrating on infibulation.

Infibulation

Immediate complications include hemorrhage and severe pain, which can indeed lead to shock and death[3]; blood loss, which can result in anemia and affect the growth of a poorly nourished child (Toubia, 1994, p. 713); and septicemia and tetanus from operations under unhygienic conditions (Aziz, 1980; Boddy, 1982; Dareer, 1982; Gruenbaum, 1982; Toubia, 1994). But death from the operation is less common than long-term complications, several of which may contribute to maternal and child mortality. Add to this a cultural preference for male children, and it becomes clear why in Mohamud's (1991) demographic study of Somalis, a reversal of natural advantage was found to occur, with mortality of females *beginning* to exceed that for males at the ages when circumcisions are performed. Medical doctors sometimes undertake the surgeries in hospitals or clinics, believing children will suffer less (Hall & Ismail, 1981, p. 99). The paradox is that once the operations are medicalized, their perpetuation seems assured, and WHO strenuously discourages the involvement of health professionals except remedially (WHO, 1986, p. 35).

Long-term complications stem from interference in the drainage of urine and menstrual blood, causing frequent urinary infections, even when the woman is married and thus "opened." (Shandall, 1967, suggests that some 28% are infected at any time.) Especially in cases of tight infibulation, voiding is excruciatingly slow; moreover, the vagina may act as a secondary bladder, and if a woman is pregnant, the fetus can be poisoned by accumulated urine, and miscarriage can result. Painful menstruation is a common complaint. A backup of clotted menstrual blood can occur particularly in girls before marriage, causing abdominal swelling that requires surgical intervention; this and the apparent cessation of menses may bring suspicion of premarital pregnancy for which the consequences can be dire in patriarchal societies where virginity is a key expression of family honor (Dareer, 1982, pp. 36-37; Dorkenoo & Elworthy, 1992, p. 8; WHO, 1986, p. 32). During childbirth, inelasticity of the scarred vulva may prolong the second stage of labor, the contraction phase when the baby is expelled from the womb, and even when a midwife is present to cut through the fibrous tissue, the outcome can be death or brain damage to the child. For the mother, a lengthy delivery can cause fistulae (passages) to develop between the vagina and the bladder or rectum, resulting in incontinence for which she may face ostracism and divorce (Dareer, 1982, p. 38; Toubia, 1994, p. 713). Dermoid cysts have been reported to develop in the line of the scar, and keloids sometimes form, complicating the necessary anterior episiotomy (Abdalla, 1982, p. 23). Maternal death can result from blood loss and exhaustion or revisitation of the unsanitary conditions attending the original operation. In order to avoid problematic childbirth, some women in their third trimester eat less than they should, resulting in low birth weights and a precarious start to life for the child (Mohamud, 1991, p. 208; Van der Kwaak, 1992, p. 780). Beyond this, Mustafa (1966, p. 304) estimates that between 20% and 25% of sterility cases in northern Sudan can be linked to infibulation, due either to chronic pelvic infection or the difficulties of sexual intercourse. It is a sad irony that the operation that is designed to safeguard women's reproductive capacity, whether by enhancing natural fertility or by regulating its use, can so readily precipitate its ruin. Yet despite the health problems for some individuals, infibulation seems to have no deleterious effect on overall fertility levels in Sudan, where women average six to seven live births each (Boddy, 1989; Gruenbaum, 1996; Sudan Government, 1982, p. 63).

These observations beg consideration of the consequences of infibulation for sexual relations and psychological well-being. In societies where virtually every girl is circumcised, there is considerable support for those who experience the operation; indeed, it is deemed necessary to becoming a full adult, to become marriageable, and to become normal: "beautiful," "clean," and "pure" (Barnes & Boddy, 1994; Boddy, 1982, 1989; Talle, 1993). Thus, *not* to be circumcised may be the more traumatic condition, and girls have been known to beg reluctant parents for the operation (Hall & Ismail, 1981, p. 98).

Yet when infibulations are performed on immigrants living in the West, the psychological consequences may be negative and profound. Gone are both a sympathetic environment and the perception of "normal" genitals; rather, the child is seen as different from uncircumcised peers and may have serious difficulty developing her sexual identity as a result (Thiam, 1983; Toubia, 1994). Even in countries where the surgery is prevalent, rapid urbanization may be weakening community support, and controversy over the appropriate form of the operation may be detrimental to those already circumcised in a more radical manner.

Toubia (1994) notes that in Sudan, many infibulated women are chronically anxious and depressed "from worry over the state of their genitals, intractable dysmenorrhea, and the fear of infertility" (p. 714). Doctors in Khartoum report seeing increased numbers of women apprehensive lest their lack of sexual sensation and response prevent them from becoming pregnant (Lightfoot-Klein, 1989b, p. 384). This suggests that concern over fertility rather than sexual pleasure per se has been fueling women's incipient questioning of the practice.

Two frequently reported medico-psychological effects of infibulation are pain during sexual intercourse (dyspareunia) and lack of satisfaction from the act (Abdalla, 1982; Dareer, 1982; Dorkenoo & Elworthy, 1992; Hosken, 1982; Kouba & Muasher, 1985). Pain may be transient, as when caused by a tight infibulation, or severe, the result of neuromas that develop when nerve endings are trapped in the scar (Toubia, 1994, p. 713). Certainly the pain of deinfibulation can be traumatic, particularly if the husband resorts to brutal means (see Abdalla, 1982; Barnes & Boddy, 1994; Dareer, 1982). Where marriages are typically arranged between families who stand to gain from the match, chances of brutality may be reduced; they may be further diminished when, as is often the case in Sudan (Somalia less so), spouses are close kin who have known each other from birth. Yet infibulation constitutes an implicit test of virility, and failure to live up to the norms of virility is deeply shameful for a man, who, like his bride, is fearful and apprehensive at the prospect of "disvirgining" her (Abdalla, 1982; Barnes & Boddy, 1994; Dareer, 1982; Lightfoot-Klein, 1983, 1989a, 1989b).

> Not only do men tend to get severe abrasions of the penis in their attempts to penetrate, but they must also maintain the fiction that throughout this ordeal their potency never fails them. Unquestionably, under such conditions, as they often are, men will not discuss this. Failure to penetrate reflects negatively on the man's self-image to the highest degree. A recurring story told particularly by psychiatrists concerns men who commit suicide when this happens. (Lightfoot-Klein, 1989a, pp. 95-96)

Similarly, for a man to oppose his wife's postpartum reinfibulation would signify masculine weakness, despite the fact that in Shandall's (1967) interviews with 300 men, each having two or more wives only one of whom was infibulated, 266 stated a clear sexual preference for the less radically excised partner.[4] Something other than men's sexual satisfaction must be at stake in continuing the practice.

The Clitoris: Sexuality, Biology, and Discourse

Few studies deal with the issue of marital sex, and those that do are equivocal. This, however, has not prevented a deluge of intuitive lay conjecture, often negative and clearly exhortational in tone (Walker, 1992). Research conducted by two Egyptian psychologists (Karim & Ammar, 1965) suggests that sexual response is affected by the extent of the surgery and the degree to which a woman has internalized the social constraints on sexual expression. Shandall's (1967) study of over 4,000 Sudanese women found that few who were infibulated had experienced orgasm, and many claimed not to know what it was. On the other hand, through interviews with some 300 Sudanese women, most of them infibulated, Lightfoot-Klein (1989b) discovered that despite an expectation of sexual passivity (for a woman to move or seem to enjoy sex is deemed animalistic and a potential sign of past infidelity), nearly 90% regularly experienced sexual climax or had done so at some time in their marriages. They did, however, need more time to become aroused. Dareer (1982, p. 48) notes that over one fourth of her respondents enjoy sex all or part of the time, and Gruenbaum (1996) reports infibulated women's descriptions of "finishing" (orgasm) (p. 462). My own informants, like Gruenbaum's and Dareer's, are equivocal, some saying that sex is but a painful necessity for maintaining their marriages and having children (both representing economic security), others that they enjoy it; all, nevertheless, regularly signal to their husbands that they are sexually receptive, albeit indirectly, by using culturally coded cosmetics and smoke baths (Boddy, 1982, 1988, 1989).[5]

Western commentators should not dismiss reports of positive sexual response by circumcised women just because they appear counterintuitive. Some midwives, in an effort to prevent excessive blood loss, may leave the clitoris relatively intact beneath the infibulation seam. Moreover, the closeness of the marital bond may mitigate partial loss of the organ responsible for orgasm and heighten the cerebral components of sex (cf. Hite, 1976; see also Bonaparte, 1953; Lightfoot-Klein, 1989a, 1989b). If we take seriously the idea that bodily experience is interactively shaped through processes of culture and is not simply culture's natural base (Geertz, 1973; Grosz, 1987), we must also allow that desires and pleasures will be culturally and historically specific (cf. Butler, 1990; Foucault, 1990; Kirby, 1987, p. 44).

We need also to consider the challenge these findings pose to Western expectations: *Why* are they counterintuitive? What is invested in the clitoris that its removal excites such horror, leading some writers to insist that infibulated women are "castrated" and entirely alienated from "the essence of the female personality" (Hosken, 1982; cf. Hashi & Silver, 1994; Walker, 1992)? The answer is, I think, complex but comes down in the end to what Gunning (1992) calls "arrogant perception": the individualistic situatedness of Western observers, however feminist and humanitarian their motives might be.

Gender constructs in the contemporary West are typically formulated in simple binary terms—as presence (male) and absence (not-male, female)—and closely tied to anatomy. In biology and psychology—scientific discourses freighted with cultural import—such distinctions have focused on the sexual organs of the male, on having or not having a penis. They are reflected to some extent in language, as when the male stands for the general category and the female is a departure from it. Such societies also evince a deep-seated division between "culture" and "nature," to which gender and other salient precepts are linked: Hence, "culture" (presence) is typically associated with social creativity, mind, reason, agency, self, and maleness, and "nature" (absence, the precultural or primitive) with body, procreation, passion, passivity/receptivity, "the other," and femaleness (e.g., Bordo, 1993; Grosz, 1987; Mascia-Lees & Sharpe, 1992b). When tied to anatomical difference, such models implicitly naturalize asymmetric gender attributes and inequitable relations of power. Though anthropological, philosophical, and feminist research has exposed them as culturally specific ideological formulations (e.g., MacCormack & Strathern, 1980) that operate in support of male supremacy (Bordo, 1989, 1993; Butler, 1990; Mascia-Lees & Sharpe, 1992a), these insights have not unseated the model's reign. Some feminists suggest that the fact of the clitoris serves to disrupt established gender hierarchies, intimating a vision of the world in which neither sex prevails (see Mascia-Lees & Sharpe, 1992b, pp. 149, 162). Thus, if the clitoris is the female analogue of the penis, both sexes are marked by "presence," creativity, agency, and so on. Such observations are linked to the "rediscovery" of the clitoris as a site of sexual pleasure by the women's liberation movement of the 1960s and 1970s, which made this body part a powerful symbol of women's emancipation. However, it is questionable whether arguing along these lines subverts the original formulation or indeed sustains it by again valorizing the male, subsuming the female, and renewing a model of gender that claims "presocial" anatomy as its cultural ground (cf. Irigaray, 1985). Still, for those who take this approach, amputation of the clitoris represents an irreparable diminution of feminine value, a violation of natural female "essence" emblematic of all women's suffering under global patriarchy (Hosken, 1982; cf. Fraser, 1995).

The objection must be raised that essence is always a *social* attribute; we are speaking of a meaningful clitoris—not (were it possible) a precultural, unmediated one. As Grosz (1987) points out, "human biology must be *always already cultural,* in order for culture to have any effect on it" (p. 7, emphasis in original). Even cherished scientific understandings are culturally informed. The conceit that biomedical discourse allows for ideologically neutral and historically transcendent descriptions of our bodies is a deeply troubled one (see Ehrenreich & English, 1979; Gallagher & Laqueur, 1987; Martin, 1987, 1991). Yet much of the literature on female genital surgery pits biomedicine as "savior truth" against a demonic horde of deracinated local explanations (e.g., S. Armstrong, 1991; Hosken, 1982; Koso-Thomas, 1987; Kouba & Muasher, 1985; Slack, 1984; "Mutilation by Any Name," 1992). "Scientific facts" are marshaled to refute "cultural misconceptions" in the faith that exposing local concepts as "superstitions" will hasten the demise of such customs; the remedy is "education." There is no doubt that the practices have negative consequences for women's health, but "social customs . . . are not 'pathologies,' and such a view is a poor starting point for change, since it is not one necessarily shared by the people whose customs are under attack" (Gruenbaum, 1982, p. 6). Several groups assert that the operations performed on males and females complete the social or spiritual definition of a child's sex by removing visual traces of anatomical ambiguity: the "masculine" clitoris and/or labia in the case of females, the "feminine" foreskin for males. Male and female children undergo their respective operations at about the same age, between 6 and 10 years in the Sudan, when they have a minimal degree of reason (*'aql*) or "social sense" and are expected to understand that their bodies are being "purified," brought under socially ministered control. The female reproductive organ is "covered," while the male's is opened or "unveiled." Locally, the operations are deemed complementary (Ammar, 1954; Boddy, 1989, 1998a; Griaule, 1965; Kennedy, 1978).

Wrong, counter the analysts: Removing the clitoris is not equivalent to removing the foreskin but to amputating the penis (e.g., Hosken, 1982; Slack, 1984). Yet critics have missed the cultural point. First, their implicit assumption that gender complementarity means symmetry and equivalence (the brute antithesis of a presence/absence model) beclouds comprehension of a system in which difference is fashioned in any other way (Sacks, 1976). Second, and more significant, they mistake a moral and cosmological statement about collective and personal identity for poor scientific observation. In Western societies, this slippage is exacerbated by the propensity to map gender values onto (presocial) anatomical sex, rather than, as in Sudan, to make (potentially social) anatomical sex conform to gender. Whereas "biology" is primal to Western cultural thought, "gender" is primal to northern Sudanese (Boddy, 1989; Holy, 1991). In short, the perpetuation of female circumcision cannot be put down to a lack of scientific knowledge. Deep culturally specific resonances of both science and circumcision render such a verdict facile.

We must be willing to think ourselves outside of a Western materialist and secular discourse—a discourse no less cultural than those it presumes to oppose—in order to achieve understanding, the only foundation for respectful and truly collaborative intercession. This may be difficult to do. Biomedicine, after all, is an extremely powerful discourse, backed by an armature of efficacious practices and multinational corporate interests. There is a clear material relevance to materialist misapprehensions, one that unwittingly underwrites the continuation of neocolonialist exploitation even as it judges Africans for their "failure to modernize" (see Kirby, 1987, p. 48). A global market devoted to fulfilling people's needs and desires requires that bodies be widely intelligible (cf. Foucault, 1979, p. 136), and biomedical discourse is a strong agent of global "normalization" in contemporary biopolitics.

Historical precedent for assimilating non-Western practices to Western systems of meaning in an extravagant exercise of hegemony that obliterates historical and cultural context can be found in the Victorian use of clitoridectomy as a cure for hysteria, nymphomania, and excessive masturbation (Bonaparte, 1953; Ehrenreich & English, 1979; Huelsman, 1976; Lyons, 1991; Scheper-Hughes, 1991; Sheehan, 1985). The Victorian "invention" of clitoridectomy was suspiciously timed. According to Huelsman (1976), the procedure was first noted in European medical journals in the early 1800s, not long after European travelers began publishing accounts of female genital surgery in Africa (p. 127). Despite disparate social origins, African women were reported to undergo clitoridectomy for reasons similar to those for which doctors recommended it in Europe and the United States—to tame them, colonize precocious sexuality and channel it toward socially suitable ends. The requirement to remove the clitorises of African females was taken as evidence of some depravity on their part. Victorian mythology about the rampant sexuality of blacks provided a foil against which Europeans could view themselves as "normal," indeed "civilized" (Comaroff, 1993; Comaroff & Comaroff, 1991, 1992; Stoler, 1995). European hysterics, women who reacted against the enforced domesticity of the age (e.g., Gilman, 1899/1973), thus became "honorary Africans" in need of a civilizing hand.

Ironically, such appropriations, like those of the present day, were confounded by the rhetoric of the Empire, in which Western women occupy an ambivalent, mediatory posture: They are positioned as "other" to Western men, but simultaneously united with them vis-à-vis exotic and unruly foreigners. Here, gender dualisms familiar to feminist critique reappear in colonial guise:

> Africa is body to the West, a vacant barbaric place—a mysterious "dark continent" which has invited penetration and colonization from those more "enlightened" and "reasonable" forces that would tame its dangerous anarchy. (Kirby, 1987, p. 46)

As Western women and men are together "constituted as knowing subjects in the ethnocentric ordering of global diversity," African men and women together "must occupy the unenviable position of 'feminized other' to the West," rendering Western women "masculinized/empowered in this relationship" (Kirby, 1987, p. 46). And, as such, Western women assume masculine/imperial privilege: license to represent others, peer through the veils of 20th-century harems, objectify with their gaze (see Morsy, 1991). Numerous publications targeting Western readers, even when otherwise culturally sensitive, include photographs of African women's disembodied genitals that are virtually pornographic; alternatively, we see terror-struck little girls undergoing circumcision or suffering in its wake (e.g., Armstrong, 1991; Bonaparte, 1953; Hosken, 1982; Huelsman, 1976; Lightfoot-Klein, 1983, 1989a, 1989b; McLean, 1980; "Female Circumcision," 1982). Marginally less prurient are the ubiquitous juxtaposed sketches of "normal" and surgically altered female genitalia. In pictures as in words, African women are "othered," depicted as aberrant, whereas intact Western women have *their* sexuality affirmed as the norm. Implicitly, Western gender identities are endorsed as "proper," natural, unquestionable; without even realizing it, Western feminists' challenges to gender hierarchy are thus muted, compromised, and displaced onto women whose own concerns are disavowed.

Those who, like Hosken, see in infibulation unmitigated, self-evident violence and counsel direct political intervention seem oblivious to the entanglements of this position, its inherent ambivalence, and that of their own subjectivity. It is woefully ironic that those who properly insist they cannot be represented by men should brook so few qualms about "speaking for" African women (Gruenbaum, 1996; Hale, 1994; Kirby, 1987; Pedersen, 1991; cf. Boddy, 1991a). Other strategies are surely available, ones in which patriarchy and imperialism are less well served.

Marriageability and Identity:
Toward a Concept of Embodiment

The reasons people give for performing circumcisions are legion; they vary by society and are usually complex. No monolithic, reductive explanation will therefore suffice. Yet a common thread has to do with making women marriageable: preserving family honor by keeping women chaste, attenuating women's sexual response and conferring on them the moral right to fertility, correcting anatomical ambiguity so that an appropriate aesthetic, standard of purity, and social identity are achieved. In various locations, female circumcision is a mark of cultural belonging, of ethnic superiority, and a rallying point in nationalist and anticolonial campaigns (Boddy, 1991b, 1998b; Gruenbaum, 1991; Lightfoot-Klein, 1989b; Pedersen, 1991).

Although the practices may be antithetical to Islam, the values they underwrite are not. Indeed, their latent compatibility with religious ideals means that associated health problems have been largely ignored or deemed insufficient reason to abandon them. Many erroneously believe female circumcision to be a religious requirement (Winkel, 1995) and even with mounting pressure from Islamic revival movements, resistance to abolition is strong (Gallo, 1986; Gruenbaum, 1991). It is still widely practiced, though a marked decrease in infibulation has been noted among urban and educated groups (Badri, 1984, 1985; Gallo, 1986; Gallo & Abdisamed, 1985; Gruenbaum, 1991; Hassan, 1990). Dareer (1983) found that slightly more Sudanese men than women think that circumcision should continue (87.7% versus 82.6%), but of those who do, more women than men favor pharaonic or intermediate forms (71.2% versus 22.8%). Conversely, more men than women support the *sunna*, likely in the belief that it is religiously prescribed.

Appreciation of women's support for circumcision requires consideration of several contexts in which material and ideological issues interweave. Given the weakness of the state in societies in which the operation prevails, kinship remains the salient form of social organization. Support for the corporate family is also found in Islamic law. Specification and defense of rights and obligations, access to property, economic opportunities, health care, and social security all flow from relations among close or extended kin. The lineage—in most cases a patrilineage, whose male and female members trace descent from a common patriarch long deceased—is the source of a person's identity and economic well-being. Recruitment to a kin group is typically by birth, seldom by adoption. Through marriages, alliances are established between unrelated or distantly related lines of descent (i.e., exogamy, common in Somalia) or between close relatives seeking to intensify existing moral and economic commitments (i.e., endogamy, common in Sudan). In a kinship-based society, where most important political and economic relations are reproduced by way of conjugal ties, genealogical relatedness provides a flow chart of corporate connections, and care is taken to avoid ambiguous parentage. Sexuality therefore presents a problem. Given its capacity to generate people—labor, numerical strength, new marriages—hence potential wealth, it is a tremendously valuable resource; but insofar as it is individually housed in fallible bodies, it represents a potential threat to the maintenance of collective interests (Abdalla, 1982; Abu Lughod, 1986; Boddy, 1989, 1994; Gruenbaum, 1982; Hayes, 1975). Hence, marriage is largely by parental arrangement, and although both women and men are subordinate to the group, women's sexuality is the more vigilantly policed.

In Islamic societies, sexual restraint is a matter of family honor, and honor is vested principally in the behavior of member women—daughters and sisters rather than wives—whose premarital chastity is assumed.[6] In the absence of a strong superintending polity, a family's fund of honor gauges its ability to command human and material resources—to be seen as valued and respectable allies. A family that loses honor risks finding its sons and daughters unmarriageable, its continuity jeopardized, its economic opportunities curtailed, its political maneuverability gone. Women's lives are circumscribed physically (they should not be abroad unchaperoned), sartorially (they are enjoined to observe a modesty code), legally, and economically (they are dependent on fathers, brothers, husbands, and sons). Even today, the women of Sudan and Somalia have few options outside of marriage and reproduction. The rare unmarried woman who works in public and lives on her own is a focus of constant suspicion. The married estate is the proper one under Islam, and to be marriageable, one's morals—the fitness of one's latent fertility—must be above reproach. Thus, by continuing circumcision, women protect themselves from the consequences of possible deviance (Toubia, 1985, p. 151). In Somalia, a husband's family has the right to inspect the bride's body prior to marriage, and mothers regularly check their daughters to ensure they are still "closed"; a girl unjustly accused of sexual indiscretion will publicly uncover her genitals in order to win the dispute (Barnes & Boddy, 1994; Talle, 1993). Here an uncircumcised woman is considered a prostitute, a social and economic pariah:

> Where a most significant aspect of marriage is control of female reproductive capacity, and where circumcision has come to be the mechanism for guaranteeing the perfect condition of that capacity, to dispense with circumcision is to violate a basic condition of an essential social relation. (Gruenbaum, 1982, p. 7)

Women circumcise their daughters, not because they wish to do them harm, but because they love them and desire the best for them. Thus, tackling the practice in terms of "child abuse" is a doubtful strategy, even in Western countries, for a mother who permits the operation is neither incompetent nor mindlessly following tradition, but making an astute and contextually appropriate judgment about the future welfare of her child (see Boulware-Miller, 1985; cf. Kellner, 1993; Schroeder, 1994).

That collective ends should take precedence over individual lives is something several Western writers have rebuked (e.g., Hosken, 1982; Slack, 1984). Here, Western assumptions of the person as a self-contained locus of rights and obligations, possessed of a social identity increasingly vested in the appetites and private (but often tellingly commercialized) pleasures of the singular body, clash with African and Middle Eastern notions of self in which the person is unthinkable except in relational terms. Western feminists who condemn circumcision as a violation of the right to sexual and corporeal integrity risk being accused of presuming their own construction of self to be the ideal or "natural" human state (cf. Boulware-Miller, 1985) and of failing to censure *all* damaging gender-specific practices with similar vigor, including those in their home societies.[7]

A common perception remains that the collective ends are those of men, not women, whose interests are unequivocally violated by the practice. Few writers consider that this apparent divide may be illusory. In Sudan, for example, a woman's status increases as her sons and daughters mature and provide her with grandchildren. The position of grandmother (*haboba*) is accorded considerable respect and decision-making power in family affairs; the family is the principal arena in which the impoverished and exploited can exercise some control over their lives. But the status of respected elder is only attained through the bodies of other women and men, daughters and sons, whose marriages she and her husband arrange. The older woman's intelligence is required for social reproduction. Owing to sex segregation, her knowledge of the moral characters of prospective spouses is greater than her husband's, and this grants her considerable space within which to maneuver for her own concerns. Hence, insofar as circumcision (female and male) is a condition of marriageability, the older generation, regardless of sex, is supported in its dominance by operations performed on juniors (cf. Bledsoe, 1984). For women, power—as well as kin solidarity and assured marriageability—is derived from continuing the practice.

Under such conditions, the issue of whether women and girls "consent" to be circumcised is murky indeed. The material constraints on women's lives give them no realistic option other than to play by the cultural rules. Women know what they must do to succeed in a world whose terms they did not set but which their own actions help to ensure. The complexities of these issues are subtly explored by Mathieu (1989, 1990), who suggests that women's very consciousness is controlled and mediated in the process of subjugation; their lack of an "autonomous consciousness" makes it impossible to speak of women as "sharing" an ideology with men (see also Al-Sa'dawi, 1980). Yet if "consent" is a fallacious concept for understanding the actions of the dominated, so too is the idea that force and active coercion are the inevitable circumstances under which they experience oppression.

Although Mathieu (1989, 1990) often appears to attribute free agency to men, there is, I think, an acknowledgment that men as well as women are produced in networks of institutions, practices, and meanings that are not of their own making—which existed at their birth—but which, as these provide the very conditions of social life, they ineluctably reproduce. This is hardly a "mindless" process, nor is it immune to purposeful transformation, yet its effects clearly exceed individuals' intent. In Sudan, for example, full pharaonic circumcision has gradually been replaced by intermediate and, increasingly, *sunna,* forms. But the latest changes are responding to Islamic fundamentalist pressures, which have disciplinary implications of their own (see Gruenbaum, 1996; Hale, 1996).

To depict men's consciousness as autonomous and coherent and women's as dominated and fragmented plainly overstates the case and unwittingly replicates Western constructs. If women are not free agents, neither are they powerless or blindly submissive. The same holds for men, whose systematic privileging is in no way denied by this observation. Materialist understandings of constraint and dominated consciousness are useful but insufficient to comprehend the intricacies of power relations and their continuous reproduction and transformation. For the issue is not so much how men oppress women, but how a system of gender asymmetric values and constraints is internalized by both, with their active participation, and as such becomes normalized, self-sustaining, and indeed unself-consciously "real." We need, as Elizabeth Grosz (1987) suggests, "a corporeal feminism," a feminism that takes the body seriously, not as a biological given, fixed identity, psychic essence, or cultural limitation, but as the subject of culture and the product of power. In what follows, I sketch one such approach by elaborating on what I call "embodied cultural aesthetics"—as culturally normalizing processes of the self—in the hope of finding some terrain on which fruitful empathy and strategic alliances across cultures can take root.

On the Politics of Aesthetics

Deeper insight into female circumcision can be gained by regarding it not as radically different from practices that inform women's bodies in the West, but as similarly produced, from below, through situated orders of practice and signification. This project continues to displace theoretical emphasis from oppression to discourse and context and calls for a shift of temporal orientation from cause and effect to immanence and simultaneity. It requires the bracketing of a "commonsense" Western assumption: that the objectified world is external to or independent of its representations, and cultural symbols are "purely expressive," without material consequence (cf. Feldman, 1991, p. 165; Mitchell, 1991). It means looking beyond Western foundational distinctions between "nature" and "culture" and between "body" and "mind," and imagining instead their integration. The approach marshals conceptual tools derived from Foucault's insights on power and biopolitics (1977, 1979, 1980, 1982, 1990), Bourdieu's corporeal ethnography (1977, 1990), and Gramsci's (1971) concept of hegemony but, in the final analysis, owes more to feminist understandings that "the personal is political" than to any of these.

According to Foucault (1979, p. 24), "modern" power broke with preceding forms by changing the relationship of the human body to the state. Beginning in 18th-century Europe, power began less to be exercised *upon* the human body—in corporal punishment, for example—than channelled *through* it; the body was transformed from the object of a power requiring external obedience (to power "from above"), into the medium and ultimate effect of a power that works more diffusely, through internal domination and subjugation (Foucault, 1979, pp. 136-139; Foucault, 1980, p. 96; Foucault, 1990, p. 94). Such power exercised "from below" works to normalize bodies through an array of noncentralized, nonauthoritarian apparatuses and institutions that constitute "a micro-physics of power" (Foucault, 1979, p. 26); the products of such techniques—our bodies, our selves—may be experienced positively even as they serve prevailing relations of dominance and subordination (Bordo, 1993, p. 26). Thus, in modern states power "is not the 'privilege,' acquired or preserved, of the dominant class, but the overall effect of its strategic positions— an effect that is manifested and sometimes extended by the position of those who are dominated" (Foucault, 1979, p. 26). Analysis, therefore, "should be concerned with power at its extremities, in its ultimate destinations": bodies, techniques, and local institutions with investigating power "at the point where its intention, if it has one, is completely invested in real and effective practices" (Foucault, 1980, pp. 96-97). The body is thus "the inscribed surface of events" (Foucault, 1977, p. 148)—a living register of history, culture, and power.

The utility of Foucault's perspective is not confined to analyses of the West, his historical reference point. As anthropologists well realize, power in all societies works from below to some extent, as selves are formed and bodies shaped in dynamic interactions among human agents, social institutions, cultural meanings, conventions, and constraints; between subjects and their humanly constructed environment of objects, spaces, others; through one's practical engagement with the world (Bourdieu, 1977, 1990). Foucault's "modern" techniques and disciplines have less exacerbated, diffuse, and bureaucratic parallels in the so-called "traditional" practices of non-Western societies. These are imbued with "power in the nonagentive mode": "power [that] proliferates outside the realm of institutional politics, saturating such things as aesthetics and ethics, built form and bodily prepresentation, medical knowledge and mundane usage" (Comaroff & Comaroff, 1992, p. 22). When female circumcision is seen in this light, rather than as a form of coercive restraint, its apparent intractability can be better grasped.

Foucault has been criticized for holding to the existence of a precultural body beneath the social skin (Butler, 1990; Mascia-Lees & Sharpe, 1992b), a view that the trope of "inscription" would seem to support. But cultural practices are not simply impressed on bodies from without; they are anticipated by those bodies' socially tuned physical and cognitive sensibilities. Bodies and selves are conditioned through interaction with a conventionally meaningful world and with others whose similarly embodied dispositions are inculcated from infancy on (Bourdieu, 1977, p. 15). This nexus of structured and structuring dispositions Bourdieu (1990) refers to as the *habitus:*

> a product of history, [which] produces individual and collective practices—more history—in accordance with the schemes generated by history. It ensures the active presence of past experiences, which, deposited in each organism in the form of schemes of perceptions, thought and action, tend to guarantee the "correctness" of practices and their constancy over time, more reliably than all formal rules and explicit norms. (p. 54)

Comaroff (1985) justly reproves Bourdieu for his apparent determinism, for "leading us so far into the domain of implicit meaning that the role of consciousness is almost totally eclipsed" (p. 5). True, a hegemonic order appears to dominant and subordinate subjects alike as natural, taken-for-granted (cf. Gramsci, 1971; Williams, 1976). Yet persons are not robots; they must be credited with an intimate knowledge of their societies, knowledge that is both tacit and conscious, "rational." Socialization, after all, requires our active involvement. However inattentive to the process most of the time, we are aware to varying degrees at different moments, of contradictions and experiential paradoxes in our lives; and we adapt to them or subvert them as best we can. But it is always misleading to confuse agency with "freedom." Even when choice seems possible, one's economic security and personal well-being may depend utterly and irrevocably on compliance.

When disciplinary power is at work, subjects are schooled to self-surveillance and self-control rather than coerced from without.[8] Here power invests the body and is not only or necessarily experienced as repressive (Bordo, 1993, p. 27). The point remains: Power is constitutive, productive of bodies and selves. It is both intentional (exercised with a series of aims and objectives) and nonagentive. (These aims do not result from the choice or decision of an individual subject.) Moreover, the interplay of power relations opens up multiple points of potential resistance. Yet resistance rarely transcends culture; to assume so is to misjudge the subtly informative nature of human "culture," or as articulated by Comaroff and Comaroff (1992, p. 23), the hegemonic "order of signs and practices . . . drawn from a historically situated cultural field" (p. 23). Thus, resistance is seldom unequivocal; it may reconstitute power relations even as it contests their effects, implicating subjects in practices that sustain their oppression even while recasting its terms (Abu-Lughod, 1990; Boddy, 1989; Bordo, 1993; Comaroff, 1985; Comaroff & Comaroff, 1992; Feldman, 1991; Foucault, 1980, 1982; Foucault, 1990, pp. 94-96).

Practices and disciplines adhere to cultural logics that are woven deeply into the fabric of daily life and inform its most mundane and intimate details. Cultural knowledge is sedimented in the bodies and minds of human actors, the simultaneously experiencing and signifying selves that Scheper-Hughes and Lock (1987) call "mindful bodies." Surely unwritten and perhaps inarticulable, it constitutes an embodied aesthetic: a historically and culturally specific system of meanings that fuses morality and concepts of person, space, and time, with concrete, material images and that engenders a sense of propriety in participants and provides them with implicit criteria by which people, bodies, and objects can be judged and understood. Thoroughly naturalized in the dispositions of the habitus, it is more felt, intuited, than thought. The notion of an embodied cultural aesthetic as a dimension of hegemony is admittedly heuristic; but I think it enables us to speak—for now—in less problematic ways than before of how visceral sensibilities are both culturally shaped and politically informed. Aesthetics, of course, are never neutral; they are judgments of value, form, and conduct, suggesting suitable—natural, normal—dispositions toward the world. Here ideological, practical, and sensory realms converge. In northern Sudan, ethics and morality are tacitly yet tangibly embedded in an aesthetic of "interiority" that enlists women in enforcing their own subordination. Importantly, the subjective implications of a cultural/political aesthetic vary by gender as well as by age and social position.

In what follows, I draw from my earlier work (Boddy, 1989) in order to foreground women's bodily experience and knowledge in the Sudanese village of "Hofriyat," where I lived and conducted research for 2 years. I do not propose to "explain" women's support for infibulation, which was, until recently, unanimous (see Hale, 1996) or indeed to "name" its meaning, so much as to locate or contextualize the practice by tracing logical connections and exploring interlacing practices, facets, and representations. Analysis is therefore systemic rather than explanatory. The approach takes women's words and actions seriously, regarding them as windows onto their world. Discussion centers on situations in which consensual notions of propriety—purity, integrity, "closure"—govern not only behavior but also ideals of physical form, food, architecture, odors, and the objects of everyday life. Their tracings in seemingly disparate domains converge toward a horizon of intelligibility that opens up the meaningfulness of villagers' lives (see Boddy, 1989, for a fuller discussion). I then juxtapose this analysis to a consideration of embodied aesthetics in contemporary North America that speaks suggestively to issues of "violence" and "oppression" as well. Though reported in literature as not strictly ethnographic, this case provides further illustration that the acquisition of culturally appropriate aesthetic sensibilities is ultimately a political matter, in the course of which the social order is internalized "by the hidden persuasion of an implicit pedagogy" (Bourdieu, 1990, p. 69) and, power embodied, made self.

Sudan

In northern Sudan, the surgical alteration of the physical body in prepubescence profoundly affects the body-as-lived. Genital operations respectively orient the mindful bodies of girls and boys to their incompletely shared social world, establishing differences in their sensibilities and adult perspectives, thus obviating the compromise Bourdieu suggests is inevitably made "between the real body and the ideal, legitimate body" (Bourdieu, 1990, p. 72). The female body is considered purified, feminized by the removal of external genitalia, then enclosed by infibulation and the courtyard walls behind which the girl should now remain; the male body is masculinized, uncovered, opened to confront the world. Each sex is beautified and made pure by its respective operation. It is the female body, however, that is both metonym and icon for village society, guarded against external threat by its own scar tissue, compound walls, and the defensive efforts of local men.

Domiciles and infibulated bodies heed a common aesthetic form; indeed, they are homologous. This is expressed both practically—as in the burial of miscarriages within the courtyard's walls—and linguistically, for the men's door to the courtyard is called "the mouth of the house," a term that also denotes descendants therein sired and housed, while a woman's vaginal meatus is "the mouth of the house of childbirth." The front of the courtyard is the men's area and place where guests—strangers—are entertained; like the vagina, it is the part of the house (body) that is penetrable under controlled conditions from without. Its protected inner part—its "belly" (*buton*), by implication its "womb"—is women's domain, a private space where kin and close friends gather. The honor and integrity of the family are preserved when women stay within courtyard walls, and outside forces are kept at bay. Then too is the village safe, protected. Importantly, women are housed within their own bodies when they are bodily present in the house.

For life to continue, houses, families, and bodies must have openings; but this requirement makes them vulnerable: to other humans, including foreign colonizers, and to powerful spirits, some malevolent, some capricious, that cannot be kept out by walls, human skin or closed doors. Illnesses result when physical and architectural defenses are breached and spirits, especially, intrude. Still other physical disorders are held to be caused by bodies "opening" inadvertently. Headache, for example, is an "opened head," curable by binding. Bodily "closure" is considered health promoting, curative.

Infibulation, by enclosing the womb, contains and safeguards uterine blood, the source of a woman's fertility and her village's well-being. Local concepts of procreation stipulate that a child's bones and sinew (hard parts) are formed from the semen or "seed" of its father, while its flesh and blood (soft parts) are formed from its mother's blood (cf. Holy, 1991). Such contributions are complementary, if differently weighted; flesh and blood, after all, are ephemeral, and bones are relatively enduring. Like the skeleton that structures the body, patrilineal descent structures human relationships in a lasting way. While preferred marriages are patrilineally endogamous, in practice, marriages traced through close female kin are considered highly appropriate, even should prospective spouses belong to different local lineages. Indeed, relationships traced through flesh and blood—through women—link the village's skeletal descent groups, providing integument that eventually succumbs to entropy and decay unless renewed by successive intermarriages. The social body—the endogamous village—is thus also homologous with the physical; both are moral entities.

These images round back again to the house, which is physically linked to childbirth and the womb through practices that accompany failed pregnancy. Stillbirths are buried outside the "mouth of the house" against the courtyard wall; miscarriages are placed in impervious rounded pottery jars and buried inside the enclosure near the kitchen. Importantly, this type of jar is also used by women for mixing flour (male seed) with water (female fluid) to produce the staple wafer-thin bread that nourishes human life with the fertility of the land. Similarly, men are responsible for producing grain for the household while women provide its water.

These practices and objects of everyday life are implicit media of socialization. They converge to shape and sustain a woman's profound identification with her fertility and persuade her of the need to protect it at all costs. Her preeminently practical sense of self is nonetheless supported and made coherent by explicit ideology. The sexes in northern Sudan are said to differ in the relative amounts of *nafs*: animal life force, lusts, passions—and *'agl*—reason, self-awareness, the ability to control one's emotions and behave in socially appropriate ways—that each will develop as it matures. Women's childbearing capacity binds them more closely than men to their *nafs*. Yet circumcision is an act of *'agl*, and girls must have attained a minimal amount of it prior to their operations. Circumcision attenuates and balances the forces of *nafs;* it socializes a woman's fertility, transforming it from a physical attribute into a moral accomplishment. Through it her body becomes, with the house and the village, a moral space, reproductive, bounded, and "impenetrable."

There are further implications here for social relations and a person's sense of self. Bodies are at once "closed" and integral, and interdependent, intimately and complexly relational. Indeed, one can regard the village as an organism in which physical substances—flesh, blood, bone—circulate and are shared by individual members to varying degrees. Consubstantiality maps potential social alignments that are, in a very real sense, embodied, physical. Closely related women experience dimensions of their shared selfhood acutely, and not only through the institution of the sororate, a common practice in many kinship-based societies whereby, if a married woman dies, her sister assumes her place in order to continue the marital relationship. (The corollary for men is the levirate. Both practices highlight the significance of marriage as political and economic alliance.) It is also common that a woman whose daughter has died in childbed or from some other cause will fall gravely ill herself from a malady called *du'f,* "weak" or "diminished blood." Her illness ultimately may be attributed to a *zar* spirit that had earlier plagued them both by "seizing" or "tying up" their (common) blood.

Gendered consubstantiality intersects with ideals of harmony, balance, and purity in bodily constitution. If health is propriety, and propriety relative closure, they also require an internal balance of complementary forces: cold and hot, light and heavy, wet and dry. All are controlled to some extent by ingesting appropriate foods or smelling suitable odors (e.g., perfumes and incense associated with males or females, opening or closing). Both impure odors and impure foods—those that are neither white nor enclosed by skins, jars, or tins—can precipitate illness and render the body assailable by spirits. Certain smells (of human sweat or blood) are idiomatic of physical openness, hence spirit intrusion, and whenever they occur can occasion possession trance. Indeed, any untoward experience or act, like walking alone through village streets at night, endangers a woman's health, for bodies out of place are "open," vulnerable to *zar* spirits and other *jinn*. So, too, a woman with fertility problems, whether menstrual difficulty, sterility, miscarriage, or an infant's early death, might consider herself possessed. For none of these experiences is "self": All are cast as alien, the work of external agents.

A concern for physical harmony is, not surprisingly, matched by a desire for social harmony. Relational selves are constrained to express negative emotion in the presence of close kin. Yet this injunction applies to women more than men, who are expected, within limits, to externalize anger in defending their own and the family's honor. Women are more liable to internalize conflict, which they legitimately express and physically experience as dysphoric illness. Illness, after all, is ultimately sent by Allah, not humans, and Allah enjoins us to seek its cure; its recognition thus mobilizes community concern and family resources, the more so if spirits are deemed its proximate cause.

In a limited way, Hofriyati culture may be described as a "culture of pain" (cf. Lightfoot-Klein, 1989a). In contrast to Western societies in which pain is to be eliminated through profitable medical management, severe physical pain is, in certain contexts, normative and positively valued and enforces ideals of personhood. On ceremonial occasions, men, for example, engage in mutual whipping to build and test their relative stoicism. And pain is a fact of the infibulated woman's life, an embodied referent supporting her sense of who and what she is. Instructively, the symptoms of somatized conflict and women's excessive "openness"—seen as departures from or failures of the normative self—entail radical *diminution* or denial of sensation: temporary blindness, loss of appetite, aphonia, paralysis of one or more limbs, depression. If possession is diagnosed, a woman will undergo a spirit cure that bombards her with sounds, rhythms, smells, sights, tastes, and physical movement. Gradually she is drawn to participate bodily in these during moments of possession trance.[9] The ritual manipulates the cultural aesthetic both sensorially and through vivid spirit imagery, as when ideals of bodily closure and behavioral propriety are satirized by wanton spirits who appear in humanly embodied form. Because spirits are alien beings who exemplify what villagers ought not to be, participation in these images is an aid to reflection, encouraging the reestablishment of bodily order; here possession is a conservative force. Yet such embodied images also defy the existing aesthetics of "health," enabling, if not overt resistance, at least self-recognition, perhaps creative doubt.

Still, the pull of the habitus is strong. Social conventions anchored in visceral sensibilities render the former—and the gendered power relations there contained—natural, inevitable, unquestionably real. An embodied aesthetic is indeed productive of specified bodies, selves, relationships. Hence its political, as well as therapeutic, efficacy. Its technique—like that of possession, which is constructed on its terms and which addresses its ruptures in Hofriyat—is mimesis, an epistemic style entailing profound subjective identification and investment "below the level of consciousness" (Bourdieu, 1990, p. 73; cf. Kramer, 1993; Taussig, 1990). Embodied knowledge claims no Olympian privilege; instead, knower and known are collapsed, engaged in reciprocal and reversible relationship. This is knowledge not that one *has*, notes Bourdieu (1990, p. 73), but that one *is:* never detached from the body, evoked only through the body, that is, mimetically.

North America

Female circumcision is a lucid, practical symbol of Hofriyati culture that draws deeply on embedded ideas of group and gender identity. It is not a symptom of what is wrong with that culture but of what its adherents deem normal and correct. Despite contextual differences, practices that bring the female body to accord with an elusive ideal of womanhood in Hofriyat formally parallel the normalizing disciplines of Western femininity. Both derive from a presumption that female bodies are in need of improvement and continuous monitoring; both enlist women as agents of their self-modification and enjoin them to self-surveillance and restraint; both work to instill in women a desire to conform, to become what they "ought" to be. Today as in the past, Western body techniques at their most extreme have included surgeries and other physical interventions: in Victorian times, clitoridectomy to reduce "excessive female sexual appetite" and removal of the bottom ribs—revived in 1990s Argentina and Hollywood—to ensure a tiny waist, plus corsets that displace the internal organs causing violent indigestion, uterine prolapse, perpetual weakness, immobility, and shortness of breath; in the contemporary West, cosmetic surgeries of all types—liposuction, lip enlargement, breast reductions and implants, tummy tucks, face lifts—in which the risks of disfigurement, discomfort, infection, and impairment of social and physical functioning are clear (Bordo, 1993; Ehrenreich & English, 1979; Morgan, 1991). Even far less radical procedures (tweezing, waxing, electrolysis) involve pain, much of it "self-inflicted." My aim in this litany is *not* to trivialize female circumcision but to detrivialize and expose as equally political—subordinating *and* productive—the disciplines of Western femininity. If Western women resist placing our practices in the same light as infibulation and persist in seeing there a form of violence absent from our own, it is because Sudanese notions of gender are denaturalized for us, exotic, distanced from our selves in a way that our own constructions of gender can never be (cf. Bordo, 1993, p. 50; see Gunning, 1992; Hale, 1994).

Still, one might object that Western women can choose to approximate their culture's aesthetic model, whereas Sudanese girls cannot. Yet surely that choice is illusory. If we fail to meet minimum but ever-shifting standards of feminine "normality"—in slenderness, skin color, facial features, even age—our social and economic chances, including marriageability, may be sharply curtailed (Morgan, 1991). Our competence may become suspect and even our morality, as racial minorities, the disabled, and the obese can attest. The myth of "choice" stems in part from the Western ideology of autonomous individualism but owes much to the proliferating repertoire of body modification techniques available in industrial capitalist societies as well. We *can* choose, yet from an array of "treatments" all directed toward normalization. Further, like Sudanese girls, we are schooled to prevalent images of femininity from an early age. Indeed, studies show that increasing numbers of girls as young as 7 or 8 engage in rigorous dieting and exercise (Bordo, 1993, p. 61), practices that can impede their development and reproductive health. The issue of choice is obscured by the fact that we spend hard-earned money to normalize our selves. In our hierarchy of resort, the most dangerous and least reversible of techniques—surgeries—are generally the more costly. Increasingly, and incrementally as our bodies age, we "purchase" our femininity (Morgan, 1991). Doubtless we may experience the result as positive, indeed liberating (cf. Davis, 1991, 1995), unmindful that the work we do and the money we invest sustain our subordination

> through the pursuit of an ever-changing, homogenizing, elusive ideal of femininity—a pursuit without a terminus, requiring that women constantly be attuned to minute and often whimsical changes in fashion—female bodies become docile bodies—bodies whose forces and energies are habituated to external regulation, transformation, "improvement." Through the exacting and normalizing disciplines of diet, makeup, and dress—central organizing principles of time and space in the day of many women—we are rendered less socially oriented and more centripetally focused on self-modification.
>
> Through these disciplines, we continue to memorize on our bodies the feel and conviction of lack, of insufficiency, of never being good enough. At the farthest extremes, the practices of femininity may lead us to utter demoralization, debilitation, and death. (Bordo, 1993, p. 166)

Parallel constraints increasingly encumber Western men yet rarely affect their lives to the same extent. Nor do they carry precisely the same material consequences or rewards. Still, these observations must be weighed against the fact that men in Western societies have, at various times, been disciplined to perform willingly acts that jeopardize their lives, like obeying orders to advance from the trenches in World War I. However, for those who survived, acknowledgment that they had lived up to society's masculine standards confirmed their gender privilege. Culture costs everyone, but its costs and rewards are not evenly shared.

The most extreme expressions of the normalizing techniques of Western femininity are pathological ones: anorexia nervosa and bulimia. These are culture-specific disorders whose symptoms until recently were seldom encountered beyond North America. Anorexia nervosa is an illness of plenty; it is foreign to Sudanese who regard corpulence as a measure of economic and marital success and a sign of potential fertility. But, like possession dysphoria in Hofriyat, occasioned as it is by experiential breaches of femininity, eating disorders appear to be produced by experiential paradoxes that both challenge the cultural order and expose the politics of its embodied aesthetic. Anorexia, at times, bears uncanny resemblance to possession.

Susan Bordo's analysis is particularly instructive, and I condense but a few of its points. She situates anorexia in a culture historically informed by profound distinctions between the corporeal or material and the mental or spiritual, in which the body is experienced as alien, "not-self." The body by this aesthetic is a cage; it confines and limits; in the strong language of Augustine, it is "the enemy," locus of all that threatens our attempts at control (Bordo, 1988, 1989; Bordo, 1993, p. 144). For women, the body—fleshy, menstrual, sexual, reproductive—is both source and ineluctable evidence of their subordination (Ortner, 1974). Anorectics' embodiment of the dualism is unusually pronounced: They experience not only hunger but other bodily sensations—pain, cold, heat—as invasive, coming from outside the self (Bruch, 1973, p. 254). Indeed, self-mastery is attained by denying sensation; refusing to eat becomes an act of creation, wherein, like medieval ascetics, the mind dictates to nature, actively produces the body's design, and experiences in the process the (ultimately destructive) pleasures of control, physical transcendence.

Anorexia nervosa is a complex phenomenon. Though virtually all North American girls are trained to its underlying aesthetic through television, film, and peers, relatively few go on to develop the full-blown syndrome. Yet its symptoms illustrate commonplace patterns writ large. Here dramatically embodied are the politics, the ethics, of female restraint, a contemporary ideal of thinness that women are enjoined to enforce in themselves. Mimetic internalization of impossibly slim "normality"—as of perfect fertility in Sudan—grants a woman little space, little distance from which to critique. Should the embodied aesthetic contradict her body, she feels compelled by her growing dysphoria to achieve their accord. Thus, like being reinfibulated or acknowledging possession, refusing or limiting one's food is, paradoxically, a self-therapeutic endeavor. The politics and aesthetics of self, overdetermined yet crystallized by the illnesses of bulimia and anorexia nervosa in the present moment and in earlier times by female maladies like hysteria or agoraphobia (Bordo, 1993), resonate provocatively with the "normal" situation of women in northern Sudan. Despite their culturally specific configurations, both compellingly counsel women's social and physical containment and self-control (see also Guillaumin, 1993; Kanner, 1993).

Conclusion

A concept of embodied aesthetics—as an effect of mimesis and a dimension of hegemony—gives us novel purchase on how gender constructs and their political entailments are rendered self-evident, routine, and banal. It enables us to contextualize this process according to cosmological and moral concerns in local contexts and to problematize agency and intention, "consent" and "desire." But it is important, I think, that cultural aesthetics, both embodied and articulated, be interrogated also for their *anaesthetic* properties, their potential to distance selves from their own, and others', pain. Ironically, Westerners' horror when confronted with female circumcision arises not only because of the challenge it poses to their internalized corporeal aesthetic but because their anaesthetic capacities are attuned for that habitus as well. Conversely, this is also in part what prompts African feminists, distanced from Western body politics to some degree, to accuse Western feminists of hypocrisy when they fail to include their own gender technologies in the same critique or neglect to acknowledge their global privilege (see Gilliam, 1991).

The stance of this essay has been unabashedly relativist—in a cultural and historical, not moral, sense. Contrary to popular impression, by adopting it I do not condone the harmful practices here discussed but seek instead to comprehend them; this is, I believe, the only way to foster truly collaborative impetus for positive change. As Renteln (1988) perceptively notes, cultural relativism is a *meta*ethical theory, a theory *about the nature of* moral perception. It is not, she argues, a defense of tolerance or, for that matter, intolerance. Nor does it deny the possibility of human universals, including universal human rights. Rather, as a precursor to contemporary post-structuralist critique, its most valuable feature is "its ability to challenge the *presumed* universality of standards that actually belong only to one culture" (Renteln, 1988, p. 58, emphasis added). It stresses the role of enculturation in making one's judgments *appear* universal, warning that ethnocentrism is inevitable and requires hard intellectual work to surmount.

Rather than serving as rhetorical whips for our own peculiar form of mutual flagellation, perhaps feminists' simultaneously positioned yet culturally critical selves can be oriented to more productive ends. By directing attention to the corporeal groundings of identity within specific societies, we can begin to appreciate the subtle connections between violence and normality and explore with genuine empathy a terrain that Western women share with women everywhere. When we relinquish insistence on "explanation" that presumes to speak from an objective, culture-free position and instead take seriously the realization that analysts are also subjects embedded in specific cultural and historical frameworks, not only may we hear what others have to say, we might also start to listen.

Notes

1. I use this term as it is preferred by Sudanese and Somali women with whom I work, rather than "female genital mutilation" (FGM), which is more common today in the Western press.

2. Dareer (1982, pp. 55-65) suggests that reinfibulation is a recent urban innovation. Lightfoot-Klein (1989b, pp. 381-382) hypothesizes that reinfibulation is "a bastardization of the Western vaginal tuck procedure, since it was first practiced by educated upper-class women with exposure to the West." In the Nilotic village where I lived, reinfibulation was a long-established custom performed frequently and meant to reinstate a woman's social virginity after giving birth and when contemplating remarriage after being widowed or divorced (Boddy, 1989; Hayes, 1975). Mohamud (1991, p. 208) notes that in Somalia, reinfibulation is regularly performed after the first birth, but not after subsequent ones.

3. Lightfoot-Klein (1983) reports that some Sudanese doctors estimate that one third of all girls die from the operation in areas in which antibiotics are not available (p. 356). Thiam (1983) gives an estimated 6% annual death rate among some Somali groups, and in a study of 7,505 women in Khartoum, 95.9% of whom were pharaonically circumcised, Aziz (1980) reports 17 cases of severe bleeding that were reported to hospitals.

4. Many couples resort to anal intercourse, which, along with bleeding that may occur during vaginal sex, has prompted concern over a possible tie between infibulation and the spread of HIV (Dorkenoo & Elworthy, 1992, p. 9; Van der Kwaak, 1992).

5. Lightfoot-Klein (1989a, 1989b) makes much of the Sudanese *dukhana,* or smoke bath (a dry sauna that imparts a smoky fragrance to the skin that remains for several days despite frequent bathing). She assumes that using it to signal readiness for sex also signifies enjoyment of the act. I am not so sanguine. Women know that to preserve their marriages—their economic security—they must please their husbands and provide them with heirs.

6. An adulterous wife dishonors her natal family; she shames her husband, who has dishonored himself by his failure to control her and/or by losing her respect.

7. The popularity (even fetishization [Abusharaf, 1996]) of "female genital mutilation" as a cause also reflects a contemporary interest in female sexuality and female victimization. We seldom hear about the equally severe "male genital mutilations" practiced by some aboriginal groups in Australia, where the penis is subincised, slit down the middle of the underside, and the urethra exposed, nor of those in Yemen and Cameroon, where during circumcision the penis is partially flayed as a test of virility and, in some cases, also the inner thigh.

8. Coercion and physical restraint may well be present and, where they occur, act to reinforce the "normalization" of selves. Such might be the "function" of rape in Western societies, a point well developed in the feminist literature.

9. It is tempting to contemplate whether the propensity to experience a dissociative state, such as trance, is linked to the trauma of circumcision in childhood. Although there is no space to develop the issue here, it merits investigation in light of Bordo's (1993) treatment of the dynamics of anorexia nervosa and Lundgren's data on ritual wife abuse (e.g., 1995a and this volume). Also crucial is the link between child sexual abuse and burgeoning "multiple personality disorders" in North America.

5

Violence Against Women in Societies Under Stress

Monica McWilliams

W hen the United Nations Conference on Women met in Beijing in September 1995, the issue of violence against women formed a key part of the discussions. The growing importance and recognition of violence as an issue at the international level were the result of almost two decades of organizing by women's groups in various parts of the world. As a result of these campaigns and discussions, the knowledge on the various forms of abuse to which women have been subjected has steadily increased. Despite this increase, there are still relatively few documented studies on violence against women in societies under stress. Most studies point to the universality of this violence, but they also note the variations in frequency due to the nature of the conflict in various parts of the world (Heise, 1994; Levinson, 1989; Richters, 1994). Less is known, however, about the impact of political conflict on violence against women and the various forms of gender-based abuse that may result. The need for this to be more rigorously documented is reinforced by the recent systematic rape of women in places as far apart as Bosnia and Rwanda.

Clearly, one needs to be extra vigilant when attempting to make comparisons about violence against women in societies that are themselves in conflict. The extent to which political conflict affects women's "telling," detracts attention from "private" acts of violence, distorts data-recording systems, and diverts help-seeking—all are important features of the way in which victims of different kinds of violence are counted. Studies that do exist are also limited in accuracy due to the lack of national accounting mechanisms, particularly during periods of intense conflict.

The kind of violence used against women in societies under stress should ultimately be discussed with reference to actual cases. What is needed is an analysis of the "universal forms of abuse" that attempts to differentiate between the various contexts that give rise to them. In seeking to find linkages and patterns in violence against women in societies under stress, it is also important to identify the various responses to the violence: how women deal with the violence and what consequences they suffer. How are violences "problematized" and "resisted," and how are they "normalized" or made "acceptable"? (See also Kelly & Radford, this volume.)

The term *societies under stress* itself requires some conceptual clarification. It could, for example, include those societies that are undergoing a process of modernization; those experiencing the effects of colonization; or those in which civil disorder, terrorism, or war has occurred. In this chapter, attention is focused on those societies that have endured serious political conflict, but there may also be inter-actions between high levels of societal change and communal strife. So too, the political conflict may not be the sole determinant in the nature and scale of the violence against women. Religious and ideo-logical belief systems may have a significant role to play, particularly in determining the legitimacy of such violence. Attitudes toward the perpetrators and victims as well as the strategies available to prevent and combat it may be dependent on both the political and ideological "forces" that exist.

What Constitutes Violence Against Women in Conflictual Societies?

In September 1992, the United Nations Declaration on the Elimi-nation of Violence Against Women produced a definition of violence against women: "any act of gender-based violence that results in, or is likely to result in, physical, sexual, or psychological harm or suffering to women, including threats of such acts, coercion, or arbitrary deprivations of liberty, whether occurring in public or private life" (Richters, 1994, p. 2).

The declaration is concerned with violence directed against women and makes it clear that violence affects women disproportionately because they are women. Violence enacted by women against women, although less frequent, is nonetheless important, but whether such abuse should be characterized as "gender violence" is debatable. The extent to which women collude with men in "violating" other women, as in situations of war, or cause harm to other women when acting as accomplices to men may indeed be perceived as gender violence. The definition becomes slightly more problematic when attempting to apply it to women who become directly responsible for administering forms of torture to female political activists or to female prison officers who carry out humiliating procedures on women prisoners. In the latter context, a pertinent example is the tactic of "strip-searching," which was used against female "Republican" prisoners in Northern Ireland and which will be referred to later.

Despite these reservations, the United Nations Draft Declaration (1992) is useful in that it specifies the gender-specific nature of the violence. The declaration also sets out a typology that can also be applied to conflict situations. Article 2 (p. 4) states that violence against women should be understood to encompass, but is not limited to, the following:

1. physical, sexual, and psychological violence occurring in the family,

2. physical, sexual, and psychological violence occurring within the general community, including sexual harassment, trafficking in women, and forced prostitution, and

3. physical, sexual, and psychological violence perpetrated or condoned by the State, wherever it occurs.

In situations of conflict, the categorization of violent acts in the context of the family, the community, and the state may be even less appropriate, because the locus for the abuse is not tied to any single category but instead becomes a pervasive and interactive system for legitimizing violence. To highlight this interaction, I will turn first to the more global picture of violence against women before focusing on the various forms of violence within the family. The final section uses Northern Ireland as a concrete example to examine the social, political, and cultural conditions impacting at the familial, community, and state level and to assess the extent to which these are accentuated or ameliorated during periods of conflict.

Violence Against Women
in Conflict Situations

The appropriation of women's bodies, for sexual gratification or as a symbol of "victorious conquest," is a common theme in the literature on violence against women in war or other situations of conflict. Outside the home, gang rape, trafficking in women, and forced prostitution are aspects of the violations against women that have been accentuated in situations of conflict. Young women and girls have been enticed by promises of jobs to move to other areas, only to be forced to work in brothels near army encampments or large reconstruction sites in places like Phnom Penh and Manila.

The use of women's bodies to carry drugs is a relatively new form of abuse. Jo Fisher (1994) highlights the case of Colombian women imprisoned in the United Kingdom for drug-carrying offenses and shows vividly how poverty and the fear of violent reprisal can drive women into dangerous situations. It is reminiscent of a similar use of women's bodies, particularly in guerilla warfare, to shelter weapons or to carry messages. In any war, there have been female activists who willingly act as carriers, but there have also been those who have had no other choice. The latter are often the most vulnerable and, like the drug carriers, are blackmailed into dangerous situations.

It is women's added vulnerability to rape and sexual abuse in times of conflict that is the most common theme to emerge from the available literature on forms of violence perpetrated on women. Women have been raped in every war—as retaliation, as damage to another man's property, and as a message to the enemy. Rape is an efficient weapon for demoralization and humiliation. In World War II, Russian and Jewish women were raped; Soviet soldiers raped German women during the "liberation" of Berlin; and Chinese women were raped by the Japanese. In more recent wars, Vietnamese women were raped by Americans; Serbian men raped Bosnian Moslems, and Hutu men raped Tutsi women in Rwanda, while Tutsi men raped Hutu women in return.

The extent of rape is such in war that "women's bodies become like letter boxes" (Warner, 1994). To apply Levi-Strauss's concept of "objects of symbolic exchange," rapes can be interpreted as messages signed on women's bodies from one fighting side to the other (Rener, 1993). The rape of women in Bosnia is also seen to have a visible political aim. According to Slavenka Drakulic (1994), it is an organized and systematic attempt to clean (to remove, resettle or exile) the Muslim population out of territories the Serbs want in order to establish an ethnically clean nation-state of great Serbia. Zajovic (1994) claims that when "territory" is cleansed, women, as part of the property of enemy males, are seized and colonized. She sees rape as an effective instrument of territorial cleansing, because men will not return to the place where they have been humiliated by the rape of "their" women. When women are raped, it is experienced not as women's pain, but as male defeat on the grounds that they were too feeble to defend their own property.

Women who have been raped by soldiers can be victimized again by the male members of the family who make it known that their sense of personal honor and dignity have been attacked. This is particularly the case when the latter is conceived as directly related to and dependent on the sense of moral propriety of the women in their family. Examples of this are to be found not just in Bosnia but also in Pakistan, Sri Lanka, India, Bangladesh, Latin America, and Palestine (Al Fanar, 1995). Turned out by family, community, and society, they become the dispossessed in both war and peace.

The appropriation of women's bodies is also exemplified by the assaults and murders of women during the political conflict in Northern Ireland. One of these occurred on April 6, 1994, when Margaret Wright was lured into a social club on the supposition that she was a Catholic. Her body was found dumped in a garbage bin at the back of a derelict house in an overwhelmingly Loyalist (Protestant) area of Belfast. She had been stripped naked and beaten before being shot several times through the head. The previous year, Anne Marie Smyth was kidnapped by a gang of men after she found herself in an unfamiliar part of Belfast. The gang tortured her for several hours, then cut her throat and dumped her body in a car park. The sectarian motives of these men became even more apparent during the subsequent court case, when the women's deaths symbolized the interaction between sectarianism and male violence in Northern Ireland (McWilliams, 1994).

The abuses to which these women were subjected were made worse by the fact that others stood by and let it happen. McCollum, Kelly, and Radford (1994) argue that conflicts, in Northern Ireland and elsewhere, foster behavior by men in groups where all are participants or some watch and encourage. They argue that male bonding has been buttressed through resort to rape and sexual violence as a deliberate strategy of war. In such situations, the range of permission from the dominant group—military or paramilitary—to subordinate the "other" is so extensive that, for women caught up in the conflict, religion or ethnicity offers a second incitement.

In Northern Ireland, arson attacks by Loyalist (Protestant) paramilitaries on the homes of female single parents have also resulted in the deaths of women and children. Because the women have been specifically singled out because they are Catholic women living in "another" man's territory, the sectarian and sexist nature of the violence once again overlaps. There have also been gang rapes in Northern Ireland, albeit on a much smaller scale, in which the women's religion has formed a further pretext for the sexual assault, freeing the perpetrators in their minds from individual responsibility.

Bargaining Sex for Survival

Cultural norms, together with women's social and economic dependency, limit a woman's ability to negotiate safer sex with her partner. In conflict situations, this is even more accentuated in that a woman can be forced to barter sex for survival. For example, aggressive and dominating sexual behavior among South Africa's young black male population has meant that the incidence of rape has increased at an alarming rate in recent years (S. Armstrong, 1994). In Soweto, a feature of these rapes is that the female victims are frequently young teenage associates of these men. Girls are being raped for the first time, on average, at about the age of 14 years (S. Armstrong, 1994). One explanation put forward by local community workers is that these male adolescents are looking for women who are relatively AIDS-free (see also Kelly & Radford, this volume). The tragic irony of this is that the sexual exploitation of girls and young women can result in higher rates of HIV infection because the surface cells in the immature genital tract are less efficient a barrier to HIV than the mature genital tract of older women (S. Armstrong, 1994).

The "sexual" search by men, either as soldiers or civilians, for girls free of disease can also be linked to the mobilization of Korean women as enforced sex laborers (comfort women) during the Japanese invasion of China in 1937-1938. The purpose of the "institutionalization" of the supply of prostitutes to the Japanese Imperial Army was to arouse soldiers' fighting spirits, to provide them with an outlet for the frustration and fear fostered by hierarchical military life, and to sustain a military morale.

Initially, Japanese prostitutes were used, but many of them were found to be suffering from venereal disease and were infecting Japanese soldiers. Japanese brokers were used to find Korean village girls from poor families who were lured to brothels under the pretext that if they agreed to be drafted they would be able to earn money in textile companies. A more indiscriminate kidnapping of women, aged 14-30, including married women, took place later in order to increase the supply of women. By 1943, under the Enforcement of the Military Compulsory Draft Act, 220,000 young Korean women were taken by the Imperial Japanese Army, among whom 70,000 to 80,000 were sent as comfort women to the front lines in Asia. The sexual slavery of Korean, Taiwanese, Filipino, and Dutch women by the Japanese Imperial Army from 1937 to 1945 reinforces the idea that these women were the common property of soldiers. An advertisement hung on the entrance to a brothel exemplifies this: "We welcome courageous soldiers who are on duty for the holy war; yamatonadeshiko, Japanese-like obedient women dedicate their mind and body to you" (Watanabe, 1993).

What these examples from various countries show is that the appropriation of women's bodies can impact on women's lives in different ways. In war, rape may become a form of booty as well as a sexual invasion of the enemy's women on a mass scale. Cultures may differ in how this violence, or its impact, is problematic or how it manifests itself in later years. Rape takes many different forms and has different repercussions for different victims. War tends to intensify the brutality, repetitiveness, and likelihood of rape. War also intensifies men's sense of entitlement and social license to rape. But marital rape, the most private of all rape, shares some of these characteristics. It is repetitive and brutal, is used to assert authority, and forces a woman to flee her home and community. Violation by a state or enemy soldier is not necessarily more devastating than violation by an intimate (Herman, 1992). We know that cultural beliefs about the role of women in society can also accelerate or moderate the levels of violence used against women as well as its impact. But what we also need to know is the extent to which these cultural beliefs can interact with particular conflicts to determine the extent and types of violence used against women, and it is to this that we now turn.

Violation of Women's Roles

Forms of torture used against women in Latin America draw on the cultural attributes surrounding the role of women in the family and the cult of the Virgin Mary within Catholicism. These attributes provide the foundation on which the edifice of the Latin American woman's self-perception and self-respect is built. Given these cultural antecedents, when a woman is sexually or physically assaulted or imprisoned in her home:

> The protection and refuge of the home that she represents is shattered and the control and coherence she maintained in the intimate sphere of the household is shattered as well. The assault on the woman's sense of self and the manipulation of her traditional role as wife and mother are used by the torturers to break, punish, and ultimately to destroy her. (Bunster-Burotto, 1994, p. 164)

In his book *It's Part of Life Here,* Robbie McVeigh notes a similar gendered nature of harassment by the security forces in Northern Ireland. One interviewee reported that mothers were frequently threatened that they would

> have their kids taken away and that is very frightening for a woman, as for many their kids are all they have. Usually, single parents are picked out for harassment. They get it worse especially the house searches . . . but no woman I know has ever officially reported this harassment. . . . They are afraid of drawing attention to themselves. . . . They would rather lie low. (McVeigh, 1994, p. 133)

The men who police women in this way do so in the knowledge that this has a particular significance for women in these countries. It means that the women can no longer be looked up to as the "pure mother figure." "There seems to be a willingness not only to violate cultural notions of what the 'natural' social order is, but in fact to direct torment with excruciating precision just to those areas of societal definition" (Bunster-Burotto, 1994, p. 166). It is also the case that different kinds of harassment are meted out to politically active women who have dared to engage in public struggle as a way of teaching them that they should be fulfilling the real or potential role of wife and mother. The general rule appears to be "the more politically active the woman, the more sexualized the violence."

The idea of subverting the political will of women by reducing their self-respect is also evident in the enforced strip-searching of female political prisoners in Northern Ireland. The Republican women who experienced this believe that strip-searching was implemented not as a security precaution but more as an attempt by the prison authorities to break the morale of the female prisoners— particularly the politically "strongest" members of the group. Given the extent to which Irish women have internalized notions of personal modesty about female nakedness, these women felt that strip-searching was a gendered form of torture leveled at them by other women. Their repulsion at being forcibly stripped was accentuated by the fact that male prison officers were allowed to stand by with dogs barking at their heels, observing the women being dragged from their cells (Cullen, 1994).

Irrespective of the conflict or the culture, it is now generally accepted that violence is a part of life directly, or indirectly, for women in almost all societies and that it is perpetuated by dominant beliefs, traditions, and institutions wherever it occurs (Borst, 1992; Counts, Brown, & Campbell, 1992; Wilson & Daly, this volume). The extent and the impact of domestic violence are better documented than other forms of violence, and it is to this that we now turn (Dobash & Dobash, 1979, 1983b, 1992; Johnson, this volume; Statistics Canada, 1993).

Violence Against Women in the Family

In an extensive cross-cultural study of small-scale and peasant societies, wife beating was the most common form of intrafamily violence, occurring in approximately 85% of the societies studied (Levinson, 1989). In countries like Sweden, where equal opportunities and welfare provision have been placed relatively high on the political agenda, women still struggle to lead lives independent of domestic violence (Elman & Eduards, 1991). Given this, the question we need to address is whether political conflict accentuates the scale of domestic violence or whether it adds other dimensions to it.

We know that a particular dimension of male violence is the attempt by some men to control the reproductive rights of their female partners (see Wilson & Daly, this volume). Asserting control over fertility can be the cause of much real or potential violence. For the purposes of this exploration, we need to know more about the significance and impact of this in societies under stress. For example, does a policy of enforced pronatalism, which is strongly correlated with postconflict situations, increase violence against women as well as decrease the opportunities for women to escape from violent relationships? In Croatia, for example, following independence in 1991, families with many children were favored in the country's subsequent taxation and social policies, and fathers' and husbands' power within the family was legally and economically reinforced. Rederlechner and Ratz (1993) note that women's roles were to be defined thereafter as "birthers" of children so as to create the "nation" of Croatia (demographic renewal) and as full-time mothers to raise these children into nationhood (spiritual renewal). In such countries, the forced impregnation of women becomes an additional dimension to the reinforcement of this subordinate role.

A common theme of these pronatalist policies is the influence of fundamentalist religious beliefs and postcolonial attitudes in countries recovering from political disruption. In Iraq, for example, contraceptives were declared illegal during the 8-year long Iran-Iraq war, and the declaration was reinforced after the Gulf War. The pronatalist policy has been modified slightly since 1991, but the current economic sanctions mean that contraceptives remain unavailable except on the black market (Bhatia, Kawar, & Shahin, 1992). When women do attempt to assert control over their fertility, assaults are frequently reported in the context of the family but are also often sanctioned by the state authorities to whom the women turn for help.

In conflict situations, the transference of inheritance through the male line is also perceived as crucial, and following marriage there is immense pressure on women to give birth to sons. An example of a husband's attempt to control the reproductive process is provided by the Northern Irish man who threatened his wife to "have a son or else" as she went off to the hospital to have their second child (McWilliams & McKiernan, 1993). Such language is also reminiscent of the advice to Irish husbands in the 1930s. For those married to infertile women, the advice was "to bounce a boot off her now and then" (Arensberg & Kimball, 1968).

"Traditional" forms of violence, such as these assaults on childless women, may be accentuated during conflict situations, whereas others simply continue as before. There is some evidence to suggest that even where the violence is related to a particular cultural tradition, it can also be influenced by the national/civil strife within that region. For example, increases in dowry-related violence against women have been associated with the demand for higher dowries in order to replace possessions that have been destroyed during civil upheavals (Njovana, 1994). Wives can also be threatened with divorce in the knowledge that they can be replaced by higher-income-generating women. In Iraq, impoverishment caused by the recent militaristic campaigns against Iran and Kuwait and the internal conflict against the Kurds in northern Iraq have led households to sell their assets, "beginning with women's jewelry" (Bhatia et al., 1992). The jewelry was the dowry, and for poor women, it guaranteed some financial security. Its sale has increased Iraqi women's dependence and vulnerability within the household, marital discord has increased, and in some cases, women have been driven to begging and prostitution (Bhatia et al., 1992).

Increasing materialism that leads to demands for higher dowries to be provided may also account for the increase in dowry-related violence in India (Matsui, 1989). Dowry murders are predominant among middle-class families and usually take place in situations in which the wedding has been arranged too quickly (Schenck, 1986). In examining the processes of capital accumulation in a number of countries, Mies (1986) stresses that accumulation (as a condition for capitalist development) has a direct relationship with the violent oppression of women in the home. She argues that men try to maintain their traditional culture by keeping their women at home while becoming obsessed by an international consumption economy (Mies, 1986). In an attempt to accumulate or maintain capital, dowry systems develop and expand to new areas. This leads to a significant increase in dowry disputes, dowry-related murders, and suicides. Research also shows that most Indian women who commit suicide have been abused for many years before they die (Kishwar & Vanita, 1984).

Elderly women are also more likely to put pressure on their families for material support when traditional income-generating systems break down. This can be the result of a range of factors— among which is civil or national political strife. Parental demands leading to intergenerational conflict give domestic violence another dimension.

El Bushra and Piza-Lopez (1993) also note the detrimental effects of structural adjustment programs on women's employment in certain parts of Africa. Where external aid has been provided following civil conflicts, it can impact in such a way that it displaces women's role in agricultural production, leaving them more dependent on other forms of "male" income, which can give rise to increased levels of domestic violence.

Challenging Culture-Specific Forms of Gender Violence

Categories and practices of violence against women inside the family other than domestic violence, such as sati and bride burning, remain associated with particular cultures, societies, or regions in the world. Feminist researchers have recently begun to deconstruct the meaning of these "culture-bound" or "culture-specific" forms of gen- der violence (Richters, 1994). They dispute that "culture" is the all-encompassing factor that explains the "why" and "how" of the particular practice. In particular, these writers have been critical of law enforcement agencies that refuse to penalize men who perpetrate violence on their partners in case the judicial system is seen to interfere with "culturally sensitive" ways of doing things (Razack, 1994) (on such cultural differences, see Boddy, this volume). When these sensitivities are applied to domestic violence, the solutions are generally more "offender-centered" than "victim-centered." As Razack (1994) notes, "The eagerness with which theories of cultural differences are taken up in the justice system is treacherous ground to travel" (p. 28).

In the same way that women have begun to challenge the judicial system, they have also learned to challenge demands that implore them to return to the "old ways of doing things." Such "ways" often have gender-specific scripts attached to them and have little to do with what the women consider to be their "traditional ways." McClintock (1993) makes a similar point in what she refers to as "the temporal anomaly within nationalism," which she describes as veering between the nostalgia for the past and the impatient, sloughing off of the past. She believes that this temporal anomaly is typically resolved by figuring the contradiction as a "natural division of gender." She notes:

> Women are represented as the atavistic and authentic "body" of national tradition (inert, backward-looking and natural) embodying nationalism's conservative principle of continuity. Men, by contrast, represent the progressive agent of national modernity (forward thrusting, potent and historic), embodying nationalism's progressive or revolutionary principle of discontinuity. Nationalism's anomalous relation to time is thus managed as a natural relation to gender. (McClintock, 1993, p. 66)

Following the War of Independence in Ireland in 1922, the emerging national narrative gendered time by figuring women (like the colonized and the working class) as "the conservative repository of the national archaic." Marriage bans were written into the Irish Constitution that denied married women the opportunity of paid employment. When DeValera became the president of the newly Independent Ireland, he called on women to adopt the role of the self-sacrificing and unquestioning mother. As Mary Holland (1988) laments, "We have apostrophized the country itself as mother. The concept of 'Mother Ireland' has met with whole hearted national approval. The message has been unequivocal. The proper place for a woman apart from the convent is the home, preferably rearing sons for Ireland" (p. 5).

For single women, the imagery was no less conservative. The metaphor of the "comely maidens dancing at the crossroads" was used as a signifier for the new anticolonial legislators to maintain at all costs the chastity and purity of these young women. McClintock (1993) argues that within these emerging national narratives, "women did not inhabit history proper but existed like colonized peoples in a permanently anterior time within the modern nation as anachronistic humans, childlike, irrational and regressive—the living archive of the national archaic. White, middle-class men, by contrast, are seen as the forward thrusting agency of national progress" (p. 67).

Such thinking helped reinforce the inferior and subordinate status of women. Indeed for women considering moving beyond their ascribed role, the potential threat of abuse was sufficient to contain them within the established roles of the status quo. Women acting as agents of social change in the transitional stages following independence often question the cultural specificity of such roles. Traditions are both the outcome and the record of past political contests as well as the sites for current contest. In any discussions following a period of conflict, both men and women should be empowered to decide which traditions are outmoded, which should be transformed, and which should be preserved. In wanting to reclaim the positive features of their traditions but not wishing to be forced back to what was for them the dysfunctional side of their culture, they are often caught between "a rock and a hard place" (Razack, 1994).

Researchers such as McCollum et al. (1994) and Kelly and Radford (Chapter 3, this volume) point to the legacy left by colonization in the form of institutionalized violence, which is gendered. In Canada, Aboriginal women are much more likely to experience domestic violence or to be murdered than any other group of women in the country. Maori women in New Zealand argue that as a result of the historical process of colonization, which resulted in the establishment of a British-based monoculture, they can no longer live their lives in accordance with their own cultural traditions that they believe valued women highly (Oudes, 1992). In a similar vein, the Ontario Native Women's Association stressed in their report on domestic violence "that the continuing colonization and the devastating impact of past domination are the contexts in which Aboriginal family violence must be examined" (cited in Razack, 1994).

The question that needs to be posed here is how does colonization transform gender relations in such a way as to exacerbate, introduce, or, alternatively, reduce violence against women. In some instances, it may be that colonialism has an amplifying effect on the violence and/or subverts existing cultural prohibitions and reactions that formerly acted as a control on the potential abuser's behavior. On the other hand, by attempting to impose their own "superior" morality, colonialists may have outlawed practices that involved forms of gendered violence. Such colonial intrusions may have helped reduce violence against women in some instances. There is also the possibility that these practices can be relegitimized in postcolonial times through claims to "authentic" precolonial culture. In noting that "some of our worst abusers are community leaders," Canadian Aboriginal women identify the endemic nature of the problem and, simultaneously, note as problematic the community denial of the abuse that does exist. Victimized in their own communities and outside them, they have put forward strategies that recognize the twin realities of racism and violence.

Community Denial and Postcolonial Silencing

One of the features that colonized women experience is their collusion in the silence surrounding violence against women from men known to them in their communities. Following the plantation of Ireland in the 17th century, abused women were silenced by the cultural representations of the English media, which continued to depict Ireland, or Hibernia, as a virginal young maiden, fair-haired and helpless, besieged by a group of bestial, ape-like Irish men (Innes, 1994). The role of the colonialists was to woo the young Hibernia away from the grasps of these men so that she could be joined in "Union" with John Bull, or England.

To contest the colonial narrative of the feminization of Ireland, Irish nationalist discourses adapted the signifying use of women to put forward their own version. In their literature, they portray Ireland as a "woman wronged" or as a sorrowful mother whose children (land) have been usurped. Women were typically construed as the symbolic bearers of the nation but were denied any direct relation to national agency. As Boehmer notes, "the motherland" of male nationalism may thus "not signify home and source to women" (as cited in McClintock, 1993). She notes that the male role in the nationalist scenario is typically one in which men are contiguous with each other and with the national whole. Women, by contrast, appear in a symbolic role in need of protection. This is similar to the Algerian situation in which Fanon (1965) notes that the imperial intervention frequently took shape as a domestic rescue drama. "Around the family life of the Algerian the occupier piled up a whole mass of judgements . . . thus attempting to confine the Algerian within a circle of guilt."

Similar judgments were made about the family life of Irish women who could not be seen betraying their partners by speaking out. This would only have lent credibility to the image of the "Fenian Franken-stein." The dream of the "total domestication of the colonized society" frequently haunts colonial authorities, and the domesticated, female body often becomes the terrain over which military conquests are fought. The analogy of peacetime is the way in which judicial and police authorities attempt to find ways of "domesticating" and "tam-ing" those who come before them charged with domestic violence—particularly when the individuals concerned come from a different cultural background.

What the imagery of the anticolonial "Irish" warriors did was to create a crass, sentimental, and ultimately offensive stereotype of Ireland as a tragic but stoically dignified woman whose honor was defended by her brave sons fighting against perfidious Albion. In addition, it silenced the much stronger imagery of the sovereign goddess figures and female Celtic warriors of early Irish tradition. The separation of women as helpless maiden or as a woebegone mother was a minor ideological distinction in which the "honor" of both were deemed in ideology (although rarely in practice) to be deserving of protection.

In many different contexts, this issue of defending women's "honor" becomes a common theme in the literature on violence against women in societies under stress. Women have been expected to internalize or to submit to this imagery even when it was far from reality. Rather than protecting women, the notion of "honor" as understood by the men in these communities can, in effect, destroy them. Moreover, in Palestine, the "Al Fanar" [lighthouse] women's group could not get any media coverage for their campaign of oppo-sition to "honor" killings that were carried out by family members on women who had been raped. None of the West Bank Palestinian newspapers would touch the subject, steering clear of any criticism of Arab society that could be used as propaganda by the Israelis (Al Fanar, 1995).

To create subversive spaces in which to name "their oppressors" as wife-beaters and murderers, particularly when some of them were regarded as local heroes, has been an intensely difficult process for women in both postcolonial and conflict situations. In an aptly titled report *Unheard Voices*, Iraqi women point to the same difficulties in talking openly about abuses leveled at them by husbands returning from the battlefield (Bhatia et al., 1992). Women married to veterans face many hurdles in exposing their "war heroes" as domestic terrorists.

Colonial Legacies and Unholy Alliances

An interesting feature of the postcolonial discourse in Ireland is that it assigned a spurious sense of authority to Irish women in their portrayal as the "matriarch" in their own home. Women were led to believe that if they lacked power in other areas of the new Ireland, at least they had held on to its reins within their home. To subvert that view was to remove the last vestiges of authority from them. As Kate Shanahan (1994) notes, "Women would go to their graves without telling anyone what has happened to them" (p. 6).

When the women's movement attempted to explode this false consciousness in the 1970s, both the church and the state went to extraordinary lengths to prevent its effectiveness. One example of this is provided in Northern Ireland by a local magistrate's reaction to the introduction of injunctions that permitted police officers to exclude violent offenders from their homes. When the magistrate first encountered "exclusion orders" in 1980, he had to adjourn court proceedings until he read the actual legislation and was convinced, in his words, that "a man could be put out of his home." He spoke of regret that a time had returned to Ireland when men could be thrown on to the street. Not being disposed to understanding the reasons for such legislation, the magistrate was erroneously equating exclusion orders with the penal times of 19th-century Ireland, when tenants were evicted from their homes by English landlords (McWilliams, 1993). Similar responses were also encountered in England, but in Northern Ireland a history could be used, which gave perpetrators a stronger claim to "unfairness." In contrast to this, the concept of exclusion gives some abused women a sense of justice, because, through its proper enforcement, they no longer become the ones on the run.

Both the churches and the judiciary formed an unholy alliance in attempting to place restrictions on these exclusion orders when they were first introduced. The constitutional ban on divorce in the Republic of Ireland until 1996 is another example of this alliance that established the view that the family must be kept together at all costs. The Irish Constitution, following the tradition of postcolonialism, reinforced the position of the church and thus the inferior status of women. Until the mid-1960s, it succeeded in silencing the voices of pluralism and in maintaining its predominantly fundamentalist religious ethos.

Forms of control of women were condoned and sanctioned by a set of cultural beliefs that upheld the sanctity of marriage even in the face of violence. It was understandably difficult for women to challenge such ideology when it was so widely supported and when their personal identity and sense of worth were seen to be dependent on successfully maintaining their marriages. For some Irish women, a major part of their cultural identity was tied to being married—even at the cost of violence.

Going Underground

When cultural values subscribe to keeping the family together, particularly at times of community conflict, the introduction of alternative approaches to domestic violence can be problematic. Until relatively recently, those who attempted to create some kind of sanctuary for abused women and children within their local communities were themselves sanctioned for doing so. Often the price was too costly, with the result that many Irish women had to leave their communities completely or emigrate to England.

One of the ironies of the conflict in Northern Ireland is that the "troubles" have provided a "place of safety" for women fleeing persistently violent partners. Studies have shown that in cases in which women have been killed, the triggering event was often the women's threat of withdrawal (Wilson, Johnson, & Daly, 1995). "Getting away" can be extremely dangerous, and finding a safe place to live can become crucial. The extent to which some women have to go in order to protect themselves and their children from their former partners is evidenced by the small number of women who deliberately chose to come to Northern Ireland in the expectation that the political conflict would deter their partners from following them. Similarly, some women from Great Britain and the Republic of Ireland selected particular communities within Northern Ireland in which to resettle in the hope that their husbands would find it too dangerous to follow them (McWilliams & McKiernan, 1993). The things that place sanctions on men's mobility in Northern Ireland, such as the threat that a man from the Irish Republic may be identified as a stranger and killed in a sectarian attack or that an English man could be "done" for being "in the wrong place at the wrong time," can help provide the kind of sanctuary that women and children need in order to start a new life.

Women who had been exposed to life-threatening situations and who finally leave their relationships more often remain in their own countries. However, this can be at the expense of breaking all of their connections with communities and families and by disappearing "underground" into a community where they may be able to remain anonymous. This option presents enormous difficulties for women who have previously had a family and social network for support. It proves to be particularly problematic for women from Traveler/Gypsy and ethnic-minority communities. The feelings of separation from their distinct cultural groups and the loss of friends and social network are exacerbated by the experience of moving into a settled or different language-speaking environment. There is much to link these women with those who seek political asylum or become refugees. The feeling of displacement from the rest of the community or alienation from the dominant culture can influence some to return to the sites of conflict in the same way that it influences abused women to return to their abusive partners.

The displacement of millions of women and children from their homes because of military conflict causes social and economic disruption that requires the setting up of alternative institutions. For example, there are presently around 20 million refugees worldwide who have fled their home countries in the face of persecution: Over 80% are women and their dependent children (El Bushra & Piza-Lopez, 1993). Another 25 million are displaced within their own countries. Women's Aid, the organization in Dublin responsible for offering refuge facilities to abused women, reports on the plight of Bosnian women who were made to seek refuge twice—once from the Serbian army who had displaced them from their homes and again from their husbands who used domestic violence as a means of venting their frustration at their own "powerless" situation.

To seek refuge from their violent partners, these women faced institutional barriers layered with racism and sexism. In addition, refugee women face the barriers of immigration law that frequently demand that they remain with their husbands even when there is knowledge of the violence. They are often forced to run to a situation that is as bad as the one from which they fled. The gender implications of the displacement of women and children and the institutional responses to women who experience domestic violence in situations in which societies themselves are under stress have recently started to be addressed by the United Nations.

Finally, I outline the implications for abused women and children living in a society that was dominated by a high level of social disruption and examine the state's response to domestic violence when it occurs in the midst of political violence. Attention is centered on whether or not there are any special problems encountered in such a situation and whether these have particular implications for women elsewhere.

Political Conflict and Domestic Violence: The Example of Northern Ireland

Between 1969 and 1996, approximately 3,200 people were killed and 36,800 seriously injured in the conflict in Northern Ireland (Royal Ulster Constabulary, 1997). It has been argued that the scale of the conflict in Northern Ireland has been relatively low when compared to the 700 Palestinians killed during the 2-year Intifada or the 65,000 killed in one decade in El Salvador (Ditch & Morrissey, 1992). However, there are two significant features that have made Northern Ireland distinct. First is the relatively small size of the country: Northern Ireland has a population of 1.6 million people. If the numbers killed and injured proportionate to the population were to be applied to Great Britain (population approximately 54 million), then the figures of 108,000 deaths and 1,188,000 injured give us some idea of the scale of the problem. The second notable feature of the Northern Ireland situation is the length of time over which the conflict has been sustained. The "troubles" continued unabated for 25 years until the Republican (IRA) and Loyalist cease-fires in 1994, which were followed by 18 months of relative peace that ended in February 1996, when a bomb was planted at Canary Wharf in London. The IRA cease-fire was reinstated in July 1997.

Against this background, there have been additional factors determining the quality of women's lives in Northern Ireland. One such factor is the less-public nature of the private violence that women have experienced from men known to them. The difficulties that women have encountered in making domestic violence more public are partly, though not entirely, the consequence of the political conflict. Police resources, for example, are almost entirely taken up with combating paramilitary activity, and media attention is similarly focused on the political situation.

The "public" and "private" juxtaposition of violence can also lead to contradictory messages about what constitutes "acceptable" and "unacceptable" forms of violence. For example, when a woman is the target of a sectarian murder in Northern Ireland, invariably there is a great sense of outrage. This outrage exposes the gendered nature of public morality in its opposition to the murder of women in political conflict. However, when a woman has been murdered in a "domestic" assault in the "sanctuary" of her own home, there is less of a sense of violation. In Northern Ireland, as elsewhere, there is a kind of continuum that ranges from the least- to the most-acceptable type of murders, which is perhaps best symbolized in the way in which murders not related to the political situation have been euphemistically referred to by police officers as "ordinary decent murders."

Between 1991 and 1994, at least 25% of these "ordinary" murders were related to domestic violence. In this 4-year period, 20 women were officially recorded as having been killed by a husband or common-law partner (McWilliams & Spence, 1996). This is more than one half the number of women who have died as a result of political violence over the equivalent time period. Yet, in contrast to the deaths of women resulting from the political conflict, the domestic violence incidents have received minimal attention. It is apparent that the "public" and the "political" nature of the violence determines the response to these homicides. In the present competition for resources and attention between political terrorism and domestic terrorism, the former will always win out.

The use of the word "terrorism," in the context of interpersonal violence, can pose difficulties, because the term itself is contested even when associated with the political conflict in Northern Ireland (on the importance of definitions, see Kelly & Radford, this volume). However important as it is to raise questions about how violences are problematic or to juxtapose violence against women (which is gendered) against that which is not, this does not tell us about the ways in which the wider social conflict itself impacts on those experiencing domestic violence.

Domestic Violence and the Availability of Weapons

The number of domestic-violence-related homicides proportionate to the number of married and cohabiting relationships gives us some idea of the size of the problem in any particular country. Using the spousal homicide ratio that calculates the average number of domestic violence homicides per million couples in the population each year, Northern Ireland's figure of 26 per million can be compared to that for other countries. It is, for example, higher than the spousal homicide rate of 17 that Wilson and Daly (1994; see also this volume) report for Canada. Comparisons with some regions of Great Britain and the Republic of Ireland also show Northern Ireland to be higher (McWilliams & Spence, 1996). Because the Republic of Ireland is adjacent to Northern Ireland but has not experienced political conflict in the same way as its northerly neighbor, does the conflict explain why the homicide rate for domestic violence is higher in Northern Ireland than in the Republic?

In ongoing research, work is being undertaken to establish the proportion of domestic violence homicides that have been caused by the use of "legally held" weapons. What is clear is that the use of such firearms introduces a special dimension to domestic homicide that does not exist in the Republic of Ireland or Great Britain. A significant feature of the incidents in which guns had been used in homicide or assault cases was that the majority of victims have been married to members of the security forces. As a result of the "troubles" in Northern Ireland, members of the security forces (police, prison service, and army) are able to apply for personal protection weapons that they can keep at home. When this is added to the number of politicians, members of the judiciary, and businesspeople considered eligible to carry weapons, one starts to build a picture of the large number of households holding such firearms.

The extent to which these guns impacted the types of abuse that women experienced was one of the main features of a 12-month study on domestic violence that I carried out in Northern Ireland in 1992 (McWilliams & McKiernan, 1993). It confirmed the findings of other research (Evason, 1982; Montgomery & Bell, 1986) that showed the increased availability of guns in Northern Ireland meant that more dangerous forms of violence were used against women within the context of their own home. Women spoke of their experiences when a gun was pointed at their head, and they did not know if it contained a bullet. One woman reported how her partner would recall episodes from the film the *Deer Hunter*, in which the Russian roulette scene was evocative of a man living on "the edge": "It was both mental and physical. You know, I am thinking of times when he would put a gun to my head (and play Russian roulette with me) . . . but there was no physical harm done then" (McWilliams & McKiernan, 1993, p. 36).

Refugee workers also recall seeing women who had circular bruising on their necks caused by the pressure point of the nozzle of a gun. Some women reported being subjected to this kind of abuse over long periods of time. For women threatened in this way, there is the additional problem that the physical marks, if any, are difficult to detect. This meant that they had greater difficulty in being believed by those from whom they sought help. Men who did not keep guns in their own houses (mostly members of paramilitary organizations) were still able to threaten their partners by suggesting repeatedly that they knew where they could get guns. Whether or not the gun was produced was often not relevant because the threat was enough to induce high levels of anxiety.

For women faced with the difficulty of reporting to the police the abuse of men who were themselves police officers, some found that their concerns were not taken seriously. Following incidents of domestic violence in which police officers had their guns removed temporarily, the men were able to retrieve them from their workplace the next day. The women who had been repeatedly threatened by these "personal protection" weapons argued that rather than protecting the family's safety, these guns constituted a potential risk to their own lives.

Individual choice has existed throughout the "troubles" on the issue of taking guns home, and some police officers concerned about the potential threat to their children have chosen not to do so. However, when concerns were raised by women's groups and researchers about the use of weapons in cases of wife assault, senior police officers discussed the possibility of introducing a "fit person" category in relation to carrying weapons. That is, a "fit person" is a police officer against whom no report exists of having used a weapon for any purpose other than personal protection (in the context of the current security situation). Clearly, one further dimension in the Northern Ireland conflict is the problem women face when living in an "armed patriarchy." The interaction of militarism and masculinity in Northern Ireland means that there is a much wider tendency to use, or to threaten to use, guns in the control and abuse of women within the context of domestic violence. For a proportion of women within these households, the availability of guns has provided the additional fear that they or their children could be shot in conflicts involving domestic violence (on firearms and violence/homicide, see Johnson, this volume; Wilson & Daly, this volume). Firearms are commonplace in North America, whereas they are very unusual in most homes in Britain, except in Northern Ireland.

As part of the ongoing discussions of the peace process in Northern Ireland, there has been much heated debate over the decommissioning of paramilitary weapons on the one hand and the demilitarization of the security forces on the other. However, despite this lengthy debate in the current multiparty negotiations on decommissioning, the Women's Coalition has been the only political party to raise the issue of the use of weapons in situations of domestic violence. Sharoni (1992) argues that the strong link between guns and military/paramilitary identities among Israeli men might lead one to suggest that it is with great reluctance that men finally relinquish their arms following the cessation of a political conflict. In Northern Ireland, the discussions about relinquishing weapons have led to serious political recriminations by the paramilitaries' representatives and the government negotiators, but little mention has been made of the issues that Sharoni raises, which is the link between masculinity and militarism.

Contested Issues in Policing Domestic Violence

Despite the fact that there is a struggle for legitimacy around the role of policing between the security forces and the paramilitary groups in certain areas of Northern Ireland, there is some similarity in the way in which both the official state police and the paramilitary policing groups carry out their roles. Judgments are made on what constitutes real crime and on how best to handle this within the community. Decisions are made on the type of "justice" that best fits the more public forms of crime, such as *joyriding*—a term used to describe the often reckless driving of stolen cars by children as young as 11 years. However, there is a good deal of ambiguity about what is involved in a more "just" response to violence in the home. This is partly because neither group considers domestic violence to be a real crime, but also because it reflects the contradictions of trying to police such crime in the context of a community that is experiencing other forms of conflict and violence.

In the Northern Ireland study, when abused women in nationalist communities were asked if they would contact the police for help, some felt reluctant to do so because the question of who policed their community was such a strongly contested issue. One respondent noted: "In this area the police are not people that you normally go to. . . . We look after ourselves. . . . When we look for help, the police are never included. They are always seen as the harasser" (McWilliams & McKiernan, 1993, p. 56).

This has also been noted in South Africa, where "no black woman would go to the police station. . . . Just to be seen near a police station might mean you were perceived to be an informer, your home would be burnt down and you would be killed" (cited in S. Armstrong, 1994, p. 36). In such situations, women's resistance to the violence may be curtailed, and they may have to find other strategies of resistance (on forms of resistance, see Kelly & Radford, this volume). Occasionally this means involving unofficial forms of community policing, such as the local paramilitary groups, but this can also create serious repercussions for abused women.

The destabilizing effects of conflict situations often result in the breakdown of structures of law and order. As noted above, some women may find it difficult to contact the police—police refusal to answer domestic violence calls, a feature familiar to peacetime situations, becomes even more accentuated by the wider conflict. In Northern Ireland, due to a perceived risk to their security, the police do not respond to calls in certain areas. This lack of police response subsequently undermines court restraining orders that depend on police action for enforcement. When police officers do respond, they have to be escorted into these communities by the British Army. This arrangement usually entails a convoy of six to eight heavily armored vehicles with the personnel wearing flak jackets and carrying submachine guns. Not only does this draw considerable attention to the offense, but it adds to the anxiety of having to ask for police help. On occasion, in order to respond to domestic violence calls in rural nationalist areas, the police have had to use helicopters for protection against sniper fire or remote-control bombs in the more open countryside. At particularly tense periods of conflict, they seek out intermediaries, such as local priests, to respond on their behalf. The attitude of the clergy toward victims of domestic violence in Northern Ireland becomes a crucial factor in whether or not these women find the help they require at such times of crisis.

Paramilitary Involvement

Do these women who are reluctant or unable to contact the police seek alternative sources of help from paramilitary organizations? One such organization is the IRA (the military wing of the Republican/Anti-British movement), which over the years has been taken to task by people within the community for exercising a form of *machismo* in the types of punishment that its members have handed out. One example of this is the tarring and feathering of women accused of going out with British soldiers. In the late 1970s, Women's Aid provided practical support for some of these women, arguing that the paramilitaries were mirror images of the forces they were supposedly combating (Harkin & Kilmurray, 1985).

It is also worth noting that although "tarring and feathering" was used against women in Northern Ireland, this form of public shaming has never been suggested for the perpetrators of domestic violence (for a history of public shaming, see Dobash & Dobash, 1981). In other conflict situations, variations on public shaming have been proposed. In Nicaragua, for example, women recommended that men who battered their wives should be publicly named and denied active participation in political projects (Collinson, 1990). In Northern Ireland too, women have begun to break the silence around perpetrators by naming men who have systematically abused women and children. In some cases, they have approached the offenders to issue them with unofficial "exclusion" orders that have time limits attached stating when to leave the area and when to return. They know that if these orders remain unheeded, they may have to use the heavy-handed tactics of the paramilitaries.

However, the paramilitaries have, like some police officers, adopted a method for deciding what constitutes acceptable and unacceptable forms of behavior. Within the continuum of more serious forms of crime, they set priorities and act accordingly. For violence within the family, child abuse has received a more immediate response than domestic violence. Several women knew they could go to paramilitaries for help, but one woman concluded that certain members of the IRA in her area "didn't like getting involved" (McWilliams & McKiernan, 1993, p. 56); not wishing to invade the privacy of the home has often been the pretext for the lack of statutory intervention for domestic violence. From the evidence above, it seems that the unofficial agents operate the same kind of gendered response. In relation to violence in the family, it is dominated by men, either at the state or community level, who have the power to decide what is or is not a violation.

For women who have experienced the controlling influence of their partner's abuse, the decision to involve "other dominant men" is riddled with contradictions. The outcome may involve the women being asked to hide weapons or personnel in their homes or to respond with sexual favors at some later stage. What they may be exchanging is one set of controls (familial) for another (community). The actions of the paramilitaries can also leave abused women vulnerable to retaliation by partners and friends who interpret it as "informing." If the abuser happens to be a member of a paramilitary organization, then exposing him to the police is not acceptable, and the policing by paramilitary organizations of their own members is unlikely. One woman who was abused by a Republican ex-prisoner pointed to the duplicity involved when paramilitaries were willing to police others but not members of their own organizations.

Other abused women disclosed that when their husband's behavior was brought to the attention of the paramilitary group, then action would be taken if the partner was wanted for some criminal offense. Here the strategy utilized in peacetime by police officers is mirrored in conflict situations. In these cases, the domestic violence incident would be the pretext for getting back at the man for some other offense. Those who had considered asking for help were also concerned that their partners would be physically harmed or permanently disabled through a punishment shooting. In a Protestant area, when a woman found no support from the police, the Ulster Defence Association offered to do something about her husband, but she declined their offer, "so that he can't claim I did him any harm" (McWilliams & McKiernan, 1993, p. 56).

What all of this shows is that the masculinity and militarism of both the paramilitaries and the police are reflected in their various responses to domestic violence. Punishment with weapons is seen by paramilitaries as the appropriate response, but it is this same punishment that makes many victims reluctant to seek help in the first place. Similarly, the accompaniment of the police with the symbolism of their military focus makes some victims reluctant to come forward and identify their plight. Where these difficulties exist, some women find support from paramilitary organizations, whereas others make clear decisions to use neither the police nor the paramilitaries. Those advocating community policing in situations of political conflict need to be sure that they are not simply replicating inequitable responses to crime.

What Does Northern Ireland Tell Us?

The concrete example of Northern Ireland highlights the differences in responses to domestic violence that can occur in the context of ongoing conflict in the wider society. The availability of weapons leads to a heightened intensity of domestic violence both in terms of its serious impact and the increased number of fatalities. Certainly, the assaults on women may more easily result in murder because of the proximity of firearms among army and police personnel. Moreover, the level of the conflict can also determine the range of protection and policing afforded to women and children. As Northern Ireland moved from a conflict situation to a more peaceful one and then back to conflict, resources were simultaneously diverted from the security side of policing to the domestic violence units and then back again. As police training and attention became focused on domestic "terrorism," rather than political terrorism, then women and children were afforded better protection and safety within the family. However, this provision has been retracted with the breakdown in the cease-fire, with the consequent shift from providing some level of protection back to toleration of domestic violence. The forms of intimate violence and its intensity expand with the lifting of some of the limited controls on men's behavior created by the conflict situation and overall lack of "escape" opportunities for abused women.

What the examples from Northern Ireland also show is that the political conflict imposes considerable constraints on women experiencing domestic violence. The alternatives available to women elsewhere cannot always be assumed as options when a country experiences a period of political turmoil. If women's ability to resist the violence is curtailed, then they become more vulnerable in their homes with fewer options open to them. As in Northern Ireland, Nevo (1993) also notes how domestic violence soared in Israel during the height of the Gulf War. She also notes how the Israeli men felt justified in using domestic violence because the government had implemented a one-week curfew that confined them to their homes rather than calling them up to fight as they had initially expected.

Conclusion

This chapter shows that violence perpetrated in the family, community, or by the state is used to keep women in their place; to limit their opportunities to live, learn, work, and care as full human beings; and to hamper their abilities to organize and claim their rights. It is a major obstacle to women's empowerment and to their full participation in shaping the economic, social, and political life of their countries. Conflict situations, such as in Northern Ireland, further complicate a society already riddled with difficulties. In countries in which the "security" services have a heightened perception of their "military" role and the police culture predominantly subscribes to traditional views about the subordinate role of women, the more laissez-faire attitudes toward domestic violence add yet another set of barriers to the help-seeking process.

Given that women are faced with choices that are dependent on these cultural and political factors, abusive partners may be in a more powerful position within these communities because they know that women cannot pursue help through the normal channels. It is clear that abused women who belong to particular communities endure a process of triple victimization—as outlined in the earlier typology of the United Nations Declaration: first, by the perpetrator of the assaults within the family; second, by both those in formal organizations such as the police and other professional help-providers within the community; and finally, by state institutions, which through their responses or attitudes either minimize or rationalize the abuse. Such collusion sends gender-stereotyped messages with the combined result that the abuse itself is maintained longer by the perpetrators and endured longer by the victims.

In societies under stress, there are fewer options for women and fewer controls on men. When controls, either cultural or institutional, are levied on men's use of violence, then that violence may be mediated or tempered. When those controls are lifted or when they disappear, as in situations of war or political conflict, then permission is granted, metaphorically speaking, for men to assert or reassert their power and dominance.

A hierarchy of controls may exist in which women from the "other" side, such as the rape victims of Bosnia or the comfort women of Korea, may experience this control most directly. Women on the same side of the conflict who live with men either as soldiers, conscripts, or civilians may also experience a heightened level of violence during periods of intensive conflict. Women married to these military men experience a different kind of control than the Bosnian, Korean, or Vietnamese women, because the violence is instigated by their own men. If one models these controls as concentric circles, according to whether the perpetrators are known or unknown to women, whether they are soldiers or civilians, then the model should also include those women who live in a constant state of fear but have learned to control their own behavior in return for a provisionally safe sanctuary. Depending on how drastic the change in their situation, there may be some flexibility as they move around the model.

This model could also represent the continuum of violence (also discussed by Kelly & Radford, this volume) ranging from the threat of physical abuse to marital rape and homicide perpetrated by men known to the women. The "extra" abuses that occur in situations of conflict and social disorder, when the "controls" get lifted, would determine where one is situated within the model.

Community activists have recently decided that women should no longer be subjected to the unending control of abusive partners or, on the other hand, become subjected to the control of those to whom they turn for help. They have begun to challenge the more laissez-faire responses within the community and the state and are finding ways of holding accountable those who are resisting any change to their gender-specific cultural beliefs and practices that permit men's use of violence to dominate and control women in intimate relationships. Those in the positions of providing help are being encouraged to move away from their advocacy of simple explanations for domestic violence and to locate the causes of the violence within a wider cultural framework.

Community women activists recognize that in order to make domestic violence an unacceptable part of their culture, they have to change the conditions and the attitudes in which it thrives. Consequently, they have set up alternative structures within their own communities. These include support networks that enable women to make decisions within a framework of choice as well as involving the community in discussions around gendered power and masculinity. When peace is declared, it is these women who work to ensure that any incoming funding from the peace dividends should establish innovative projects for young people that challenge the gender inequities within relationships and that young men become socialized into ways of resolving conflict without resorting to political or domestic violence. Women in conflict situations know that a cessation of military/political violence does not bring a cessation of all violence. But they also know that they have to find ways to challenge those who have used violence in the past: Men should not be allowed to rationalize its use, but likewise they should not be excluded from the possibilities of change. As the victims of this violence in both the domestic and political fronts, women have learned to face fear but also to leave open a space for change (on changing violent men, see Dobash & Dobash, this volume).

In their imaginative ways, local women are left to create an alternative cultural environment, one that will put in place a more democratic set of structures, which should ensure that women are written into, and not out of, the multiplicity of national narratives that take place after periods of conflict and colonialism. They are insistent, in the same way as Eleanor Roosevelt once was, that a family life free from violence is a fundamental human right. In engaging the cultural dimensions of the problem at the grassroots level, women have few misconceptions about the struggles involved in implementing the aspirations of Human Rights Declarations.

6

Violent Men
and Violent Contexts

Rebecca Emerson Dobash and Russell P. Dobash

P opular conceptions of violent acts and those who commit them often reflect the notion that this is mindless, incomprehensible, unpredictable, and unpatterned behavior enacted by the alcoholic, the mentally unstable, or the socially desperate. Such notions are less uncomfortable and less challenging than the notion that violence might be functional, intentional, and patterned. If violence is a form of random deviance rather than a reflection of recurring social relations, then one need not worry about the shape and form of everyday social life but only about deviations from it. The concern about violence and its attending circumstances can thereby be removed from the concerns of those who have had no direct experience of it and expect none. It is the problem of others, the behavior of others, and an issue for others. If, however, violence is seen as intentional acts undertaken in order to achieve ends that are deeply embedded in the circumstances of daily life, it becomes an issue for us all, may affect anyone, and is about daily life. This conception requires a detailed

AUTHORS' NOTE: This research was undertaken with Kate Cavanagh and Ruth Lewis, and Dan Ellingworth assisted with computer analysis. We wish to acknowledge support from The Scottish Office (Edinburgh) and The Home Office (London), which funded the research reported here; The Harry Frank Guggenheim Foundation, which supported the international seminar meetings in Carmona and Madrid, where earlier versions of this and other chapters were presented; and The Rockefeller Foundation, which supported our stay as visiting scholars at the Villa Serbelloni, Bellagio, Italy, where ideas had time to develop.

account of violent actions and the circumstances and contexts in which they occur. Locating violence in the midst of daily life demands a focus on the mundane, the ordinary rather than the extraordinary, the conflicts of interest embedded in daily life, and the rationales and justifications of perpetrators as well as the reactions and responses of victims.

Here, we shall focus on the men who perpetrate violence against a woman partner in order to examine their notions of the sources of conflict in which they use violence and to gain insight into their definitions, motivations, rationales, and justifications. Close and careful engagement with the perpetrators of violence, with the acts themselves, and with the contexts in which they occur is essential if we are to grapple with a meaningful explanation of when and why such violence emerges, how it is used, and why it might continue or cease. Although building knowledge about men's behavior, rationales, and justifications forms an essential part of developing a more comprehensive explanation of this violence, it by no means implies an acceptance or tolerance of such behavior nor should it be used in an attempt to explain it away. Quite the contrary, it is not possible to effectively address men's violence if we know nothing about it.

The findings presented form part of a 3-year study of criminal-justice-based programs for violent men, The Violent Men Study (Dobash, Dobash, Cavanagh, & Lewis, 1995, 1996, in press), and also draws on our earlier research, the Violence Against Wives Study (Dobash & Dobash, 1979). The Violent Men Study uses a panel design to compare the effects of abuser programs with other forms of criminal-justice intervention (fines, probation, etc.) across three time periods (at intervention and 3 and 12 months later). Depth interviews with violent men ($n = 122$) and with women partners ($n = 134$) were conducted at Time 1, followed by postal questionnaires at Times 2 and 3. The sample included 95 couples. Both quantitative and qualitative data were gathered at Time 1, and primarily quantitative data were gathered at follow-up. Most interviews at Time 1 lasted between 60 and 90 minutes for men and between 2 and 3 hours for women. They were tape-recorded and transcribed for qualitative analysis and coded for quantitative analysis. The Violence Assessment Index (VAI), the Injury Assessment Index (IAI), and the Controlling Behaviour Index (CBI) were used along with the qualitative data to build an extensive picture of specific violent events and the immediate contexts in which they occur as well as of the overall "marital" relationship of which they form a part.

Following our earlier research, an "event analysis" was used to examine violent events as a whole, and the three indexes were used to gather data about the *prevalence* and *frequent* use (five or more times) of violence, injuries, and controlling behaviors throughout the life of the relationships and during a 1-year period (Dobash et al., 1995, 1996) (for earlier use of event analysis, see Dobash & Dobash, 1979, 1984). Scales based on the three indexes have high levels of internal validity and are reported elsewhere (Dobash et al., in press). Overall, the Violent Men Study provides a combination of qualitative and quantitative data and uses the "context specific approach" (Dobash & Dobash, 1979, pp. 27-30; Dobash & Dobash, 1988) and an "event analysis" (Dobash & Dobash, 1979, pp. 97-123; Dobash & Dobash, 1983a, 1984; Dobash et al., 1996). The three indexes— (VAI), (IAI) and (CBI)—will be used to examine a constellation of factors forming violent events and violent relationships. We shall present the evidence about various forms of physical and sexual violence, injuries, and different forms of controlling and intimidating behaviors. For comparison, we shall present evidence about the same incidents provided by violent men and by women partners. As shall be seen, this raises considerable doubt about the voracity of survey research concerning "symmetry" in the perpetration of violence by men and by women. While this controversy is examined elsewhere (Dobash, Dobash, Wilson, & Daly, 1992) and will not be detailed here, these findings further strengthen the claim of *asymmetry*, provide some insight into why this might be so, and introduce research instruments that yield fuller accounts of the overall phenomenon of violence and thus overcome some of the well-documented problems of the CTS. Finally, with the focus on men and their use of violence, we conclude with reflections on "masculine identity" and how this cultural construction might articulate the ways in which men use violence and rationalize and justify its perpetration.

Violent Acts and Violent Actors

"Marriage": A Context of Violence

At once, men and women in marital and marital-like relations have common interests and are in conflict. Interactions occur against a backdrop of expectations and responsibilities that include common cause as well as competing and conflicting interests. Parents and children as well as husbands and wives obviously share common goals within the context of the family but are also in competition for the resources of the domestic arena, including time, physical space, freedom of movement, and the fruits of domestic labor. Conflicts of interest between men and women as well as those between parents and children are a part of the social construction of the family and underpin the negotiations between its members. While the specific sources of conflict between marital partners are writ large in the arenas of domestic labor and personal possessiveness, they are played out against a background of the differing interests and responsibilities of men and women in their respective positions as "husbands" and "wives" and "fathers" and "mothers." These cross-cutting interests and responsibilities bring a complexity to every exchange such that it is sometimes difficult to examine them all in action simultaneously, although this idea must be grasped if we are to have an understanding of this form of violence.

Personal exchanges, interactions, and daily conflict form the seedbed of specific violent events, yet these occur within wider cultural contexts that affect the general position of husbands and wives in a given society or subgroup. Historical, anthropological, and contemporary evidence suggests that the social positioning of marital partners supports men's control and domination of women through various means, including the use of force (Dobash & Dobash, 1977, 1977-1978, 1979, 1981, 1884). If so, this should be discernible in the specifics of everyday life and the discourses about such relationships and their inherent conflicts.

Conflicts of Interest Between Husbands and Wives

Most violent events begin with arguments and confrontations about everyday life that are of significance to the individual men and women concerned. They argue about all sorts of things, but evidence from our previous research on Violence Against Wives (1979) and data from the Violent Men Study (1996) reveal four general themes: men's possessiveness and jealousy, disagreements and expectations concerning domestic work and resources, men's sense of the right to punish "their" women for perceived wrongdoing, and the importance to men of maintaining or exercising their power and authority (Dobash & Dobash, 1979, pp. 83-106, 124-33; Dobash & Dobash, 1984, pp. 272-274; Dobash & Dobash, 1992, p. 4; see also Kelly, 1988, p. 131; Eisikovits & Edleson, 1989). Domestic issues involve standards of housework, preparation of meals, child care, the allocation and uses of household income, and friends and relatives. Conflicts often involve the man's general sense of possessiveness as well as specific feelings of jealousy that focus on real or imagined transgressions. The right to punish wrongdoing, like the exercise of authority and power, is vested in husbands and not wives, thus allowing men to be violent simply because of their position.

Sources of Conflict Leading to Violence

A range of specific issues may be in dispute prior to a violent event. As might be expected, couples do not always agree about "what" is in conflict or "who" is at fault, and disputes often cover more than one contested area. However, in the Violent Men Study and in the earlier Violence Against Wives Study, the specific issues usually identified by men and women as sources of conflict leading to violence included the woman's domestic work, the man's jealousy, money, the man's use of alcohol, and assorted issues relating to children, other family members, and friends. The accounts of men and women are both similar and different. Although the broad outlines are usually the same, men and women are often at variance about the sources of dispute and the nature, severity, and consequences of the violence. Although they share the marital relationship and specific violent events, they often differ with respect to the interpretations and consequences of both. They converge on certain points but differ on others; for example, women complain that men are not prepared to listen or to try to understand their points of view or concerns, while men complain that women fail to meet and/or anticipate their personal needs and accuse them of all manner of wrongdoing that "caused" his violence against her. In this attempt to understand and explain how men conceive of their perpetration of violence, we shall focus primarily on their voices as they discuss specific conflicts of interest in dispute prior to violent events as well as some more general issues such as power and authority.

Domestic Work

"We always have steak on Saturday, so where is it?" (a line from the film *Shirley Valentine*).

Numerous aspects of domestic labor are important, recurring sources of confrontations and conflict that end in violence. Historically and today, the marital relationship is one in which women carry out scores of domestic duties deemed to be "their" responsibility, and men have the right to oversee, direct, and judge this work. Housework is continuous with meals to prepare, children to bathe and dress, washing, ironing, shopping, and cleaning. Women can easily "fail" in these tasks, particularly when standards are capricious and/or impossible to achieve. Men are there to judge women's work and may punish her failures to meet his standards or anticipate his needs.

A man speaks about how he was "provoked" to use violence because of his wife's performance at housework:

> 114: [How did she provoke you?] I come home from my work and she's never vacuumed or dusted the place.

From other studies, women speak about conflicts over domestic work:

> He started accusing me of things, you know, stupid and ignorant things. I'd cleaned the living room maybe and dust, and maybe one of the kids would come in and have a biscuit or something and I would leave what I was doing and go and get them a biscuit, and when I came back naturally you think you've finished dusting the mantelpiece and you just leave it. He would come in and he would say, "Have you done this room today?" And I'd say, "Yes." Maybe there was a radio sitting on the mantelpiece, and he would say, "Well, you haven't dusted under that then." And I said, "I have done." And he lifted it up and he'd say, "Well look at that." And that's what used to cause fights. (Dobash & Dobash, 1979, p. 199)

> "I could not stand another day of him saying, 'Have you done the vacuuming, have you dusted?'" (Lees, 1997, p. 170)

Some men are particularly concerned about household work, especially when tasks are associated with servicing their personal needs. The content, preparation, and timing of meals constitute a particularly sensitive area for criticisms and verbal confrontations that sometimes end in violent attacks. Men demand that household chores conform to their wishes and expect their personal needs to be given priority in the woman's routine. Women protest that other tasks, financial constraints, and inappropriate requests often make it impossible to meet such demands even as they try to do so.

> He was late and I'd started cooking his meal, but I put it aside, you know, when he didn't come in. Then when he came in I started heating it. I was standing at the sink and he just came up and gave me

a punch in the stomach. I held on to the sink for ages, and the pain
in my stomach and trying to get my breath, and that was the first time
I remember that he ever touched me. It was only because his dinner
wasn't ready on the table for him. (Dobash & Dobash, 1979, p. 101)

The nuclear family is an arena in which most emotional needs are
to be met, and women are primarily responsible for this emotional
labor. Arlene Hochschild (1993) has examined how the "caring"
qualities of women have also been diffused into the realm of wage
labor. Nurses, female airline staff, and secretaries are expected or
contractually required to exhibit these caring qualities and may be
penalized if they do not do so. In a more direct, personal, and
potentially brutal fashion, women living with violent men may be
punished for not anticipating, interpreting, and fulfilling men's physical, emotional, and sexual needs. Men may not articulate these
needs—they may just feel uneasy and "unhappy"—but they nonetheless expect women to anticipate their needs, interpret their moods,
and understand even that which remains unarticulated. Such needs
can be extensive, and men's perceptions of women's failure to meet
them may "provoke" arguments and altercations that end in violence.
Women interviewed in the Violent Men Study and in the earlier
Violence Against Wives Study indicated that they became sensitive to
men's "moods" and anticipated "demands" but also complained that
it was impossible to accurately anticipate all such moods and to meet
the varied and changing demands. Men, they argued, had little or no
appreciation of the demands of children and household work. For the
most part, women recognized the importance of fulfilling a myriad of
responsibilities to children, husband, and household, whereas violent
men generally elevated their own personal requirements above all
others and remained inflexible with regard to them.

Money

Money and the allocation of resources is a recurring and important source of conflict in many relationships. Women generally view
money as belonging to the family as a whole to be spent on children,
the household, men's personal needs and recreation, and, lastly, on
their own personal needs and desires. Men, on the other hand, tend
to feel that financial resources belong solely or primarily to themselves. With little understanding of domestic expenses, men "allocate"
some portion of "their" money for such expenditures and retain the
rest for their own use. The allocation may be too small or taken back

during the week for additional pub money or personal expenditures. There may not be enough in the first instance, and no amount of careful planning or arithmetic will make the sums meet the demands. Differing perceptions provoke arguments as women seek to renegotiate the allocation of money or manage unanticipated needs. Men may acknowledge the need to pay the rent or buy children's shoes but view the "lost" money as a personal deprivation, a loss of well-earned leisure, and/or an irritant to be ignored or brushed aside. For men, such irritations are deemed to justify their anger and violence.

> 053: We argued about money that night and I punched and kicked her and she went down to her Gran's. . . . I went down to her Gran's . . . [because] I wanted to borrow her bank card [to return to the pub]. . . . Her brother came to the door and he punched me and I didn't realize what I had done. I was angry because he punched me, you see I didn't realize what I had done. I knew I'd done something [to her] but I didn't realize it was as bad as it was, but it was bad.

A woman speaks about conflicts over money:

> 1017: These days I'm bad with my nerves. I can't think straight because he loses his temper with me if there is not enough food or we run out of something like milk, etc. or if there are no [cigarettes], that's when he really starts ordering me to go and borrow money. If I can't get any he goes mad, that's when the threats start and the hitting me.

Children

Conflicts over children take several forms. Some involve the amount of time and energy women spend in child care rather than husband care. Some involve conflicts about what to do about children in trouble or about the usual troubles of adolescents. Some involve the "invasions" of the woman's children from another relationship who "spoil" the man's desire for an exclusive relationship with his partner and "their" new family.

> 023: I think the only time we nearly came to blows when I've been sober was over the kids.

> 016: I thumped [her teenage daughter] and [she] got up to try and stop me and I thumped her. [He wanted her daughter to leave the

house as he saw her as an interference in their new life with their new baby.]

Alcohol

The excessive use of alcohol exacerbates other problems and is also a source of conflict in its own right. The use of household income for drinking, time spent at the pub instead of at home, and the talk and atmosphere of the male group may all contribute to violence. Men reflect:

> 036: You see them here. They don't work but they've always got a can of Pilsner or a can of lager in their hand and they get drunk and go barmy [crazy].

> 058: If I was to stop drinking, [she] would never have a black eye. It's only been with alcohol, that's all it is.

The following quote shows how one man used alcohol and the woman's sense of responsibility for child care to control her mobility and access to a social evening with friends:

> 062: I knew she was going out with her pals so when I came in from my work . . . she's still working and I thought, "She's going out with that lot tonight—no chance, she's not going." So when I'm on my way home I'll get a bottle of vodka somewhere . . . and I'm sat here maybe half way through the vodka when she comes in from her work and she sees I'm that drunk so she will not leave me with four kids. Not that I would do anything to the kids but just the fact that she's not going to leave me drunk in charge of four kids. [So you deliberately kind of sabotaged it just to stop her?] Yes.

For a recent discussion of alcohol use and sexual violence, see Schwartz and Nogrady (1996).

Possessiveness and Jealousy

Possessiveness and jealousy play important roles in the conflicts and arguments associated with violent events (for a discussion of the distinction, see Wilson & Daly, this volume). Many of the men who used violence were very possessive. Sexual transgressions, real and imagined, were seized on and used as rationales to confront, interrogate, and seek admissions of guilt. In some relationships, arguments about sexual fidelity were common and recurring. Although the source of many of the conflicts might seem "minor" to the casual observer, they were taken very seriously by the men concerned:

> 045: (re: former girlfriend) She once told me that she had held hands with another boy. . . . I went seriously mad about that.

> 007: If she's cheeky and is drunk I'll hit her and if she's been unfaithful while I've been away. [What would prevent you?] Nothing.

> 062: [You said earlier that she used to go out more; why does she go out less often now?] I suspected she was seeing somebody else and she was denying it. Now she knows I don't like her going out. My idea is that she's going out to meet this bloke or whoever it is. . . . [Do you have disagreements about friends?] Yes. I don't like hers. [Why not?] Well, they're always wanting to borrow something. [Any other reason?] One of them, she likes the men. [So you don't like your wife associating with her because she likes men?] That's right.

Isolation and Restriction of Mobility and Social Life

Apart from specific concerns about infidelity, some men took a more general view that married women should be at home or have restricted contact with others:

> 064: Well, it's not so much that I detested the idea of it [her going out with her friends] but, well I was annoyed. I was annoyed when she used to just run about with her pal when she was married. I mean I tried to get that over to her a couple of times.

> 116: [How often does she go out socially with her friends?] Not very often, not at all maybe once or twice a year, a girl's night out or something. [Why does she go out so infrequently?] I don't know probably because she doesn't trust me cause if she goes out I will sit down and have a drink . . . but then again, she doesn't go out unless she wants to.

Although men's anxieties about fidelity and restrictions of women's lives might be related, they do not always or easily see the connection. They do not see restrictions on women's lives as engineered or imposed by themselves but simply the ways things are, a shared agreement rather than an accommodation to his wishes that might reflect differing views.

126: I would say I went out once or twice a week. . . . It just depends on how I really felt and how the money was [she disagrees]. [Thinking back to when you were together how often did she go out on her own or with her friends?] She maybe used to go out once a week to bingo that's about all, maybe twice a week if we had money but that was all. [What did you think about her going out?] I didn't mind her going out much. [What would you think if she went out to the pub with friends?] She never really asked. I suppose if she wanted to go out I would let her, I would think we would probably have a discussion about it. [Do you think you would give her permission to go?] As long as she would ask me first. [Would you say you were quite jealous, possessive of her?] Yes, I am quite jealous. Yes I do get jealous. [Would you prevent her from going to a place that you thought she shouldn't go?] I have never prevented her from going anywhere that I am aware of, she was at the bingo a couple of nights ago. [Bingo is quite a safe place.] That's right, it is the only place that she ever wanted to go.

Sex

There are disagreements and arguments about men's access to women's bodies. Some men demand or coerce sex from women, while others disagree about the amount or type of sexual activity in the relationship.

038: [Can you remember the very first time (you hit her)?] It was on the Sunday afternoon about [noon]. I came in and I told her I was going down to the pub to have a couple of drinks. She said to me, "Well, mind your time because you've not had anything to eat and your dinner will be ready at 4 o'clock," but I didn't come in till about [midnight], and I was really bad drunk. I don't remember whether she was in her bed or up the stairs but I tried to have sex with her, pushed myself a lot if you know what I mean, but she wasn't wanting it and I just started hitting her. . . . [What sort of violence?] Headbutt. [And did you force her to have sex?] No, I was trying to but she wouldn't so I just got mad with her. [Injuries?] Broken nose and two black eyes. . . . Well if she'd let me do it [have sex] I wouldn't have punched her.

054: Sex. I wasn't getting enough. Once a week's no good to me.

023: We argue less than we used to but I mean the basis, the whole thing all happened because of [her] attitude toward sex. That was the bottom line.

Men's annoyance regarding sex may constitute an important backdrop to confrontations and arguments that appear to be related to other issues yet also involve stated and unstated debates about sex. In some incidents, men are not prepared to negotiate about sexual access. Three percent of the men in the Violent Men Study said they had physically forced their partner to have sex, while about one quarter of the women said they had been physically forced to have sex.

Responsibility for Violence: Blaming the Victim

Men usually say they have a good reason for using violence, and it lies somewhere in *her* behavior even if the detail of violations remains vague or unspecified:

> 047: [Have you ever wanted to stop being violent?] I wouldn't really say I'm violent. I've been given reason to be violent. I'm not just violent for the sake of it.

> 045: I was sometimes justified in hitting [her]. I never hurt her badly physically—I never cut her or beat her senseless. . . . She'd always [argue] until there was really no alternative [to hitting].

> 054: [Why do you think men do it?] What? Bang women? I don't know. I know why I did it, I was pushed to it.

> 006: [What do you think of men who hit women?] I don't agree with it but it all depends. It depends what the circumstances are. Unless you're fully aware of the circumstances, you don't really have the right to criticize. I suppose it's not alright for a man to hit a woman, but I mean there are certain circumstances when it's inevitable—it's going to happen. Well, I hit [her] for a reason.

Some do not articulate a specific complaint for using violence but express a more "generic" view of women as "no good" or "not to be trusted":

> 058: Of course hitting a woman and turning her black and blue is bad but there's some women are just bloody rotten. There's a lot of bad women out in that world.

> 005: It's not right to scalp her but in saying that, there are times and places. Women do a lot they shouldn't do.

> 054: I mean I'm not the type that ties them up and does this and stops giving them money and doesn't feed the kids. There's guys like that, I know that, but there's also women that just take the piss out of guys.

Some men become obsessive about the possibility of infidelities. It becomes important to guard and monitor "their" woman and keep her under close surveillance. Their movements are scrutinized, they are interrogated, and their mobility is curtailed. Women's access to individuals outside the family may be strictly limited, and a few are even locked in the house when the man is away. These men have strong anxieties regarding the possibility of sexual infidelities and at the same time often see women as "only good for one thing." In some male environments, attitudes toward women are stark:

> 016: [What do your friends think of women then?] That they're here for one thing and that's it. [Do you not think that men's attitudes toward women are changing?] Not in the pub that I go to.

> 036: [How acceptable do you think it is today in society generally for a man to hit a woman?] There's that much of it going about that it's accepted. I mean round about this area it happens all the time. . . . I would say it's acceptable. . . . In this area a lot of it is drink-related and unemployment and drugs.

Several things may be at work at once. While attempts to isolate women do in fact limit their access to other men, they also constrain women's mobility outside the home so they are constantly available to provide domestic service. Isolation also cuts women off from contact with others who might become aware of the man's violence and intervene on her behalf, thus challenging his ability to act as he pleases.

Male Power and Authority

It is clear that these men do not believe that women have the same right as men to argue, negotiate, or debate. Instead, it is a nuisance and a threat to his authority, and violence is often used to silence debate, to reassert male authority, and to deny women a voice in the affairs of daily life. Frequently, men cannot remember the source of the argument, just that she wouldn't stop talking/arguing/negotiating when he wished it to be over. Nagging, "going on and on," and failing to "shut up" are frequently given as reasons for violence. The exact nature of the conflict is forgotten or ignored; what counts is that she went on about "it" and would not shut up when he wished her to do so. Authority is at stake.

038: [Why did you hit her?] I was wanting to show her who was the boss.

017: [How does she try to stop you being violent to her?] Shuts her mouth. . . . She used to carry on the arguments and I wanted to let it drop but she'd carry it on and that's when I ended up, I would turn round and hit her. [Can you understand why she needed to continue with the argument?] Not a bit.

006: [Why did you hit her?] Because she knows how to wind me up, basically. Sometimes she doesn't take "no" for an answer. Sometimes she'll go on and on and on about different things.

019: [When you think back to when you actually hit her, can you think what you were hoping to get?] Well it was just actually to get her to shut up.

063: [Is there something she could have done to stop you being abusive to her?] Yes. Keep her mouth shut. [Have you wanted to stop being violent to her?] No. She's my wife.

005: I have no violent behavior. . . . She knew she deserved it. She does my head in. [Is there something she could have done to stop you being violent toward her?] Yes. Shut her mouth.

062: (She should stop) doing things I don't want her to.

007: [Do you think there is anything (she) could or should do to stop you being violent?] I've battered her that many times, she should know when to stop her crap. She knows when I get annoyed because I sit and clench my teeth. . . . Why do I hit her? I don't know. Sometimes she just really nips my head. And it doesn't matter what I say, she won't shut up. . . . [Did you feel that you were right to be violent to her?] Yes. She was being cheeky (showing disrespect). . . . [When do you think it's okay for a man to hit a woman?] I don't like it. A slap, yes, now and again . . . if it's needed. [What do you mean "needed"?] If you're sitting in a pub with all your pals and she comes in and gives you a load of cheek. To put her in her place verbally, and if verbally doesn't work, physically.

A couple speaks differently about isolation, restrictions on her daily life, and men's authority:

Him (091): [What do you think has brought about this change for the better in your relationship?] Because [she] let's me get on with what I want to do. [Do you think that this violence can be stopped?] If she just shuts up and accepts what I say and do.

Her (1091): Women feel they have to make up lies to say where they have been because men just don't believe us or like to rule us. It's one set of rules for them. We are just here for their wishes. We give in just to save a hiding or [to keep the] peace.

Although violent events are not always preceded by verbal arguments and confrontations, most of the events in the Violent Men Study did begin with an argument. It is not easy to pinpoint the specific moment when an attack is likely to begin. Men do, however, describe a number of intense emotions and specific orientations that accompany their decision to use violence. They often describe themselves as intensely angry and usually blame the woman for their anger and their subsequent violence. The point at which the man enters the narrative about a violent event is invariably the point where "she did or said something" that "caused" the violence, even if he doesn't remember exactly what it was. In interviews, the men tended to offer sparse accounts of their own behavior while providing more complete descriptions of the actions of their partner. They say women complain too much and nag and harass them for no good reason. Men say they don't understand what women want or that women's attempts to curtail their "freedoms," use of money, or consumption of alcohol are out-of-bounds and warrant being put down.

The Constellation of Violence:
Violence, Injuries, and Controlling Behaviors

Within this field of study, surprisingly little attention has been directed at describing and understanding violent events as a whole and even less on the contexts surrounding such events and the relationships in which they occur (see Dobash & Dobash, 1979, pp. 97-143; Dobash & Dobash, 1984, 1992, pp. 1-14). This is crucial if we are to understand the emergence and continuation of this form of violence. Here, we use a "context-specific" form of analysis (Dobash & Dobash, 1979, pp. 27-30; Dobash & Dobash, 1983a, 1992, pp. 253, 267, 281-284) to examine violence, injuries, and controlling behaviors as reported by men and women partners. The VAI and the IAI provide sets of indicators of different components of violent events. Men who use violence also use other coercive, intimidating, and controlling behaviors, and these are assessed using the CBI. The three scales form an overall constellation of factors composing violent events and violent relationships.

Types of Violence

Figure 6.1 uses data from the Violence Assessment Index (VAI) to compare men's and women's accounts of the different types of violence that occurred at least once in the relationship.

When examined for concordance and discordance between the accounts of violent men and women partners, four items show considerable correspondence between their accounts: pushing/grabbing, slapping her face/body, restraining her, and punching walls. The majority of men and women report at least one such act during the relationship. Such concordance is not, however, apparent on the other items assessed by the VAI. The greatest discordance between men and women occurs with respect to forced sex, hitting the stomach while pregnant, using or threatening to use weapons or objects that could do harm, and kicking the body. There are also differences between women and men concerning choking, demanding sex, and threatening to kill the woman. The overall pattern of discordance and concordance shows that men and women are fairly similar in their reporting of less serious acts, but there is more difference between them with respect to reporting more serious acts of violence. Across all items in the VAI, a smaller percentage of men report having committed such acts than are reported by woman partners. On the face of it, it should not be a surprise that men usually underestimate their use of more serious forms of violence. It cannot be to their credit that they beat a woman into unconsciousness, burned or wounded her, or hit her in the stomach while pregnant. There is no valor in violence directed at a woman as there might be in a "fair fight" between men.

The reports of women and men differ in terms of the *prevalence* of the types of violence ever used by men against woman partners, but the differences are even greater concerning the *frequent* use (more than five times) of such acts. Although reported in detail elsewhere, findings about the *frequent* use of various forms of violence, infliction of injuries, and use of controlling and intimidating behaviors all reveal considerable differences in reporting by violent men and by women partners. Men always report that they have committed less on any of the items, whereas women partners report that men have committed more (Dobash et al., 1996, pp. 66, 70, 74; Dobash et al., 1998).

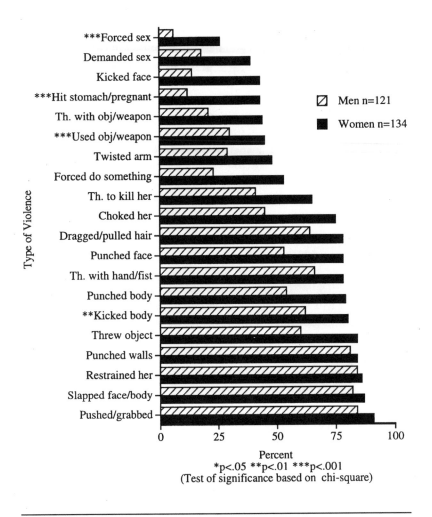

Figure 6.1. Prevalence of Violence (at Least One Incident) [reports of men and women compared]

Injuries

Men's and women's accounts of injuries reveal two clear and strong patterns: Consistently higher proportions of women than men report injuries (prevalence), and higher proportions of women indicate that such injuries occur on a frequent basis. As above, only the findings on *prevalence* are reported here.

It can be seen in Figure 6.2 that most women report experiencing black eyes and bruising on at least one occasion throughout their relationship, whereas fewer men report inflicting such injuries. Over half of the women report bruising of the body, face, and limbs, black eyes, bleeding face, split lips, and hair pulled out, whereas fewer men report inflicting such injuries. One of the most striking differences in the accounts of men and women is that well over one half of the women report feeling nauseous or vomiting after a violent incident, whereas only 7% of men report inflicting such an outcome. Forty percent of women reported being knocked unconscious on at least one occasion; only 14% of the men reported inflicting such an injury. Internal injuries and miscarriages are reported by a few women but by fewer men. One half of the comparisons between men and women on the *prevalence* of injuries were statistically significant. Although some outcomes of violence, like internal injuries, sprains, biting the inside of the mouth, and so on, are "invisible" to men and can more easily be overlooked, ignored, or denied, this cannot be said about more obvious injuries with visible markers, such as bleeding, burns, or those requiring medical attention. Other explanations must be sought for the differences in reporting between women and men.

Again, the percentage of men who report inflicting various types of injuries is always lower than those reported by women who receive such injuries. Agreement may be more likely about those injuries crudely defined by men as "less serious" and therefore more easily acknowledged by them and, conversely, those that are so serious or of a nature that they are likely to come to the attention of others (e.g., doctors or police) and therefore less easily denied. In between lie the invisible injuries (sprains, vomiting, missing hair, and the like) and those not so likely to come to the attention of others. These may more readily be ignored, denied, forgotten, or simply remain unknown to the man. Overall comparison of the reports of men and women on injuries reveals many statistically significant differences, as men persistently report inflicting fewer injuries than women report experiencing.

There were differences between women and men in their assessments of the seriousness of the men's violence throughout the relationship, from "very serious" (49% women, 28% men) and "serious" (37% women, 37% men) to "not very serious" (10% women, 25% men) and "not at all serious" (3% women, 11% men). When the categories of "serious" and "not serious" are combined, one in three men placed the violence in the lesser category, whereas just over one in ten of women did so.

Although many men claim a lack of knowledge and control with respect to their use of violence—a mystery that just happens—some do articulate what they want to obtain through its use and whether

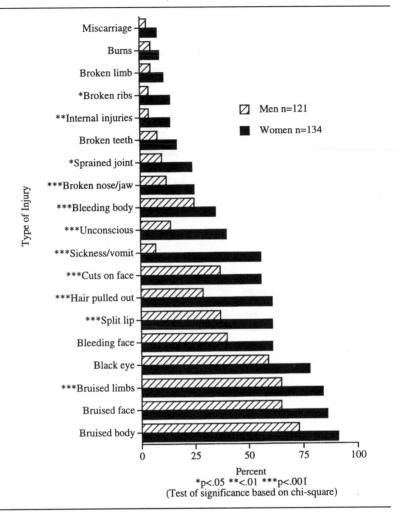

Figure 6.2. Prevalence of Injuries (at Least One Incident) [reports of men and women compared]

they have been successful. In this sense, violence is functional, is meant to achieve a specified goal, and is often successful, even though other costs may be incurred. Thus, violence both works and fails.

045: It [violence] was the thing I could do and she couldn't, the one way the situation could be controlled to my liking.

047: [Would you say you were successful in getting what you wanted; did it work?] Yes, I definitely got her attention, but I think if she had answered the door when I threatened to smash the window, there wouldn't have been any smashing, and then I would have been home and there would have been no trouble.

Sometimes violence works; sometimes it doesn't. The following man had both success and failure in achieving his declared outcomes:

016: [Did you feel justified in hitting her?] I did (because) she wouldn't let me see my daughter. [What did you hope to get by hitting her then?] To teach her a lesson. (I succeeded) because I get to see my daughter now. . . . [When you hit her, what did you hope to get?] I wanted to get (her teenage daughter) out of the house. [Did you succeed?] No.

Controlling and Coercive Behaviors

Figure 6.3 shows the proportion of men and women reporting the occurrence of at least one incident throughout their relationship of each of a range of controlling behaviors. With the exception of threats to children, over one half of the women reported having at least one experience of each of the items on the CBI. The figures show more concordance in men's and women's reports of men's use of various forms of controlling and intimidating behaviors than for violence and injuries. Nearly equivalent proportions of men and women report that men shout, swear, call names, threaten, criticize the woman or her family, and question her. There is, however, considerable disparity in men's and women's reports of men's attempts to use children in arguments, men's attempts to control and restrict the woman's life and movements, putting her down, deliberately keeping her short of money, and threatening to hurt the pets. Although there is greater concordance between men and women reporting on the *prevalence* of various forms of controlling behavior, the same cannot be said about their reports of the *frequent* use (five or more occurrences) of such behaviors. Again, the details about *frequent* use of controlling behaviors are reported elsewhere (Dobash et al., 1996, p. 74; Dobash et al., 1998), but over one half of the items revealed statistically significant differences in the reporting by men and women of the men's *frequent* use of various forms of controlling behavior.

Displaying certain "looks" and moods, pointing in an aggressive manner, swearing, calling names, and criticizing can be used by men to control women and display signs of potential danger. Threatening violence, feigning to strike, and pointing in a threatening fashion can

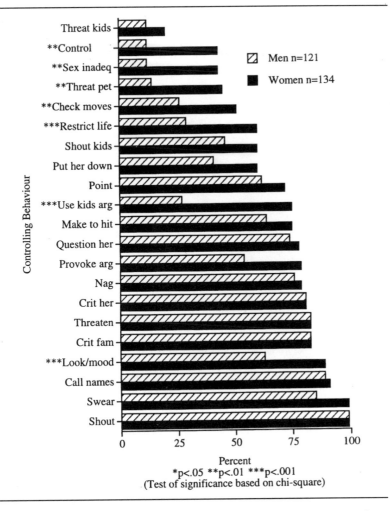

Figure 6.3. Prevalence of Controlling Behavior (at Least One Incident) [reports of men and women compared]

all be frightening, particularly when used by someone who is stronger and has shown themselves willing to use violence. Such acts take on an even greater significance for those who have been the victims of violence and have experienced what might come next. When women were asked to assess the seriousness of the controlling and coercive acts, few judged them as insignificant (9%), while most judged them as serious (19%) or very serious (65%).

Violent events change over the lifetime of a relationship. Men and women react differently to the onset of violence within a relationship.

Men may ignore their own violence and act as if it has not occurred or has no consequences for the woman or the relationship.

> 058: [How do you think she feels (about the violence)?] Well she must feel something for me or she wouldn't put up with it.

> 003: [Would you say that your violent behavior is damaging the relationship at all?] No. . . . Well it's no big deal. I'm not saying that I'm not as bad as the next one, but I know people who've actually beat up a woman like they've beat up a guy, with kicking in the head. I'd never do that to a girl.

When men do appreciate that their violence may have some effect on the woman and her well-being, this is often tempered by the notion that a cessation of the violence will automatically bring an immediate end to her fears or feelings of depression and that, in any case, it is her responsibility to leave the relationship if she is being harmed. The responsibility for change is hers and not his.

> 019: [Would you say that your violent behavior is actually damaging your relationship with your wife?] In the past it has. [Is it doing that just now?] No. I've never been violent to her for months now.

> 045: She knew what I was like. . . . She shouldn't have been around. She should have left me. She knew what I was like at that point and she had a choice. It's like if you had a dog who every time you took it out it would go and bite people, then if you walked up to that dog and it bit you, it would be your own fault.

In summary, men, in contrast to women, "forget" their violence or offer only abbreviated, vague descriptions of it. If violence "did not occur," it was only "a minor thing," and it was probably "justified" by something she had done. Men's descriptions of violent events usually begin with specific elements of the encounter that focus on the actions of the woman deemed to justify the violence and make her responsible for his violent behavior. Men complain that women "wind them up," "nag," and generally behave in ways that "provoke" arguments and violence. When men acknowledge that violence has occurred, it is usually minimized, blame is shifted, and responsibility is deflected. Men say the failures and transgressions of women are the main reasons for their violent behavior, and in a number of relationships, the men manipulate the situation to constitute themselves as moral enforcers acting merely to make sure "their" woman behaves like a good "wife" and "mother" (for an extreme example of this orientation, see Lundgren, this volume). Deflections and rationalizations allow men to see their violence as legitimate and appropriate responses to women's "inappropriate" behavior, and minimizations of the consequences of violence (injuries, depression, etc.) allow men to view it as irrelevant, insignificant, or inconsequential.

Violent acts occur within a context of conflict, intimidation, coercion, and hostility. Men need not always demonstrate such orientations in order to use such behaviors to control and dominate women. Once used, violence facilitates men's ability to control their partner through various forms of intimidating behavior as well as through subsequent acts of violence. For her part, a woman's life begins to alter in many ways. She may restrict her movements and suppress her opinions. Negotiations with her partner are likely to be greatly influenced by instances of intimidation and demonstrations of violence directed at dogs and doors as well as at her body. At this point, women can be controlled through fear and anticipation as well as through direct action.

Some of the men voiced a sense of shame, but most did not. It could be argued that these men have jettisoned normative conventions about not using violence against a woman to the extent that moral restrictions no longer play a role in their everyday behavior or their subsequent accounts of it. Other explanations might emphasize a differential masculine morality, thwarted development, or socialization into a value system less likely to emphasize self-control or self-regulation. Accumulating evidence certainly shows that men who perpetrate violence in other contexts—gang violence or child sexual abuse—generally lack empathy, are narcissistic, elevate their needs and desires above all others, and do not see their acts as particularly odious. Men who use violence may be engaged in a morality play, but their sense of morality is likely to be at odds with that of their woman partner, and they may also in this extreme form be out of step with the moral prescriptions of other men and/or the society at large while at the same time reflecting many of the general notions that underpin this behavior. Although a husband's use of violence against his wife has traditionally been condoned in most societies, there have always been limits set on when violence is "justified" and how much might be administered. For some time there have been growing restrictions on this "right" and erosions of the notion that it is a "right." At present, there are contradictory messages of principle—"it is wrong/illegal to use violence against anyone"—and practices that turn a blind eye to such behaviors, thereby indirectly supporting its continuation. Notions of the necessity of a man to have authority over a woman still remain, albeit in less stark forms than in the past. Traditional notions about the "appropriate" behaviors of husbands and wives continue to form part of men's notions about being in charge, even if that requires the use of violence (Dobash & Dobash, 1977-1978). In this and other respects, violence is used as a means of obtaining an end, as a product of men's power over women, and is deeply rooted in men's sense of masculinity.

For those who see violence against women as an "acceptable" response to women's real and imagined transgressions, this provides a context in which the behavior may be practiced, even if not explicitly encouraged, with few impediments and with little sense of shame, guilt, or a felt need to stop. Interventions directed at violent men and their behavior enter this context of mixed and contradictory messages and responses. Such interventions may serve to assist or impede the aim of reducing or eliminating violence. In turn, the responses themselves not only serve as enforcers or deterrents but also form a part of the expanding body of messages received by violent men, the women they abuse, and the society at large.

Men, Masculine Identity, and Violence

The propensity to use violence is greater among men than among women. For men, violence is embedded in a net of physicality, experience, and male culture such that it is more easily used and more readily available as a resource. Young men are risk-takers, and although male culture is variable, aggressive and violent behavior are highly valued in many cultures of masculinity. Sports and leisure activities provide arenas in which to express aggression and use the body as an instrument of force, intimidation, and success. Perhaps most important, however, is the culture of males in which violent acts may be valorized as signs of masculinity, male authority, power, and control. Certain cultures of masculinity prize and reward aggressive and violent encounters between men (see Archer, 1994, pp. 121-140). Such encounters are valuable as signs of manhood and male prowess and symbolize that men are different from women. Ethnographic literature from several countries provides persistent evidence of this pattern (Bourgois, 1996; Descola, 1996; Lancaster, 1992), and Wilson & Daly (this volume) reflect on male violence as a part of an evolved male psychology (see also Archer, 1994, pp. 324-327; Daly & Wilson, 1994). Young men learn to "do" violence, and within some cultural expressions it plays an important role in their social place and personal identity (Newburn & Stanko, 1994; Toch, 1992, 1993).

Acts of Violence Between Men: Masculine Identity, Valor, Heroism, and a Focus on the Act

Consider the conversation between men about violent encounters or fights. The conversation is filled with elaborate descriptions of "he said," and "then I said," with blow-by-blow descriptions of the violence and lurid details of cuts, bruises, and even tiny injuries. Such tales may be told to an admiring audience with excitement and a sense of pride in the very fact of participation. Winning or losing has a certain relevance, but the outcome is not everything, and even the loser or an unwilling participant gains some benefits in masculine identity simply by participating in a violent encounter. The outcome of violent acts (winning or losing) and the process of doing violence (the blows and injuries) would seem to be important features that distinguish violence between men with its "heroic" and reaffirming qualities (Archer, 1994; Daly & Wilson, 1994; Jefferson, 1994; Newburn & Stanko, 1994; Polk, 1994a, 1994b) from men's violence directed at women (Counts, Brown, & Campbell, 1992; Dobash et al., 1996; Godenzi, 1994) or, indeed, from violence by women (Browne, 1987; Jones, 1980) or between women or girls (violence between adolescent girls may have some of the same "heroic" features as those between young men, but this tends to be short-lived and does not appear to extend into adulthood; see Campbell, 1992a). In general, violence between the sexes does not have cultural *cache* nor does it affirm personal identity. Thus, violence between men and women needs to be examined differently than violence between men.

Young men offer accounts of violent encounters with other men that stress laudable behavior carried out in the defense of "higher" values and notions of masculine identity. Hans Toch (1992) offers a valuable framework for considering these accounts. The telling of tales to those who count, for example, other gang members, takes on a certain regularity and litany. Violent individuals often present themselves as "warriors" using legitimate violence in the defense of worthy goals. Tales of heroic violence permit serious reviews of "good violence" with the details of violent events in which victims are discredited because of actions, such as showing disrespect or supporting the "wrong" athletic team (Toch, 1993). In various subtle and not so subtle ways, the victim is cast as the "cause" of the encounter, inciting violence by disregarding warnings or failing to heed demands made by the aggressor. Exculpatory discourses show the "inevitable" outcome. In this way, the violence is seen both as an inevitable and commendable outcome; danger, action, and heroic exploits are highlighted (Toch, 1992). When recounted to those sharing the same perspective, violent encounters become morality plays confirming and cementing group identity in the face of the "other" and reinforcing the "rules" that support the use of violence. Recounting violent encounters builds reputations, valorizes the participants, and confirms the position of the enforcer of group norms. Whatever the outcome of such encounters between men, whether one wins or loses, simply having taken part is a marker of achievement and bravery. This validates a certain form of masculinity, and even the loser obtains some kind of badge of honor simply through his participation. Wounds provide signifiers and distinguishing markers of valiant struggles, whether won or lost.

Within the wider social context, even men who do not themselves fight or use their bodies in acts of violence against other men nonetheless receive some sort of reaffirmation of the power of men as a category or group vis-à-vis that of women. A man who would never raise his hand in anger, competition, or sport nonetheless benefits by having the power and physical superiority of men reaffirmed by those who do (on sport and violence against women, see Crosset, Ptacek, McDonald, & Benedict, 1996; Messner & Sabo, 1994). Thus, all men benefit in a variety of ways by the violent displays of their fellows that provide powerful signifiers of the potential of them all. All men vicariously benefit from the violent acts of the few insofar as such acts illustrate the potential of men to do violence and use it to resolve conflicts. They also illustrate the effectiveness of physical blows in subduing others and the utility of violence as an instrument of intimidation and coercion. Finally, they also illustrate that, for the most part, violence is a man's activity and that men are more willing and capable of using it.

Acts of Violence Against Women: Masculine Power and a Focus on the Outcome

When the men in the Violent Men Study spoke of violence perpetrated against another man, they often projected a sense of heroic achievement, stressing prowess and masculine identity; these accounts differed from those about their use of violence against their woman partner. By comparison, accounts of acts of violence against women were impoverished and abbreviated, containing no blow-by-blow descriptions with heroic flourishes and reaffirmations of masculine identity. Instead, they were morality tales of a different order, in that women had "done something wrong" and deserved violent treatment, and they confirmed masculine identity to the extent that a man is not "subordinated" to a woman and certainly not a husband to his wife. It was the ultimate outcome, the "winning" or defeating of the woman, that was valued and not the process of the violent encounter itself with its blows and wounds. Men could usually articulate why the violence was "necessary" or "warranted" by referring to the point at which it was used ("she was in my face") and whether it achieved its purpose of "shutting her up," getting a meal, or having sex. Unless questioned extensively, they rarely articulated the nature of the conflict prior to the moment when she "was in his face" or "would not shut up"—was it money, children, sex, jealousy?—nor did men readily or easily provide detailed, blow-by-blow accounts of the act of violence itself. Here the comparison of accounts of violent encounters between men is particularly striking.

Men's accounts of their use of violence against their woman partner were usually animated by anger and supported by rationales but not by a general sense of male pride. The evidence of masculine identity lay not in the encounter per se, but rather in the outcome of not letting a woman/wife win, of putting her in her place, or showing her who was boss. Unlike encounters with other men, there was no sense of personal pride or reaffirmation of masculine identity embedded in the very act of doing the violence itself but only in the outcome of obtaining some desired end, inflicting punishment for some wrongdoing, or maintaining authority over her. Again, the vocabulary of elaborate and detailed descriptions, of blow after blow, of blood, cuts, wounds, and injuries gave way to near silence or monosyllabic and restricted accounts in which almost nothing seemed to have happened, there is little or no meaning, and the consequences are of little importance. Minimization and denial are characteristic of men's accounts of their violence to women. Elaborate accounts are difficult to obtain; elements seem to be forgotten or are not counted as "real" violence. Partial or total amnesia, tunnel vision, and other "syndromes" seem to prevail among men violent to a woman partner.

The accounts of the women involved in such incidents are almost universally more detailed about sources of conflict, the nature of attack, injury, emotions, and effects on the relationship and other individuals in the immediate environment. Although men may not dispute the woman's more detailed account, they do not provide such complete accounts themselves. Why not? It may be that they are embarrassed by the full extent of their violent acts [the most serious] and/or that they simply do not count as violence those at the less serious end of behaviors: "Oh yes, I slapped her, but that wasn't violence." A restricted code of what counts as violence among abusers may help account for the differences in accounts given by men and women about the same event. It also seems likely that although a man may reaffirm his masculine identity through the *outcome* of a violent encounter with a woman (i.e., getting her to shut up, keeping her at home, punishing her for some wrongdoing, and the like), it is not reaffirmed through the *process* of using violence itself. Thus, whereas a violent encounter with another man, whether won or lost, may valorize masculine identity, only the *outcome* of an encounter with a woman has the potential to do so.

In summary, a focus on the process of doing violence and on the outcome of such encounters may help explain men's use of violence against women and the differences in how men and women view such acts and their consequences. Whatever the costs and benefits to the individuals concerned, in a wider cultural sense, feminine identity is not valorized by female-to-female violence or by violence to men. When men do violence to women, it is the outcome that is valued and at stake (getting what he wants, not letting a woman win an argument, ensuring that she is isolated from other men and from others who might intervene on her behalf). Unlike encounters between men, the process of doing the violence itself (the act of violence, the blows and wounds) does not reaffirm masculine pride, identity, and status. Thus, a crucial difference between encounters across genders is the differential importance of the outcome of the act of violence rather than the process of doing violence. Masculine identity, social ideals about husbands and wives, as well as personal privilege and material benefits are all at stake when men use violence against a woman partner. Violent men cannot be understood without understanding the immediate contexts of violent events and the wider social context in which such behavior is more or less tolerated or rewarding. This provides a key to understanding when and how violence is used and, more important, to the conditions in which it might be stopped.

7

The Hand That Strikes and Comforts

Gender Construction and the Tension Between Body and Symbol

Eva Lundgren

W hen women study feminist self-defense and pay lower taxi fares than men at night and the police provide abused women with alarm systems, all this can be characterized as change. But from another point of view, we can see that it cements and validates or stabilizes the very phenomenon against which women are rebelling. Do we conceive of gender power as inevitable and our only defense as self-defense, ourselves incapable of enabling change? When we analyze gender,

AUTHOR'S NOTE: This research was financed by NAVF (The Norwegian Research Council for the Humanities and Social Sciences). *Power as love and erotic domination: An analysis of empirical material on abuse with a view to developing dynamic models for an understanding of the interrelation between normality and deviation in gendered/sexual relations.* Substantial portions of this chapter were originally published in *Rethinking Change: Current Swedish Feminist Research,* HSFR, Uppsala, Swedish Science Press, 1992; used with permission. Original translation by Linda Schenck; this version edited by Rebecca Emerson Dobash. Only references available in English are cited here; all others are in the original publication.

including feminist research, we must begin by understanding the interplay between *change* and *continuity,* both in actions and in research, including theories of gender. This interaction is related to the fact that the social and cultural framework in which we act and contemplate is, in a multiplicity of complex ways, also a power-coded framework. Moreover, in the process of learning what it means to be a woman or a man, and in our analyses of the prerequisites and limitations of gender construction, our bodies are ever-present both as an arena of interest and action and as a point of departure. Yet the body is concomitantly inherent in the social power relationship; it is a bearer of intentions, interpretations, and symbols.

The theme of this chapter is gender construction seen as a lifelong process in the field of tension encompassing "body" and "symbol," "stability" and "change." My aim is to contribute to a more open theory of gender than is represented by the ideal type of "gynocentrism," in which gender is fixed as a static concept with a given content (see Lundgren, 1995a, part I). Gender construction may, of course, be analyzed using a variety of tools, especially different cultural frameworks; sets of norms for cultural circles, national cultures, partial cultures, and subcultures all provide good points of entry to such analyses (see Lundgren, 1995a, part III, chap. 2 and 3). Here, I illustrate my theme using a set of empirical data on sexual abuse of women in the context of a small group of Christian couples. My analyses interweave biological and symbolic gender and then go on to an in-depth study of this interplay in the light of the difference between the concepts of "constitution" (fundamental rules) and "regulativity" (applied rules). The empirical material provides a basis for more abstract reflections on gender theory.

My work on abuse began with a pilot study of religion-based abuse and included in-depth interviews with a sample of women with whom I had maintained contact over a long period of time. I gradually extended my contact with four groups of women and have followed 10 women from each of these groups over a number of years. I have also been able to contact and interview their present and sometimes their former male partners, a total of 40 men. The focus is on understanding legitimization activities around violent behavior and creating an understanding of abuse as a *process.*

Based on the interviews, I have developed what I analytically refer to as the *normalization* process of violence: how violence is seen, justified, and experienced as "normal" and/or "acceptable" behavior in the life of a man and a woman. One important aspect of this process is the *internalization* of violence; on the part of the woman this is expressed, *inter alia*, as the effects of physical and mental isolation and on the part of the man, by control and intentional switching between violence and warmth ("the torture effect"). Another important aspect is the *externalization* of violence; the man gradually ceases to behave simply as an individual and instead becomes his ideal type of "Man/Husband" ("it is not my hand that strikes") or "God" ("then I become the Lord," i.e., the one who controls life and death). (For a somewhat analogous conception see Wilson & Daly, this volume, on men who actually do kill themselves and their entire family [familicide] based on what appears to be a notion that as he cannot go, nor can they.) In my latest analysis of the normalization process, I studied this as a *process of gender construction;* the man gradually creates his masculinity by symbolically "becoming" God, and the gender construction of the woman takes place on the terms of the abuser. Through this process of compulsory adaptation, the woman's space for femininity is reduced to a minimum, and she is gradually effaced and "killed" as an individual woman. (At another level, this may be thought of relative to the power and control of men over women, husbands over wives, and particularly abusers over the abused. See Dobash & Dobash, this volume, on violent men and the context of violence.)

The Symbols of Violence or the Aesthetics of the Gender Battle? A Symbolic Field Based on Bodily Movement and Contact

Sexual violence is intense corporeality, religion is a concentration of symbolic dynamics, and gender demarcations stubbornly remain in the socialization process. All are intimately intertwined in many if not all societies, including our own. Because analyses of the *interrelation* between the bodily and the symbolic have not been extensively applied to empirical materials to date, this undertaking is relatively novel and, as such, is tentative and delimited.

My point of departure is a series of interviews with one of the couples in my study, Karl and his wife, Margaret. The initial purpose of the interviews was to understand the context of their linguistic imagery (metaphors) and its interplay with corporeality. Karl and Margaret are part of a group of fundamentalist Christian married couples I have interviewed over a period of several years. I have also followed three other groups, mainly composed of nonreligious couples, and have applied the same methodological approach—interviews characterized by strong interaction. For all of the couples, I have interviewed both husband and wife several times. In all four groups, the husbands physically abuse their wives. Here, I use quotes from only two of these couples as a means of illustrating the general, theoretical points being made.

Karl and Margaret consider themselves committed Christians. They are members of the Norwegian state church, the western Oslo (upper-middle-class) congregations that have been strongly influenced in recent years by the charismatic wave from the United States. This movement has had a major impact on religion in Norway throughout the 1980s, both in its conservative and more extreme forms.

The "charismatic" doctrine and its theological teachings are characterized by a reinforcement of the traditional dualist view of reality, in which "God" and "Satan" comprise the universal—cosmic and ethical—poles of existence. This duality is often referred to in terms such as the "authority principle of God" and "the rebellious principle of Satan," and it is no coincidence that the "authority principle of God" tends to be represented by man and the "rebellious principle of Satan" to be domiciled in a woman. Furthermore, just as God is superordinate to Christ, the relationship of man to woman is one of superior to subordinate, with man representing the authority as delegated to him by Christ. (On the history of such notions in early Christian thinking as they relate to the relationship of husbands to wives and the use of violence in the management and control of wives, see Dobash & Dobash, 1979, pp. 40-45.) Thus, the subordination of woman is seen as subordination to the authority of God, not man. Ultimately then, "masculine" and "feminine" are complementary principles, in the sense of mutually exclusive phenomena. This makes gender polarization strong—if you are a man you must not behave, act, or think like a woman. Crossing the gender boundaries means moving into dangerous, taboo territory.

Within the theoretical hierarchy of such theological thinking, women have been diagnosed as rebellious, even "possessed," if they behave in contempt of male gender norms, such as the principle of superordination. Effective means of dealing with such women has included the use of violence, once openly tolerated or espoused by the church, and for some sects, various forms of "exorcism" have been used. Within such a framework of beliefs, "the friends" and, on occasion, Karl personally, "exorcises" the demons of disobedience and rebellion from Margaret's body. He personally does what he can to cure her, including the use of physical and sexual violence. For example, he gets the idea that she is possessed and "unworthy of being a Christian wife and mother" when she has a miscarriage about the time she is finishing her undergraduate studies at the university. This, he believes, is God's way of signaling that she "is not ready to become a Christian wife and mother" unless she sacrifices her studies in order to "prove herself worthy." The first time he realized that she needed to be "cured through beating" was when she ordered theater tickets and "quite arbitrarily had arranged my time as she saw fit."

Even a summary overview of the imagery in his language shows strong elements of metaphors based on bodily-physical movements such as "press," "crush," "beat," "life," "hold," "avoid," "push," "carry," "move," "knock," and so on. He makes constant metaphorical reference to parts of the body, even when discussing apparently "spiritual" subjects. Her description of one such beating on a weekend retreat and the omnipresence of "the friends" emphasize the fact that parts of the body and bodily movement are constituent elements in the symbolic imagery and in communication in general. Karl also emphasizes the bodily-sexual desires—symbolized in the phallic emblem, the penis—which stand as the main symbol for his under-standing of God and the mystery of salvation: "It (the male sexual organ) is such a wondrous image of Christ and the church, the very tool, if you like, given us by the Lord."

Let us imagine imagery and communication in the light of the theory of Neuro-Linguistic Programming (NLP). This theory empha-sizes organization and understanding of communication on the basis of which "channel" dominates: the visual, the auditory, or the kines-thetic. Karl and Margaret's main channel of communication is clearly the kinesthetic; touch and bodily movement are their dominant and metaphor-creating media. Although the focus of the interviews quoted here is on sexuality and violence, this can only explain this motor-tactile dominance to some extent. It would be equally possible to describe sexuality via the "visual" channel. In a Norwegian cultural context, the "touch-movement" categories of sexualized language are not pronounced.

Both Karl and Margaret display a clear reluctance to explain sexuality in direct communication, at least using general, secular terminology. It is revealed that each gives priority to a spiritual-religious reference of interpretation and is eager to make the researcher see the unique dynamics of their relationship and their biblically oriented worldview. Once freed from the terminology of the researcher and given the opportunity to use his own terminology, Karl

is relatively open and direct when describing his sexuality and com-
municates via the kinesthetic channel.

The auditory is a nearly silent arena in their symbolic world.
Despite being articulate and displaying a subtle verbal sense of authority, the strength of Karl's gender affiliation is rarely expressed in
auditive metaphors; nor does Margaret use this symbolic arena. In the
linguistic atmosphere of the interviews, she appears to be silenced,
with verbally impoverished communication. In one part of the interview, with extreme hesitation and marked by self-censorship and
moralistic repudiation, she implies that there is an alternative lifestyle.
On this occasion, the symbols she uses and the channel of communication do not give an unambiguous picture. In a fumbling, cautious
description of the erotic dreams of her youth, characterized by joy and
lust—a relationship she had while in France—she moves between the
tactile and auditive channels, after a visual introduction: "I remember
enjoying having the light on, being fondled and embraced, being
played with, being joked with a little . . . a mixture of fun and irony
and sentimentality." When she later turns back to her new life with
Karl, her language becomes consistently "kinesthetic" as, for example,
she tries to describe him as a nonspontaneous, structured, authoritarian spouse—in contrast with her charming, uninhibited French lover.
When talking about violence, sexuality, and when associating these
themes with their new life together and with "the friends," both use
unilaterally kinesthetic imagery with regard to symbolic types and
channels of communication. Based on my analyses of the normalization process of violence, I assume that she has gradually learned to
accept his (and "the friends") symbolic universe. Part of this process
of influence appears to be domination of the kinesthetic channel with
regard to symbolic types and communication channels. According to
theories of NLP, had Margaret operated on a visual and auditive
channel, this would have been a heavier, more conflict-oriented type
of communication, a sign of poor adaptation on her part and a
situation that might have "necessitated" even more violence from
Karl.

As I have attempted to illustrate, violence as a practice that is
strongly legitimated appears to be intimately integrated into this
motor-tactile form of communication. In this symbolic worldview,
based on bodily movement and touch, it is not surprising to find that
for Margaret, the hands, breasts, and genitals are very highly charged
concepts, both morally and symbolically. As her husband and the
religious circle referred to as "the friends" attempt to "exorcise"

Margaret from some perceived transgression, pacification of the hands and arms serves a vital symbolic function: "They held my hand and the Devil left it, they held my elbow and the Devil left my arm—particularly my hands, I think, because every now and then they are enticed to do unchaste things." There is an interesting contrast here with Karl's hands, both his freedom to open his arms (when he holds them up in praise of the Lord), to use his fists in violence, and to use his hands to comfort. By contrast, Margaret's hands are feeble and weak, useless in lust and in defense against pain and abuse.

During the tactile-dominated "ritual" at the weekend retreat, the breasts were also central: "They held onto my breasts and prayed that they might be made worthy of being a mother's breasts." The background for this is Karl's systematic and goal-oriented blows, controlled and planned: "He is supposed to cleanse my entire body, all the sinful places, and I cannot bear the blows. He no longer beats me on the back, he strikes my breasts, the symbol of motherhood." In this context, all sexuality has moved from the (pleasurable and sinful) bedroom to the bathroom, with ice-cold showers, gagging, and a leather strap. As potential erogenous zones, the hands like the breasts are "dirty"; their only legitimate function is related to motherhood, which is generally inaugurated with pain. The genitals are the final, stubborn stronghold of the devil.

> They held my genitals and expelled every ounce of resistance. And I felt the demons leave my body, I felt them flee; it was as if there were a sound in my genitals when the Devil left me. I was so indescribably tired. I was heavy. I was emptied of the Devil. I was receptive. I could receive the Holy Spirit, and I could receive that which would create the child. And I spoke in tongues when we lay together; we both spoke in tongues. It was fantastic, it was phenomenal, it was blessed intercourse.

The use of symbols and violent behavior appear to glide into one another without friction, as natural aspects of a relatively consistent symbolic universe without particular breaks or contrasts. Thus, in my opinion, making an analytical distinction between the corporeal and the symbolic in the analysis of Karl and Margaret's gender construction in the arena of violence—as many feminist researchers do via the analytical distinction between biological, social, and symbolic gender—is too shortsighted about violence as a gender-related phenomenon.

The Visual Symbolic Basis:
The Eye—God's Vision—"Guardian Eyes"

Although the kinesthetic form of communication is dominant, the visual is also a carrier of important, highly charged symbols. One of the key expressions in Karl's interpretation of his gender power is very close to the emphasis placed by Freud (and Lacan) on "the eye" and "the visible" as the basis of gender identity and linguistic power: "The very construction of the body of a man and a woman reflects this difference so clearly. A man bears his sex on the outside, while there is no sex to be seen on a woman." The visibility of the male phallus—the phallic symbol—is Karl's basis for his active development as well as the metaphorical basis of masculine power and divinity: "I was made a man, and I have the joy and the reason to praise the Lord in my sex life. A man can do that much more than a woman. She forgets the Lord, but I have him with me; I am the Lord." According to Karl, his version of their sex life is almost identical with hers. He considers that what he has to say is helpful to her, is their joint version. He is an expert at "seeing things from slightly above." His view is an overview and he relates it to God's vision: "There is the earth, with heaven above it; there is the woman, with the man above her. All these images flow together and are actually symbolized in sexuality. This is vital—it is fundamental Christian doctrine."

Although Karl tends to construct his masculinity with visible, masculine phallic metaphors and symbols, he experiences visual communication with Margaret, eye-to-eye, as hazardous. Once she was extremely low, sick, and miserable and tried to twist away, protesting desperately. He commented: "I covered her face over, didn't want to see her, just wanting to sanctify that which was holy in her, so I came inside her and sanctified her. Then I left her lying there and went into the bedroom and prayed for her, prayed deeply for the Lord to give her guidance." Eye-to-eye and face-to-face contact would be devastating to pure, physical, sexualized, and metaphorical dominance and subjection. Visual communication might be the bearer of a structure indicating equality, and this might counteract his objectification and disintegration of her. Looking into her eyes and face might destroy her role as pure object.

This interrelation of the subjection of the women as a gender object and a theological object in Karl's overview becomes even more distinct when he goes into greater detail:

The act has a value of its own, I am not supposed to have her face in front of me. She is meant to be neutral. She is open to me as a woman, as an image of the earth, as an image of the church, as an image of the soil in which God sows. . . . She is not meant to be one who looks at me with her lustful smile or with her tears. She is to be a woman to me.

[Q: So you don't want to relate to her as a concrete woman then, not as a concrete identity?]

She was given to me as the woman in my life—woman, irrespective of what name she goes by, she is the woman . . . subjection is the very goal.

The least sign of anything concrete, individual, or personal destroys this pure order of things.

One contrast with the eye of the partner is what Karl calls the "guardian eye" of "the friends" who, according to his account, kept her in isolation and guarded over her for five days and nights, woke her each time she fell asleep, and prayed over her to draw out the last demon inside her and prepare her for the calling of motherhood. She describes this as the ultimate in caring: "And I was there for five days, surrounded by people day and night. . . . They didn't take a single hour off, they prayed for me all the time. . . . They prayed and prayed and sang and spoke in tongues." This kind of "guardian eye" is a strong, effective form of influence:

In the past I had been stubborn, possibly rebellious. I had even had thoughts in the direction of wanting to leave Karl. If I slept it was the devil who put me to sleep because what I really wanted was to run away. And they woke me, gave me cold water, had me shower in cold water to sort of wake me up again. I was always so tired. I was indescribably tired. And had they not been with me and called down the Holy Spirit, the devil would have found an easy victim. But I made it through.

Total isolation from her ordinary life and contacts served to counteract her heretical thoughts and impulses: "I didn't have to receive guests or letters, to be bothered by the phone; I was protected from everything."

These are familiar techniques for breaking down and transforming a personality and are used in many contexts, from brainwashing and torture to intensive courses in management skills. The combination of being guarded over, isolated, subjected to psychological pressure and physical exhaustion can lead to drastic personality changes in a shockingly short time. This influence is even more effective when the process is seen as an expression of caring.

The symbol of the "guardian eye" thus expresses the divine, "phallic eye" with total control from which there is no escape. Because escape is impossible, one must abandon oneself entirely to this guarding eye, which is an expression of absolute love and caring. The use of symbols and bodily (violent) behavior glide—once again—into one another and integrate. In my opinion, the cultural meaning lies in this integration and infiltration and again, illustrates the fruitlessness of making an analytical distinction between symbolic and biological gender in the study of gender construction in the arena of violence.

The Masculine Symbolic Trinity:
The Hand, the Strap, and the Phallus

The few but vital "phallic" metaphors in the visual channel used by Karl and "the friends" contribute to a better understanding of the dominant symbolic foundation built on bodily movement and touch. Margaret takes over and acknowledges phallic symbolism as fundamental to her theology, the core of divine masculinity:

> The Lord himself is the marrow of our sex life; it is for the view of the Lord and for his sake.
> [Q: Do you mean that the Lord endows him with lust?]
> Yes. Hallelujah.

Thus, Margaret speaks with an effectively internalized masculine sexual theology and, in that vein, provides a definition of masculinity as embodied in Karl: "Yes, he is strength." Masculine strength and power are also the source of his wealth of symbolism. Hunting and war metaphors are frequently used, with references to battles and victories in the kingdom of God and in the sexual arena. As such, references to violent practices are neither striking nor outstanding. Instead, they glide naturally into the wealth of imagery in the kinesthetic symbolic universe. When asked directly what he, as a man, finds attractive in women, he answers quite directly, despite the risk that it might sound absurd or vulgar: "Namely, vanquishing a woman. Being the one who takes possession and owns her on behalf of God; no, even on behalf of myself. I have been given the strength, the fighting spirit of my lust, so that even if God were not there, I would do my duty as a man, as God determined it."

It would hardly be possible to describe the masculine erotic realm more directly or revealingly than in these battle metaphors. His language is filled with these strong dynamic-motor images. For example:

> We are struggling and fighting together . . . deep in the hands of Satan . . . with one blow the Lord can be hailed, if only the Devil would let go. . . . I think our marriage has been marked by this struggle . . . the fight to break it and help her onwards. . . . It is not abuse, it is love. There is a difference between breaking her lust and giving her rich, true pleasure. . . . We force her thoughts toward the Lord and by humiliating her he will uplift her. . . . Thoughts are in the flesh and so they can only be exorcised from the flesh . . . carried forth for the Lord. . . . She tried to control and seize our marriage. . . . She is so far down that I can't manage to lift her. . . . The Lord allows my wrath to rise while I hit . . . leads us in the direction of having children . . . become part of the Sacred.

In addition to the hand that fights and hits—and can also touch in comfort—a leather strap plays an important physical and symbolic role. When asked why the leather strap, Karl responded, "It was the natural thing. What would you hit with but a leather strap? I can't go into a porn shop and buy a whip! . . . . And I have a leather strap, I've got my own belt." His familiarity with biblical terminology undoubtedly makes him associate the belt with the girdle that holds clothing in place, in which one is enclosed, which orders and structures—keeps the woman in her place. A safeguard against chaos, which ties, holds tight, binds together, keeps loose things in place and flying things down.

The hand, the strap, and the phallus are tightly intertwined in practical physical use and as a masculine, symbolic trinity. This trinity plays important physical and symbolic roles as weapons. They also stand in contrast with women's hands, breasts, and genitals. These specific "women's bodily places" are associated with deep structure in the grammar of the production of symbols, and they are the most highly charged symbols for Margaret. They are polysemous and ambivalent but mainly negatively charged. The decisive "context" for Margaret's experience and interpretations is the gender construction process that takes place when she is abused in her relationship, when communication is dominated by the motor-tactile, and where the contrasts between them are so revealing. Her hands are powerless while his are free; he uses his eye visually while denying her visual communication. The eye—in combination with the hand, the strap, and the penis—provides endless sources of imagery of "natural" safeguards against chaos, of order and structure, and of keeping the woman in her place: an erotic masculine realm that disintegrates her as an individual woman. This leads to physical and psychological "disintegration"—she is crushed both as a biological and a social sexual/gendered being.

Let me emphasize two items of principle. The use of symbols and bodily (violent) behavior are, as I have indicated, intimately related and tightly intertwined. This highlights the fruitless nature of distinguishing between biological and symbolic gender in the context being analyzed here. Categorically replacing the visual, the "phallic" with the tactile, which we will also see is the strategy proposed for women by French philosopher Luce Irigaray, does not automatically appear to be sufficient to alter the basic power constellation between the sexes. In my research of couples with whom there is abuse, there is nothing to indicate that women who communicate mainly *via* the kinesthetic-tactile channel manage to break out of the pattern of subjugation any more or less than other women who communicate more visually (or auditively). This means there is no indication that a woman who invests linguistically-symbolically in the kinesthetic-tactile dimension manages to transcend the power of the phallus or gender domination. Touch *per se* does not appear to be a category of liberation, in contrast to visually constituted power. I will now discuss these two items in greater abstraction, with Luce Irigaray (1995) as my "sparring" partner.

Women's Sexual Morphology
of Touch as a Symbolic Basis

At least implicitly, Irigaray breaks down the demarcations between the biological-bodily and the symbolic and takes a stand on the widespread conception of an "ontological hierarchy," with the biological as its static basis, the social as the intermediate level, and the symbolic as the most highly derived, most dynamic "fluid" level. She builds her philosophy quite directly on the contradiction between the phallic sexuality of the man and the tactile sexuality of the woman. Irigaray goes far in binding the different sexualities of men and women: their ways of thinking, their language, their biological bodily differences, that is, their primarily sexual characteristics. When she does not build her philosophy directly on the physical differences between the male and female sexual organs, she attributes a great deal of significance to the different "morphologies" of the sexes (Moi,

1985, p. 143). Because Irigaray attributes fundamental significance to the "phallic" form, it is not surprising that Jacques Lacan, who bases his linguistic theories on the phallic, provides both a foundation on which to build and a position against which to react. Because Irigaray's ambition is to transcend all male power (the phallic), she must attempt to phase out and transcend the entirely masculine-structured language system. Before an alternative language can be established, such feminist rebels must identify themselves and relate to their own bodily attributes and their female sexuality and then gradually develop an alternative form of communication based on the "morphology" of women's sexuality.

I will now sketch some of the points at which the physical body and symbolic-linguistic structure are intertwined. The work of both Irigaray (in a feminist way) and Lacan (in a patriarchal way) uses this as their point of departure. A very brief description of Irigaray's (1985) theory of the intertwined nature of the shape of the genitals and the structure of thought, including symbols, will have to suffice. Her argument begins in the opposition between active and passive sexuality as modeled by Freud on the basis of masculine parameters. But this Freudian alternative, the choice between a masculine/clitoral/active sexuality and a feminine/vaginal/passive sexuality is fundamentally false—and must be transcended. In Freud's model, female sexuality is seen as a basic deficit (Irigaray, 1985, p. 39). The clitoris defines woman as man in miniature, bound to be characterized by penis envy and the desire for a child as a penis substitute. On these Freudian premises, Irigaray can make the subtle definition of the female sex as the sex that does not exist but that, instead, must compensate parasitically by taking advantage of the real, that is, phallic, sex of the man.

The definition of woman as deficit or vacuum also connects Irigaray with Aristotle's view of women as the underdeveloped human being and to Plato's parable of the hole. But Irigaray wants to fill this female hole, traditionally considered the domicile of ambiguous, vague knowledge, with a new content and a whole new interpretation. For Irigaray (1985, p. 24), feminine "auto-eroticism" is fundamentally distinguished from masculine eroticism. Whereas the man requires an instrument to stroke himself—a hand, the hole of a woman's body, or language—women stroke themselves automatically and constantly. The continuous rubbing of the labia allows a woman to caress and embrace herself or "one another" constantly but never defined, never delimited to one, two, or more. As opposed to the concentrated, delimited single organ of the man, the genitals and erogenous zones of the woman are all-encompassing and nonspecific: the vagina, the breasts, and far more (Irigaray, 1985, p. 28). Thus, feminine lust is more closely related to *touch* than to looks. For a woman, the one who touches cannot be distinguished from the touched as is usually the case in the erotic categorization of men.

In the tradition of Freud, language is constituted by the *visual,* and thus female sexuality is considered to have no language. Because the woman's sexual organs are plural and unseen, it follows that they do not exist. Or, as Olav, one of the abusers in my material, puts it: "[Female sexuality] is, approximately, nothing. . . . It is receiving, it is being a receiver. . . . There is not something you can point to as female sexuality, is there?" Thus, women develop an anxiety about not being seen, and female lust becomes unstructured, not clearly goal-oriented—until it is reshaped and redirected toward the child who is seen as a limited, phallic being a woman can hold and caress just as a man touches and feels his penis with his own hand or with the help of an instrumental "other" (the body of a woman) (Irigaray, 1985, p. 41).

The entire shared culture, the language that both sexes must learn and accommodate, is thus built on the morphology of the one gender, the phallic, the visible, the delimited, the explicit, the tangible, that which is defined as distinguished from the other, that which is "outstanding." What Irigaray strives to do is to abolish and transcend this ungendered monopoly on language and culture. In order to transcend the phallic monopoly on language, she must first become intimate with the morphology of the female sex, which, as a result of gender subjugation, was initially interpreted as invisible, a deficit, a vacuum, the "nonoutstanding" and indefinable. In line with the image of the "labia continually caressing one another," Irigaray creates a feminine universe, an exclusive alternative to the masculine universe based on the symbol of the phallus and using it as the *constitutive* element of its language.

Contrary to her overt intentions, it is clear that, in practice, Irigaray explicitly defines the content of the feminine in *contrast* to the system of the masculine rather than as an *exclusive* alternative to it (Moi, 1985, p. 139). She does extend herself to modify the impression of a limited definition, using literary terms, such as irony, a mimetic, imitating narrative technique (Irigaray, 1985, p. 41) and other types of emphasis of the tentative, incomplete, indirect, and groping. But despite her clear restrictions and modifications, her entire philosophy blares out the different, bodily-based values—and thus the different symbolic values—in a direction that also defines the feminine/female. This becomes even clearer in comparison with Lacan. Both Lacan and Irigaray stress that language is mainly constituted on the basis of the visual. The phallus is symbolically determined as that which is seen, strikes the eye, stands above its environment—with the tower of the church spire as the paradigm. It is natural for a negative category of the feminine to develop against this background. This notion is well formulated by Karl, with his extensive system of symbols in legitimization of the sexual dominance of the man: "There is nothing visible on the woman." In line with this definition of visual absence, woman is seen as one big deficit. Irigaray's strategy of liberation in this respect is based on filling the feminine, visually determined category of absence, applying a consistent gynocentric logic—with a positive content and a positive charge, on the basis of *kinesthetic-tactile* categories. Whereas the phallus symbolizes the visible, external, delimited, and delimiting, the symbolic basis of the female sexual morphology describes and interprets the feminine as the embracing, the self-caressing, the internal, the diverse, the fluid, the oceanic, the devoted—that which becomes part of a larger whole, the unlimited, the integrative, the mystical.

Irigaray's theory implies an interplay between body, thought, and the production of symbols. My analysis of Karl and Margaret would, however, be hard to carry out according to her theory, because she also implies that women and men have completely different symbolic bases, owing to their different genital morphologies (i.e., the kinesthetic-tactile and the visual, respectively). Moreover, when Irigaray attempts to fill the phallically determined nongender (woman) with a fluid, undefinable, oceanic, unstructured content to pose an alternative female sexuality and an alternative female language, she, like many other gynocentric feminists, runs the risk of falling into the "reflective fallacy": Inverting the phallic may, as we shall see below, only serve to validate it.

Striking and Comforting—or the Hand as a Constitutive Category

In the process of socialization, or learning what "femininity" and "masculinity" mean *symbolically*, I see more clearly that the *body* is always present as an arena and a physical point of departure, and vice versa. The body, in the "gendered" sense of the word, is more than the genitals. The sexual body also includes the hands, hands that strike and hands that comfort. Analyzing the movement of the hands in strict isolation is meaningless. Movement is always inherent in the social power relationship and is the bearer of intention, interpretation, and symbol. I refer again to my interviews to examine the distinction between the concepts of *constitution* and *regulativity*.

The diversity of arenas for developing and justifying gender norms and the many sets of norms to which we may relate give a superficial sense of flexibility, variation, and potential for change while also providing a number of contrasts. There is quite clearly a close interplay of meaning among the various areas and sets of norms, a context that makes it meaningful to discuss a basic patriarchal structure, both in a synchronic and diachronic perspective. Operating with the concepts of constitution and regulativity is fruitful when discussing the relationship between that which superficially is both extremely variable and clearly stable (difficult-to-change aspects of gender dynamics), as these concepts express the logical distinction and the difference in levels between basic and derived rules. The distinction between regulative and constitutive sets of rules is based both on general games theory and on jurisprudence and political theory.[1] Generally, the *constitutive* describes the basic terms and conditions for the application of regulative rules, their validity, and their limitations. The constitutive is a set of rules, usually implicit, that defines the basic prerequisites for behavior in various political, social, psychological, or playful games—including the prerequisites for gender construction—on the *basis* of which, but not about which, we speak and act, write, and discuss, because it is part of our selves, self-evident beyond thematized or the explicitly visible. By contrast, *regulative* rules are applied rules that can somehow be derived from basic rule. Constitutive rules are stable but not static, whereas regulative rules are more flexible and in constant flux at the "surface structure" grammatical level.[2]

The hand that strikes generally does so in violation of rules of law, social conventions, and certain ethical norms, but it does not necessarily strike in violation of the underlying structural—constitutive—rules of masculinity. The hand that strikes may be violating a serious regulative norm (e.g., laws that categorize assault as an offense) but will not necessarily be violating the cultural norms with regard to what the male hand is permitted. In other words, abuse is not always necessarily a violation of the deeper constitutive gender rules. If the hand that strikes suddenly begins to comfort, this may be interpreted as a violation of the rule of violence—the hand apparently obeying the rule of love. The woman may experience this deviation as strong and decisive, giving her grounds for not leaving a violent partner. She may interpret this as an indication that he is "really" kind and loving.

In that case, she interprets his comforting hand constitutively (i.e., regretful, gentle, and tearfully loving is what he is "really" like). But what if the very *switching* back and forth between violence and warmth is what is really constitutive to his way of being? At the regulative level, the comforting, loving hand is experienced by the woman as a real change. A week without violence is experienced as paradise. But the wife's positive response to the (regulatively) comforting hand validates the hand of her husband as a basic *symbolic category* (i.e., his power and divinity), *the source of both violence and warmth, evil and good.*

Anyone who has studied the process of abuse will have no difficulty identifying this as an expression of normalization and internalization. The man's constitutive behavior includes both beating *and* comfort, and thus he takes full advantage of his interpretative privilege, which gradually becomes the unchallenged, prevailing one. He comforts out of caring love just as he strikes out of love, and he cares his wife to "death." By rejoicing in the comforting hand and interpreting it constitutively, she indicates that she has learned a deep and basic lesson about "becoming a woman," about the framework of development for her gender affiliation, about the limitations of her sex in the process of gender construction. When taken together, beatings *and* comfort, as expressions of values with opposing (regulative) meanings, teach an implicit but effective (constitutive) lesson about gender identity and gender limits. My material on abused women and their husbands is full of examples of this learning/teaching process and illustrates how *gender construction takes place in the field of tension and interplay of "different" and "same," of flexibility and stability.*

A Violent Sex Life: Regulative
Flexibility and Basic Constitutive Patterns

Placing this in the context of the understanding of the arena of sexual violence within the small religious group under study, men generally expressed clearly and directly the theological symbols in this type of "intertwining" in the process of gender construction. When they strike *and* comfort, protect *and* isolate, they show and explain that their cruelty is not actually "abuse," but rather a firm, controlled methodology and pedagogy, steps in the paternal upbringing of the not-yet-adult, not-yet-mature woman. In this process, she is becoming a woman in the correct fashion, according to the rules. The tactical, conscious, and controlled switching that characterizes these men's regulative, norm-determined behavior is meant to show that men act in a larger context. When they abuse their wives, they do not do so in assertion of their own power, but do so in the service of a higher power as part of their divine mission. In the service of the Lord, these men become an extension of the arm of God, like God, both loving *and* punishing. Based on the model of the parent who can humiliate *and* nurture, punish *and* comfort, God can make the man little and childlike. Thus, the man becomes like God by first "crushing" and then "loving" his wife.

Both the woman and the man interpret these extreme types of behavior as part of a learning process, in which the invisible (constitutive) limits of masculinity and femininity are drawn. The woman is to be a little sexually active, but not too active. Gradually, through rewards and sanctions, the woman learns the limits of the "appropriate" sexual behaviors for a wife. She learns her place; she learns to be a woman. But too much passivity can also be a threat to the male structuring and regulation of femininity. For example, when Elisabeth complains about how tired she is (after many years of severe physical abuse), John interprets this as rejection, an assertion of female power, a sexual trick, and thus a rebellion against his masculinity. With her "rejection," Elisabeth breaks a constitutive rule, the requirement of continuous male access to female sexuality.

> First you commit to fidelity when you marry. And you have expectations of getting to act out that side in your marriage. But when the woman goes on strike for long periods of time, well, that's not the way to treat your husband. And then she can't come around afterwards and expect to be treated with satin gloves, when she has committed sabotage against everything that's important to the other party.
>
> [Q: What was this sabotage?]
>
> Oh, being tired and all that—that kind of thing. Of course you can always find an excuse. She never took the initiative.
>
> [Q: But did you?]
>
> Of course I did. Naturally. But I would have liked her to do it too. At least every once in a while.
>
> [Q: And it felt provocative to you that she never did?]
>
> Well, it was a rejection, I'm sure she meant to do me in, or to assert her power. She was the type of person who likes to extinguish a guy's fire. And she was good at that.

John had to physically punish her potential sabotage—pedagogically and in a controlled fashion.

I decided to teach her that at least that kind of sabotage wouldn't do her any good. You can't get away with that sort of thing.

[Q: Are you saying that you decided to have intercourse anyway, even if she didn't want you to?]

Yes, naturally. Are there any marriages where there is no intercourse?

(. . .)

[Q: If she had been in pain and you beat her anyway, could you still have intercourse afterwards?]

Of course you can, of course. I could and she could.

Here we can see some ambiguity about the rules on the active-passive scale, some regulative flexibility. But it is clear that a nonexplicit norm about what constitutes the masculine and the feminine, the limits of the power game, is always there underlying the negotiations. Here, too, the switching provides another illustration of the constitutive level and how, intimately, it is intertwined with the interpretative rights of the man, his epistemological privilege, in relation to female sexuality and her "upbringing" as a woman. The beatings were an effective means in a behavioral-pedagogical *process of gender construction,* in which both sexes gradually found their right (God-given) places. Gradually, John's interpretative privilege becomes inviolable and applies both to his own gender construction and to hers.

We may follow a new and tragic phase in this process of construction in Elisabeth's second marriage. In the first marriage she slept with violent John out of a sense of obligation, under the threat of rape and abuse. This obedient passivity made her wonder whether she might be frigid. She was incapable of integrating or familiarizing herself with the myth that an aggressive, violent man is a sexy one. When she finally managed to get out of that violent marriage, she met a completely different man, kind, tolerant, and mild-tempered. In their sex life, they began playing with *apparently reversed roles*. She tested the role of the active partner, took the initiative, and was fascinated with testing the limits. She could now become the lustful subject in relation to the power of which she had previously only been the lustless object:

Well, I have personal experience of the way men relate sexuality with power. And it fascinated me tremendously, how they were able to do that, but I never really understood it. But now I feel it; sexuality can be closely allied with power.

[Q: How do you feel it?]

> Because now I'm playing a whole new role. I can feel, myself,
> that it can be kind of . . . sexy to take the initiative and be the one
> who has the advantage, the one who decides what we will do.

She sees clearly that the whole thing is about testing limits and about
fear of crossing boundaries:

> That's what I am afraid of. Like with everything else, where am I
> going to be in 10 years time then? I'm actually scared about that, the
> power is so strong that I really want to keep it under control for as
> long as possible. . . . I'm afraid. Will I have to constantly extend the
> register? When will I get to the end?

The content of her sex role has changed drastically, been inverted,
stood on its head. At the superficial level, she appears to have
undergone a complete sexual transformation and feels pleasure in the
feeling of freedom to move in this "different," new, previously taboo
erotic landscape. But, indirectly, she reveals that she is waiting for her
new husband to say "stop" and send her off rejected once again,
evicted because she did not learn the silent prerequisite underlying the
new, regulative, intoxicating freedom. In other words, because she did
not learn the explicit basic constitutive pattern for what "femininity"
is and is not, even in their exciting sex games that included the power
"inversions" of sadomasochism, John's interpretative privilege goes
on haunting her, intertwining with that of her new partner—the one
with the right to establish what's what—and she goes on playing by
the "same" rules that applied in her previous marriage.

"The Stone" and "The Sea": "Different" or "The Same"?

In order to consider more theoretical considerations of the significance of the conceptual distinction between *constitutive* and *regulative* rules, I return to Irigaray. For her, it is important to replace the
main metaphor of "the stone" (the fixed and delimited) with "the sea"
(the fluid—the prevailing structural opposition between the male
phallus morphology and the continuous female touching and her
diverse "genital" morphology).

The question becomes, What is changed by this type of metaphor
and what is not? In other words, what is "different" and what is "the
same"? Superficially, "fluid, touching" language is entirely different
from "fixed, visual" language. But the male language that Irigaray

wants to estrange is also constitutively decisive for being able to use the concepts of "sameness" and "difference" at all. Using language (the phallic symbolic system) to express some kind of feminist "difference" is contingent on using the patriarchal logic of the constitutively phallic concept of "sameness." "Different" thus becomes a covert *formal* patriarchal category at the constitutive level, as the patriarchy is identified as idealization and validation of "the same." Thus, Irigaray finds herself with a problem of self-reference when she appears to mean that only the one gender, with its phallic point of departure, stands for the development of language and symbols. Also, as Irigaray explains, "the difference" in the genital-morphological symbolic patterns of the genders, the "masculine" and the "feminine," takes on a striking constitutive similarity. This constitutive similarity does not make it any easier to analyze (see also the section "Women's Sexual Morphology of Touch as a Symbolic Basis").

Seen from a different perspective, we can say that the "same" and "different" are only seemingly defined, whose meanings only apply in a closely defined context; something is "different" or "similar" in relation to some other particular thing. Anything may be "different" or "similar" depending on the rules for defining them as such. We may say that the "fluid" and the "fixed," "the sea" and "the stone" are "different" in relation to their *positive manifest content,* but they may be "similar" in relation to a *possible underlying essentialist category.* Irigaray thus violates the regulative patriarchal norms for the development of new metaphors, replacing a regulative rule (about visual, limited thinking) with a new regulative rule (about tactile, fluid thinking). But if, for example, the fundamental constitutive rule requires that gender always have a metaphorical (or perhaps rather symbolic) essence—irrespective of its content—then, in being regulatively subversive, Irigaray is implicitly validating the constitutive.

"Different" Contents—"The Same" Function?

This point is elucidated if we choose for a moment to consider the matter from the point of view of functional logic; we may meaningfully state that the two opposing elements may have one and the same function. For example, in a parliamentary system, the opposition party tends to validate and strengthen the legitimacy of the party in power. The opposition of the women in a party may, correspondingly, legitimize and strengthen the power of the men in that party. Similarly, "radical theology" may be seen as a compensatory phenomenon, beneficial and vital to the functioning of the conservative church. Such recirculating, stable functional units may be referred to as "repressive tolerance," in line with Herbert Marcuse's analysis of how instigators and revolutionaries in a latter-day capitalist, industrialist society are deprived of their negative power by being defined as "classics," well-adjusted necessary elements of the society as a whole. Without effective integration of the critics of the system, its functionality decreases. Another way of describing this phenomenon is to say that "modernist" rebels may, in practice, be well adapted to a "postmodern" consumer structure in art and literature. In line with this view, it is easy to imagine clever male strategists rubbing their hands in glee over a number of subversive feminist metaphors such as those of Irigaray and other gynocentrics. Far more hazardous revolts than this have previously been swallowed and integrated by the easily adapted, flexible patriarchy. Replacing a patriarchal rule with its opposite, a feminist reflection of it, does not automatically open up changes at the constitutive level. That is only possible under very special conditions. In an academic environment, a purely intellectual milieu, such conditions for transcendent change are seldom available.

However, it is a frequently used feminist strategy to act, think, feel, and write as differently as possible from the ways in which men do such things and in contrast with general, patriarchal norms. Julia Kristeva also bases her thinking on the model of an alternative, differing practice in her analysis of "the dissident" or the "stranger in exile." But her development of the essential term "abject" makes it possible for her to at least partially avoid falling into the trap into which Irigaray appears to tumble with respect to the development of an alternative feminist "space," which, paradoxically, has fundamental categorical similarities with the patriarchal "space": that which I refer to as the "reflexive fallacy." Her reading of the concept of the "abject" helps Kristeva bring out the ambiguity and the vacillation between being and moving outside and inside, the absence of a clearly formulated alternative "space." "Abjectification" expresses the ambiguity and the spaceless as the potential for real transcendence.

Thus, when we violate regulative rules, we may simultaneously be contributing to a defense of the very constitutive rules we are trying to reject. When something constitutive is made *explicit and clear,* so clear that it stands out as delimited, as something on which it is possible to take a stand "for" or "against," it is easy for the implicit, fundamental, structured nature of the constitutive to be lost. This kind of "trap"—the disappearance of the overall dynamics when the constitutive is transformed into something regulative—is probably also widespread in subversive, feminist games in academic settings. "Sameness," stability, and stubbornness may be reproduced in a cleverly concealed fashion when the regulative content of a norm is replaced by something "different."

Nor is the constitutive ever entirely static or ever entirely the same. Although tough, stubborn, and resistant to change, it still remains somewhat adaptable. In fact, this is the very strength of the constitutive. The ability to adapt and develop flexibly may be enlarged to the extent that fundamental change may also appear to have taken place. For example, shortly after the Russian Revolution in 1917, when large numbers of women rushed into traditionally male jobs in industry and professions such as medicine, the official interpretation was that there had been a fundamental system shift between the sexes and that the socialist revolution would automatically bring a feminist revolution in its wake. But this change in the external division of labor may also be interpreted as a way of avoiding change in the basic gender power relationship. Within the communist system, these phenomena largely prevented the development of a dynamic women's movement such as that in Western industrialized societies. Correspondingly, the existence of women ministers in Sweden and Norway may be interpreted, on the one hand, as a decisive system shift within the church or, on the other hand, as an expression of the adaptation and cementation of the "restored" patriarchy; that is, the church has developed a female-dominated ministry because it is a low-paid, low-status profession.

In summary, I maintain that the advantage of the conceptual distinction between regulativity and constitution is that it highlights the necessity of understanding the interplay of change and stability, difference and sameness for an analysis of gender construction. This distinction particularly illuminates and elucidates the reasons for which change at one level often implies validation and cementation of the point of departure at another, more basic level. Thus, from a feminist, analytic perspective, gender construction, along with many feminist rebellions, is characterized by ambiguity.

The Division Between the Bodily and the Symbolic "Self"—The Strategy of the Abused Woman

I would now like to expand on the conceptual distinction between constitution and regulativity in an effort to do that which Irigaray and the analysis of abuse have shown to be so vital, to break down the barrier between the biological-bodily and the symbolic.

"Symbolic gender" has gradually become part of feminist research—as a supplementary dimension to "biological" and "social" gender. See Sandra Harding's (1986) description of how three processes, symbolic, social, and individual gender, have come into being. As the trichotomy has replaced the dichotomy, the division of categories has become correspondingly problematic. We have begun to see that "everything is biology, everything is sociology," and "everything is symbolism" at one and the same time; that is, biological, social, and symbolic gender are so intertwined that the simplistic division into categories serves more to confuse than elucidate this extremely complex matter. A more fruitful way of analyzing gender construction than dividing factors into such categories and claiming that relationships are more or less biological, and so forth, might be to collate and integrate, *to couple the bodily with the symbolic,* as I have tried to do in my analysis of gender construction in the arena of sexual violence. Of course, this attempt is far more than an intellectual/scholarly game in the philosophy of science.

When a woman is abused, it is impossible for her to be *completely* present in her painful, violated body. She has to "break loose" from her body. Like a prostitute or a sexually abused child, she may separate her body from her "self," repress her body, make it into an *object.* She cannot feel the feelings with her "self"; that would be too painful, so she estranges herself from her body and flees to a *symbolic* world as a survival strategy; "she" is no longer her body. For the women in the religious group studied, the symbolic "self" allows the woman to integrate into her husband's theological worldview, identify with it, and become a different person. For her, the man becomes a man by becoming "God." This means that she, as a concrete, individual woman, is slowly disintegrated and resurrected in a new form; she takes on the attributes of "pure" femininity, and her body expresses pure female subjugation or "possession." Thus, the woman transforms her "self" and denies her corporeality, replacing it with a symbolic "self"—to defend herself against physical or sexual abuse by her husband. In other cultures, for example, among some North American Indians, there are rules and rituals describing how the "soul" can leave the body when it is subjected to intolerable bodily infractions or punishment. They have learned the ritual "division" between soul and body, and thus they have a religious-symbolic preparedness for such extreme situations. Thus, an Indian woman who has been raped can ritually return to her body after her soul has fled.

In my interpretative structure, when men behave violently, the constitutive power relations, normally implicit and invisible, break into the regulative level of action of "surface grammar" with such force and dominance that the modest space allocated to women's "regulative" behavior is so compressed that it disintegrates. When this happens, the woman has no place, no ability to adapt and follow the normal, regulative rules for women's behavior. She must either fight back and die (commit suicide) or shift to a different metaphysical level (allow her soul to leave her body—which remains there defenseless and lifeless, fully accessible to the abuser). Constitutive male power is no longer an underlying, latent prerequisite or structural condition for the repertoire of women's behavior. Instead, it has completely filled the woman's—regulative—life structure with its violent presence. Violence makes the body "totalitarian" as a constitutive source of gender symbolism and gender rules; the constitutive level drowns and totally permeates the space for regulative actions: The difference between the physical-tangible and the symbolic-normative has been entirely effaced.

In our Western culture, we have no similar readily accessible rituals for interpreting and channeling the flight and defense strategy implemented by some women victims of violence. Western victims of violence are abandoned to their individual, solitary, disempowered state by the effective social isolation imposed by the man. Western women estrange themselves permanently from their bodies, separate the bodily and symbolic levels, and flee forever to a symbolic world. Bodily feelings and identity are deeply and enduringly damaged, as Western women cannot return to their bodily "selves" and reestablish the contact between the bodily and symbolic worlds. The only ritual that I know of in Western cultures relating to the violation of the human body has developed in accordance with the terms of the violent man. These are the rituals or "exorcism" in some charismatic Christian subcultures. These contain ritual regulations for how the rebellious nature of women is to be broken through the bodily-symbolic, tangible, ritual "exorcism" of Satan. In these rituals, the woman "possessed" by Satan is totally subjected to the physical power and symbolic interpretations of the male "exorcist." How can she possibly reestablish contact with her body as the constitutive level for (symbolic) meaning, when the physical basis of the symbols is so painful? How can she even comprehend the meaning of the signs, when she has lost contact with the body into which the symbols have been written, physically and in blood?

The Body as a Category for Change?

One scholarly prerequisite in the theory of science for the sharp distinction between the physical and the symbolic, not only in feminist research but as one of the dominant traditions in Western thinking, is the conception of *body* as "primary" (a given, a categorical basis, the location of the primary gender criteria), whereas the *social* is considered "secondary" (derived, more mobile), and the *symbolic* tends to be seen as "tertiary" (the most fluid, stratospheric). This covert normative, "ontological" hierarchy easily loses the "dialectical" perspective by which I have attempted to interpret this empirical material: that is, the fact that the body is not only the point of departure for and the source of production of a continual stream of symbols, but it "is" *fundamentally symbolic,* the symbolic and the social "are" perpetually bodily, the social "is" symbolic and the symbolic social, and the symbols are also constantly interpreting and changing the bodily. There is no such thing as "pure" corporeality; the bodily is always mediated and shaped by the social and the symbolic.

At one time, the focus of feminist research on the difference between biological and social gender was advantageous. It was probably necessary in order for feminist research to be able to develop a strategy of change, to liberate research from the heavy legacy of attributed femininity derived from our "biology" (woman as the passive recipient, as irrational and directed by her emotions, etc.), which had entrapped and silenced us. It was particularly necessary because the massive wave of "biological" femininity appeared to be omnipresent. However, the programmatic, watertight bulkhead between biological and social gender implies that they have lost their interrelation and common context as, by definition, they *were not meant* to have anything to do with one another. Social gender received all the attention; as it was within social gender that the potential for change was seen. With a feminist strategy for changing "dynamic sociality" by ignoring "static biology," research ran the risk of losing its connection with the body.

As early as the time of socialization of the women's movement under the Marxist banner "the social is all," we feminist researchers were largely estranged from our bodies. Consistent with this, Shulamith Firestone proposed that we have our entire female biology surgically excised or subjected to genetic manipulation. When we were thus drastically "thrown back" into our bodies, we found ourselves fundamentally insecure. Had our bodies not been made irrelevant to the process of change unless we accepted Firestone's project of going to war against our biological "nature"? This, of course, is equivalent to accepting the curse of being a gendered/sexual being (McMillan, 1982, p. 154). This led to the gynocentric pendulum swing between idealization of the female body, symbols of life, and "Mother Earth."

Some gynocentric researchers (e.g., Susan Brownmiller, Mary O'Brien) emphasized the biological-bodily difference of women. "Differ"-ence was also to impact on the social-dynamic ("biological essentialism") such that the social was to support and reinforce the biological uniqueness of women rather than to neglect it—for which Simone de Beauvoir and Firestone had paved the way—but not to compensate for it. Thus, the body became relevant, but hardly for change. It was still seen as a relatively *static basic constitutive* category, albeit now in a positive light. Other gynocentric researchers (e.g., Nancy Chodorow, Carol Gilligan, Evelyn Fox Keller) stressed the social difference of women, which was not necessarily to be fought against or changed but which needed to be profiled as a qualitatively positive point of departure for an in-depth study and further development of the social (possibly combined with biological) uniqueness ("social essentialism"). But here the "static" biological gender shone through as a constitutive category for the social as well. By laying all the stress on understanding the dichotomization of the genders in relation to a social aspect (primarily the division of labor), feminist research fell, paradoxically, back on some biological constants, particularly constraints related to giving birth and breastfeeding (Chodorow). The more change we tried to promote by overstepping social and political bounds—but without touching on or problematizing the biological— the more we implicitly came to accept the reading of the body as a nonhistorical, unchanging, basic constitutive category, as a virtually static "deep structure" underlying all the "surface grammar" of social change. When feminist research focused so unilaterally on social change, it was thus damaged by its implicit confirmation of exactly what it was attempting to do away with, a biological imperative.

In the absence of a thorough analysis and "problematization" of the body, the body became far too much the bearer of the static and timeless, and this also characterized the social institutions most closely related to the body. Strangely enough, biological gender became a constitutive category for the social as well. Only by refocusing on the body can feminist research go on to apply the logic of change also to the body and biology, as I have illustrated in my interpretation of the empirical material presented here.

Now feminist research is chasing its own tail, with all its energetic examination of socially determined forms of "femininity" and "masculinity." Relative social differences have been attributed heavy symbolic meaning, and we have become the helpless hostages of the "social construction"—out of touch with the power and dynamic ability of our own bodies to change. Introducing the concept of "symbolic gender" and analytically integrating the biological with the social, including the integration of symbolic gender, may, in my opinion, serve to reestablish contact with the body in an analytically fruitful fashion.

Conclusion: A More Open Approach to Gender Theory?

First, to me, was being able to draw up the contours of a more open way of understanding the continuous, ongoing process by which we construct and shape ourselves as women and as men coming to terms with the forms of "essentialism," irrespective of whether we seek the essence in biological constants such as hormones, in socially constitutive constants such as the "object relation," or in symbolic constants such as the language-constitutive phallus versus the tactile-constitutive fluid (e.g., Irigaray's boundless swimming pool). A stubborn battle with many linguistic categories, with dichotomies of thought as well as trichotomies, and with many deeply rooted myths on the essence of the genders are all prerequisites to implementing this type of analytical program.

Second, the distinction between the biological and the social must not be drawn too sharply or absolutely if the social is to retain its "conceptual potential" in the dynamics of transcendence. When seen as separate from the biological, the category of the social tends to take on characteristics that are too firm and absolute. This speaks in favor of definitions of the social, which carry with them implicit aspects of the biological, seen as a determinative basic category. For this reason, it is important to see the social and the biological as relative concepts that may be useful, necessary tools but that are confusing when they are absolutely, categorically distinguished from one another. In relation to the social and the symbolic, the biological should be seen more as an osmotic relationship, with fluid, vague transitions, a mutually dialectical pair of concepts that cannot logically be conceived of separately. When we think about the basis of one of these concepts, the other follows naturally in its wake.

Third, another way of breaking down this dichotomy of thought is to expand the relationship, adding a third concept, the "symbolic."

In my thinking, this does not give rise to any ideologically or normatively structured conceptual pyramid, but rather suggests lines connecting all the levels in this conceptual triad. So, for example, the biological and symbolic levels interact, in principle, equally with the social and the symbolic, and so forth. In other words, I see these three concepts as relative tools in constant interaction, with no absolutely recognized hierarchy of status.

Fourth, "constitution" and "regulativity" provide another conceptual means of analyzing gender construction as an ongoing process. That which is basically stable and difficult to change—such as gender—is often analyzed using models (essentialist theories of gender), leaving too little space for the dynamic and variable aspects that must also be there. But it is not easy to avoid falling into these essentialist traps without tipping over into the opposite "postmodernist" traps. And if, on the other hand, one focuses too much on the variable aspects of gender norms, the roof (i.e., the permeating nature of synchronic and diachronic and the overall power relationship between the genders) might collapse.[3]

Fifth, one of the overall aims of feminist research must be to reclaim the body as a category of change, to attempt to see the body as changeable and as the source of psychological, social, and symbolic change, including change of comprehensive, apparently stable, extremely stubborn linguistic systems. For example, the bodily aspects of sexualized violence may be highly ambiguous and dynamic, and the interplay between physical, psychological, social, and symbolic relationships may be a complex one in which power coding plays an important role.

Contrary to the "postmodernist" critique of civilization and culture, under the influence of Nietzsche, we might conceive of the Western philosophical tradition and its basis in an ontological hierarchy of values, but in reverse: When the philosophical patterns of civilization become too rigid, the "body takes revenge," permeating the thin membrane of civilization with a stream of bodily energy, giving rise to a strong new mobility, which can also move thought. In this perspective, the bodily-biological stands out as a changing, flexible, highly ambiguous, and open category—whereas inertia, rigidity, and stability may come to characterize the social, the philosophical, and the symbolic. It is, then, possible to see the body as a point of departure for and a source of psychological, social, and symbolic change—including change of extensive, stubborn, seemingly extremely stable linguistic systems.[4]

Notes

1. I make no clear distinction below between norm and rule, but I do place some emphasis both on the difference in everyday language between these concepts—and in their narrow application, where a norm indicates "should," that is, goal- and function-oriented, and tends to span an extensive, diffuse area. A rule tends to be seen as more technical, with a more distinct, delimited area of application.

2. In order to avoid both the "essentialist" and the "postmodernist" or "gender-relativity" traps and to express the dialectic tension and intimate relation between the superficially extremely variable and simultaneously clearly stable and difficult-to-change aspects of gender dynamics, other models than the conceptual distinctions between regulativity and constitution have been developed. Briefly, these include:

a. The distinction between "surface grammar" and "deep grammar," used not only in linguistics but also in more social-philosophical or cultural-sociological contexts and sometimes also with psychoanalytic overtones, on the basis of the difference and tension between the conscious and the unconscious.

b. Norwegian social anthropologists Jorun Solheim and Tordis Borchgrevink use the critical hermeneutics of Paul Ricoeur as their point of departure for building on the distinction, decisive to gender-analysis, between the aspects of language that are *open* to new interpretations and the aspects that are extremely *resistant* to altered interpretations.

c. These same scholars have also analyzed texts/social situations/cultural patterns that display problematical, difficult-to-access, and intricate gender complexities and have found the structuralist-inspired distinction between the concepts of *the open aspects of a symbolic universe* and the closed aspects, referred to as "doxa," into which we are inherently "written" and, therefore, about which we find it difficult to theorize (Bourdieu, 1977).

As can be seen, these models share many of the features of the conceptual distinction on which I have concentrated.

3. If the sets of norms for gender are related to norm sets based on a series of (other) dimensions, such as social class, race, ethnicity, geography, religion, and so forth, the gender dimension easily loses the characteristic of "fundamental category," that is, a category fruitful and relevant to "all" analyses. The fact that woman is also always something more (e.g., black, Christian, middle class, a slave, an English speaker, etc.) does not automatically mean that we cannot meaningfully analyze gender constitution as a fundamental, deeply rooted aspect of human life.

Elizabeth Spelman's characterization of most radical feminist positions as "feminist ethnocentrism" (Spelman, 1990, p. 185) and her arguments against idealization of a generic feminist term, such as "a generic woman," or what she objects to as the illusion of being able to focus on some essential "womanness" (Spelman, 1989, p. 187) appear largely to lose all potential for fruitful analysis of gender categories.

4. In this perspective, Irigaray's statement becomes comprehensible: to transcend the phallic-total linguistic system by a temporary lack of language and return to the unique morphology of the female body. As I have tried to show, I still find this strategy problematic.

8

Lethal and Nonlethal Violence Against Wives and the Evolutionary Psychology of Male Sexual Proprietariness

Margo Wilson and Martin Daly

V iolence against wives occurs in all societies, but the rates at which wives are beaten and killed are enormously variable over time and place. The rate of *uxoricide* (wife killing) in the United States, for example, is currently approximately five to ten times greater than in western Europe. In some societies, wife beating is normative and allegedly almost universal; in others, it is apparently rare and aberrant (Counts, 1990; Counts, Brown, & Campbell, 1992; Levinson, 1989). But despite this variability, the studies of anthropologists, criminologists, historians, psychologists, psychiatrists, and other family violence researchers suggest that the contexts and ostensible motives of violence against wives exhibit considerable cross-cultural consistency. One aim of this chapter is to identify a level of abstraction at which

AUTHORS' NOTE: We thank the following agencies for funding our research on violence against wives: the Arts and Humanities Research Board of McMaster University, the Harry Frank Guggenheim Foundation, the North Atlantic Treaty Organization, the Rockefeller Foundation, and the Social Sciences and Humanities Research Council of Canada.

one may describe a cross-culturally general masculine mind-set whose periodic use of violence is intelligibly contingent on experience and circumstance. A second aim is to suggest variables that may be responsible for husbands' differential use of violence in different social and cultural circumstances.

Our thesis is that the particular ways in which violence against wives is contingent on circumstances can be understood as systematic consequences of the evolved organization of the human male mind— in particular, of the functioning of psychological processes whose normal domain is the self-interested regulation of sociosexual interactions and conflicts. A phrase such as the "coercive masculine sexually proprietary complex" might be used to describe the intersection of sexually proprietary and violent psychological processes with which we shall be concerned.

If these (or any other) psychological phenomena are successfully characterized at a level of abstraction that transcends cultural particularity, then this provides strong support for the thesis that they were "designed" by the evolutionary processes of natural and sexual selection. Accordingly, violent capabilities and inclinations arose in our male ancestors in response to the demands of male-male competition, and they have presumably been further shaped in hominid evolution by selection in the contexts of big-game hunting and collective aggression or warfare. In addition to the utility of violent prowess in vanquishing enemies and in acquiring food, assaults and threats are effective coercive tactics more generally, whether in the context of helping oneself to another's property, in the pursuit of sexual access or in any other area in which interests are not consonant. Thus, although it is unlikely that any of the basic morphological and psychological necessities for violence evolved in the specific context of marital conflict, men have presumably used assaults and threats throughout history to deter wives from pursuing courses of action that their male partners disliked. An evolutionary perspective sheds considerable light on what it is that husbands dislike, why wives may be motivated to pursue such actions nevertheless, and what personal and situational variables affect the likelihood that husbands will resort to violence.

Our premise, then, is that violence against wives is a product of self-interested male motives directed at constraining wives' autonomy by "encouraging" them to prioritize their husbands' wants rather than their own. Unfortunately, we cannot address the issue of how effective such coercion really is (or was, in premodern social environments) because there is virtually no systematic empirical evidence bearing on this issue. It seems obvious that threats and assaults would often have deterrent utility in controlling and monopolizing a wife, even though such coercion increases a woman's incentives to end the relationship. How violence against wives affects the victims' behavior and whether these effects serve the perpetrators' interests are important questions in need of further research.

Another issue that we will not pursue is that of the detailed functional organization of the psychology of coercion in general. Rather, we will simply assume that motives and emotions are usefully interpreted as adaptively contingent, that is, that their situational determinants can often be discovered by considering what are likely to be the contingent determinants of their utility for the actors. However, we stress that although we shall analyze risk factors for uxoricide, the utility of the underlying motives does not reside there: Killing wives is almost never an effective way of promoting the killer's interests, as we shall define "interests." Instead, we interpret uxoricides as epiphenomena (by-products) of the evolved psychology of the human male, in the sense that the relevant masculine psychological phenomena evolved because their nonlethal manifestations served the purposes of our male ancestors. The claim that uxoricide is an epiphenomenon rather than an adaptation in no way detracts from the relevance of evolutionary psychological reasoning for understanding where, why, and when these killings occur.

In what follows, we review some of our findings about patterned variation in the risk of uxoricide and consider whether risks of nonlethal violence against wives are similarly patterned. We discovered the empirical regularities that we shall review by considering this question: If the motives and emotions that comprise male sexual proprietariness have evolved by selection to promote the man's fitness, then what are the situational and demographic factors to which we should expect sensitivity? In brief, the answer is any variable that has been a statistical predictor of variations in the risk of loss of reproductive and productive control of his wife.

Notwithstanding cultural diversity, there are many cross-cultural regularities in men's sexually proprietary inclinations toward their women (Daly & Wilson, 1988b; Daly, Wilson, & Weghorst, 1982; Wilson & Daly, 1992a). However, the only expression of a sexually proprietary mind-set considered in this chapter will be violence against wives.

Psychological Links Between
Sexual Proprietariness and Violence

If uxoricides are epiphenomena of male motives whose function is coercion and deterrence, then lethal and nonlethal violence should be found to share commonalities of motive, causal dynamics, and circumstance, and factors that exacerbate or mitigate the prevalence and severity of one should have parallel effects on the other. These implications are testable, and we shall review evidence supporting the conclusion that uxoricides are indeed largely, although not entirely, "the tip of the iceberg" of nonlethal violence against wives.

The ostensible motivating circumstances in most uxoricides reflect what we have called male sexual proprietariness: Husbands who kill usually appear to have been moved by an aggrieved intolerance of the alienation of their wives, either through (suspected or actual) adultery or through the woman's termination of the marriage. Daly and Wilson (1988b) reviewed several studies of well-described spousal homicide cases, and in each sample, such sexual proprietariness was apparently the primary motivational factor in over 80% of the cases. For more recent studies upholding this motive's primacy, see Allen (1990), Campbell (1992a), Crawford and Gartner (1992), Daly, Wiseman, and Wilson (1997), Mahoney (1991), and Polk (1994b). Studies of nonlethal violence against wives indicate a more diverse set of motives, but the predominant one is apparently the same: When asked what are the primary issues around which violent incidents occurred, both beaten wives and their assailants nominate "jealousy" above all else (e.g., Brisson, 1983; Dobash & Dobash, 1979, 1984; Rounsaville, 1978).

Jealousy (as distinct from envy) refers to a complex mental state or "operating mode" activated by a perceived threat that a third party might usurp one's place in a valued relationship. It motivates any of various circumstantially contingent responses, ranging from vigilance to violence, aimed at countering the threat (Daly et al., 1982; Mullen & Martin, 1994). Sexual jealousy is a relatively dynamic mental state of attentional focus and readiness to act, normally aroused by imminent cues of rivalrous threat. It is most often experienced and described, by both the jealous party and others, as a transitory emotional/motivational state like anger or fear, but it can also be relatively chronic. "Sexual proprietariness" refers to a more pervasive mindset, encompassing not only episodes of jealous arousal but also presumptions of entitlement and inclinations to exercise control and prevent threats of trespass or usurpation. Men who are especially proprietary and controlling appear to go beyond jealous concern about their wives' interactions with other men, curtailing contacts even with female friends and family. However, even the most extreme claustrating tendencies invite interpretation as sexually exclusionary in motive and function. In a North Carolina study, for example, Hilberman and Munson (1978) reported that 95% of 60 rural wife batterers were so proprietary that "leaving the house for any reason invariably resulted in accusations of infidelity which culminated in assault" (p. 461).

The idea that the discovery of wifely infidelity is an exceptional provocation, likely to elicit a violent rage, is cross-culturally ubiquitous, perhaps universal (Daly & Wilson, 1988b). Indeed, such a rage is often considered irresistible, mitigating the responsibility of violent cuckolds (Daly et al., 1982). In Anglo-American common law, for example, killing a wife upon discovery of her adultery is deemed the act of a "reasonable man" (Edwards, 1954), and such violence is also considered normal both in societies in which the cuckold's violence is seen as a reprehensible loss of control (e.g., Dell, 1984) and in those in which it is seen as a praiseworthy redemption of honor (e.g., Bresse, 1989; Chimbos, 1993; Safilios-Rothschild, 1969).

Granting that adultery is a potent elicitor of men's anger, why target the wife? Of course, assaults against rival males are also frequent, and they too are apt to be treated leniently because they are "provoked." However, although much male-male violence is motivated by sexual rivalry (Daly & Wilson, 1988b), "errant" wives are targeted too. If directing anger and assaults at wives is to be understood as functionally coercive, an implication is that the sexually proprietary male psyche sometimes responds to adulterous events as predictive of further infidelities, unless the wife's inclinations are punished and deterred. But what if there is no reason to suspect her of unfaithful inclinations? Some "infidelities" are involuntary, such as in cases of rape, and we would then expect that violent anger, if it is functionally deterrent, will be directed mainly at the usurper. Even in the case of rape, however, signs of weak resistance, such as a lack of injuries, may elicit hostility directed at the "adulterous" wife too (see Thornhill & Thornhill, 1983, 1992).

If we accept that male sexual proprietariness is a causal factor in violence against wives, it is still important to ask whether those husbands who are especially proprietary and controlling are also especially violent. In 1993, Statistics Canada conducted a national survey on violence against women, interviewing a stratified probability sample of 12,300 women about their experiences of sexual harassment, threats, and sexual and physical violence by marital

Table 8.1. Percentage of Wives Agreeing to Five Statements About Current Husband (Registered and Common-Law Unions Combined) According to Type of Violence Perpetrated by Husband of Present Union, Canada 1993

	Type of Violence		
	None n = 7,060	Only "Nonserious" n = 1,039	"Serious" n = 286
"He is jealous and doesn't want you to talk to other men."	3.5	13.0	39.3
"He tries to limit your contact with family or friends."	2.0	11.1	35.0
"He insists on knowing who you are with and where you are at all times."	7.4	23.5	40.4
"He calls you names to put you down or make you feel bad."	2.9	22.3	48.0
"He prevents you from knowing about or having access to the family income, even if you ask."	1.2	4.6	15.3
Autonomy-limiting Index[a] (range 0-5)	0.17	0.74	1.78

SOURCE: See Wilson, Johnson, and Daly (1995).
a. Index: average number of items affirmed by wives.

partners and other men, including injuries sustained (see Johnson, this volume; Johnson & Sacco, 1995; Statistics Canada, 1994). Interviewees included 8,385 women currently residing with a spouse: 7,363 in registered marriages and 1,022 in common-law marriages. Several bits of demographic information were also collected, as were measures of the women's perceptions of safety and their assessments of the applicability to their own husbands of five statements about "autonomy-limiting" aspects of some men's behavior.

Table 8.1 indicates that each of the five autonomy-limiting behaviors was attributed much more often to men who were also reported to have behaved violently than to nonviolent husbands. Moreover, women who had experienced relatively serious violent incidents, as defined by their affirmation of one or more of a set of particularly violent acts, were more likely to affirm each of the five items than were women who had experienced only lesser violence (Wilson, Johnson, & Daly, 1995). (The validity of the behavioral criterion of "seriousness" is supported by the fact that among a subset of women who were further interrogated about one incident of marital violence, 72% of those who described a "serious" incident required medical attention versus 18% of those whose incident did not meet the criterion. In addition, wives reported being fearful for their lives in

Table 8.2. Average Autonomy-Limiting Index Values (Ranging from
0 to 5) According to Number of Violent Incidents
Perpetrated by Husbands of the Current Marital
Relationship, Canada 1993

	Mean ± S.D.
No violence	0.17 ± 0.53
Single incident	0.63 ± 1.01
2- 10 incidents	1.16 ± 1.33
11 or more incidents	2.19 ± 1.56

SOURCE: See Wilson, Johnson, and Daly (1995).

56% of the incidents that met the "serious" criterion versus 9% of the
violent incidents that did not.)

The women were also asked "How many different times did these
things happen?" and the more violent episodes a woman reported, the
more likely she was to verify that her husband had engaged in the
autonomy-limiting behaviors as well (Table 8.2). Thus, if these replies
are valid, it appears that especially proprietary, controlling husbands
are indeed especially violent husbands. Rather than wife assault being
one of an alternative set of controlling tactics of proprietary men, it
appears to go hand in hand with other tactics of control (see also
Dobash & Dobash, this volume; Dobash, Dobash, Cavanagh, &
Lewis, 1998; Gagné, 1992).

Those who deal professionally with domestic assault are aware
that women who leave proprietary husbands may be pursued, threatened, and even killed (e.g., Crawford & Gartner, 1992; Ellis, 1987;
Mahoney, 1991). In fact, a remarkable proportion of uxoricide victims
are estranged from their killers (e.g., Barnard, Vera, Vera, & Newman,
1982). The most substantial body of relevant data comes from New
South Wales (NSW), Australia. Allen (1990) reported that almost one
half of all slain wives in NSW in the late 19th century were separated
from their killers at the time of murder and that the proportion was
even higher in the 1930s. Similarly, Wallace (1986) reported that 45%
of the 217 NSW women slain by husbands in 1958-1983 had left their
killers or were in the process of leaving; 47% of these victims had been
separated for less than 2 months. Wilson and Daly (1993b) computed
uxoricide rates for coresiding and estranged wives at three locations,
with the results shown in Figure 8.1. Elevation of uxoricide risk in the
immediate aftermath of separation is presumably even more severe
than the contrasts in Figure 8.1 would suggest, because the denomi-
nators for "separated" uxoricide rates include all separated women

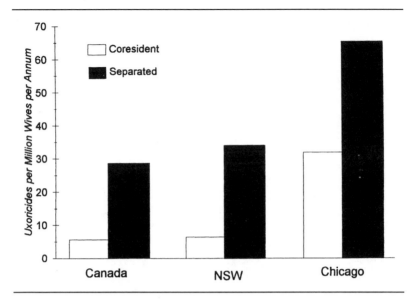

Figure 8.1.   Uxoricide Rates for Coresiding and Separated Couples in Canada (1974-1990); New South Wales, Australia (NSW, 1968-1986); and Chicago, United States (1965-1990) for Registered Marriages
NOTE: *Uxoricide rate* is defined as number of registered-married wives killed per annum per million registered-married wives in the population at large who were coresiding or separated (see Wilson & Daly, 1993b).

regardless of duration, whereas the case reports indicate that, as in Wallace's NSW data, risk is temporally concentrated.

Of course, temporal association need not mean that separation is a cause of uxoricide. The mere fact that separated couples constitute a subset of marriages with a history of discord might explain their higher homicide rates, and it is also plausible that women are especially likely to leave when their husbands are at their most violent. Nevertheless, case descriptions frequently imply that the link between separation and murder was direct. Past threats to pursue and kill his wife if ever she should leave are often on the record, and the killer is likely to explain his behavior as a response to the intolerable stimulus of her departure (e.g., Allen, 1990; Campbell, 1992a; Crawford & Gartner, 1992; Daly et al., 1997; Mahoney, 1991; Wallace, 1986; Wilson & Daly, 1993b).

But why should men be motivated to pursue and kill women who have left them? Such acts present a challenge to the evolutionary psychological premise that motives and emotions are organized in such a way as to promote the actor's interests. Killing is "spiteful"—an act that is costly to the perpetrator as well as the victim—and the evolution of spiteful motives is not readily explicable. Moreover, if the utility of the motivational processes underlying violence against wives resides in proprietary control, killing seems all the more para-doxical. Resolution of these issues is most likely to come from develop-ing theoretical understandings of the evolutionary psychology of threat and coercion (Clutton-Brock & Parker, 1995a, 1995b; Cohen, 1996; Daly & Wilson, 1988b; Frank, 1988; Gray & Tallman, 1987). In brief, a threat is an effective social tool, and usually an inexpensive one, but it loses its effectiveness if the threatening party is seen to be "bluffing," that is, to be unwilling to pay the cost of following through when the threat is ignored or defied. Such follow-through may appear spiteful—a costly act too late to be useful—but effective threat must convey that such follow-through will occur nonetheless. Thus, although killing an estranged wife seems clearly to be counterproduc-tive, threatening her can be self-interested and so can displays of "uncontrollable" anger and apparent obliviousness to costs. Effective threatening behavior does not "leak" signs of bluff, and the best way to appear sincere may be to be sincere. Nevertheless, most men who coerce, pursue, and threaten women do not go so far as to kill them, and those who do may be considered the dysfunctional overreactors in a game of brinkmanship.

An Evolutionary Psychological Framework for Understanding Links Between Male Sexual Proprietariness and Violence Against Wives

In criminology textbooks, "psychology" is invoked mainly with reference to attributes that differ among individuals, especially attri-butes that can be interpreted as deficits or pathologies. In fact, psychological science is mainly concerned with species-typical attri-butes, not with constitutional differences among individuals and pathologies. And even pathologies are best understood as defective versions of complex, functional subsystems of the brain/mind.

Violence and Jealousy as Pathology

Extreme acts of violence sometimes reflect dysfunction. We have stressed elsewhere (Daly & Wilson, 1994) that violent capability is a complex adaptation, not a pathology, but there are undeniable pathologies *of* violence. (Rabies provides an obvious example, and the almost chronic rage of some patients with limbic system damage is another.)

Violent offenders are fairly often considered insane. Some uxoricidal men (and some nonlethal wife assaulters too) are found "unfit to stand trial" or "not guilty by reason of insanity." Psychiatrists call such cases "morbid jealousy," "delusional jealousy," or "Othello syndrome," more or less synonymous diagnoses that are based on obsessive concern with a (presumably imaginary) interloper and/or a tendency to invoke bizarre evidence in support of jealous suspicions (e.g., Dell, 1984; Mowat, 1966; Shepherd, 1961; Vauhkonen, 1968). Morbidly jealous people are not always violent; they may be clinically depressed. Nor are wives and interlopers the only persons at risk of violence; some unknown proportion of suicides are precipitated by a despondent reaction to imagined (or actual) risk of losing the affection of a valued person.

Even when such pathological jealousy is the result of brain damage, it can shed light on the normal structure and functioning of the mental mechanisms of sexual proprietariness, just as the detailed characterization of deficits caused by stroke or other trauma can illuminate other aspects of the functional organization of the mind/brain (e.g., Silva, Leong, & Weinstock, 1992; Silva, Leong, Weinstock, & Wine, 1993; Young, Reid, Wright, & Hellawell, 1993). Exploration of the circumstantial determinants of extreme and presumably dysfunctional, but relatively unequivocal, forms of violence against wives may shed light on the functional organization of less extreme motives and tactics of marital conflict. The prevalence of highly focused jealous obsessions and delusions, often stroke-induced, would seem to lend some support to the notion that sexual proprietariness is a mental "module" with dedicated brain structures, but it is not yet clear whether the morbidly jealous syndrome(s) can be differentiated neuroanatomically or neurochemically from other obsessive or delusional disorders.

Violence and Jealousy as Personality Traits

There is a fairly extensive literature concerning "personality" traits of wife assaulters (e.g., Holtzworth-Munroe & Stuart, 1994). Implicated traits include (a) a proclivity to be angry and use violence, (b) a tendency to lack empathic concern, especially for women, and (c) dependency and insecurity in romantic or marital relationships. A personological or individual differences perspective on psychological traits generally assumes that the traits are characteristic of the person throughout a lifetime or at least throughout adulthood, such that his particular constellation of personality traits would account for his patterns of behavior in various circumstances. But, in fact, situational factors have been more successful predictors of the dangerousness of individuals suffering from various kinds of mental illness than have psychiatric syndrome or personality measures (Monahan & Splane, 1980), and they may be better predictors for those who are not mentally ill as well.

An evolutionary psychological approach grants the value of understanding how individual differences modulate perception and interpretation of social events and inclinations to act, but it insists that these individual differences cannot be understood except in relation to the functional design of the underlying psychological processes (Buss, 1991; Simpson & Gangestad, 1991; Tooby & Cosmides, 1990; Wilson, Daly, & Daniele, 1995). Whence the consistency of an individual's response to various social and other cues? Is this largely a result of the fact that subjective probabilities change only gradually with the incremental information gains of day-to-day experience, or of preferences for choosing courses of action that are proven and in which one is skilled, or of constrained imagination, or of adjusting one's expectations to one's assets and liabilities? The evolutionary perspective places a greater emphasis than has traditional personality psychology on the role of social and other events modulating inclinations and behavior in systematic ways as a result of the activation of evolved psychological processing mechanisms.

Evolutionary Psychology

Psychological science is primarily a quest to discover the mechanisms and processes that produce behavior and to characterize them at a level of abstraction that applies to everyone (or at least to everyone of a given sex and life stage). Psychology's constructs include things like memory encoding and retrieval, attention processes, recognition, categorization, attitudes, values, self-concepts, motives, and emotions. When postulating such constructs (and more specific and detailed variants of these), psychologists aim for a level of abstraction at which historical, cultural, ecological, and individual variability can be explained as the contingent products of panhuman psychological processes responding to variable circumstances and experiences.

All psychological explanations rest on models of the functional organization of the mind/brain: The primary goal of psychological science is and always has been the discovery and elucidation of information-processing subsystems and their domains. Evolutionary psychologists are simply those who think it useful to recall that species-typical functional parts of the brain/mind are evolved "adaptations" (Williams, 1966) and to think about how the process of natural selection operates in "designing" adaptations. Psychological adaptations are evolved solutions to recurring information-processing problems, and they entail contingent responsiveness to environmental features that were statistical predictors, on average, of the fitness[1] consequences of alternative courses of action in the past. Adaptation is not prospective. The apparent purpose in organismic design depends on the persistence of essential features of past environments. For more thorough accounts of evolutionary psychology, see, for example, Barkow, Cosmides, and Tooby (1992); Bock and Cardew (1997); Cronin (1991); Daly and Wilson (1997); and Wright (1995).

Evolutionists often refer to functionally integrated systems consisting of many evolved mechanisms as constituting a "strategy." Sprouting in response to a threshold soil temperature, flowering at a certain day length, maturing the female parts of one's hermaphroditic flowers before the male parts, and so forth are all elements in a particular flowering plant's "reproductive strategy." In this case, the metaphorical nature of the language of strategy is obvious: No one imagines that the plant has intentionality. But with animals, this metaphor can be misleading, especially with species with complex cognitive capacities, as one may slip unwittingly from claims about what the organism is "designed" to achieve into claims about what it is "trying" to achieve.

Invoking natural selection as the designer of the human psyche does not imply any particular psychological theory, and in particular, the notion that the components of our minds and bodies have been shaped to promote fitness does not imply that fitness is a goal. When the fitness consequences of behavior are invoked to explain it, they are properly invoked, not as direct objectives or motivators but as explanations of why particular more-proximal objectives and motivators have evolved to play their particular roles in the causal control of behavior and why they are calibrated as they are. When male birds continuously follow their mates closely during the breeding season, for example, ornithologists interpret the behavior as "mate-guarding" and its fitness-promoting function as paternity assurance. These interpretations have suggested numerous hypotheses about the contingent causal control of behavior. In some species, mate-guarding has been found to vary in relation to several cues of the onset of female fertility, and in relation to the proximity, abundance, and attractiveness of male rivals; and the male's success in keeping his mate under guard has been found to be predictive of his subsequent level of effort in the care of his putative offspring (e.g., Davies, 1992; Møller, 1988). These facts were discovered as a direct result of theorizing that the adaptive function of mate-guarding psychology in these species resides in paternity assurance, but paternity itself is not something that the animal monitors or responds to in any way.

Male Sexual Proprietariness Is an Adaptation That Evolved to Deal With the Problem of Paternity Uncertainty

Using a similar logic of analysis, we propose that sexual proprietariness in humans is a sexually differentiated motivational/cognitive subsystem of the human mind, with behavioral manifestations that are culturally and historically variable but are nevertheless predictably related to various aspects of the status and circumstances of the focal man, his partner, and his rivals.

The proposition that men's sexual proprietariness evolved to defend their probability of paternity implies that female infidelity has been a genuine threat to male fitness. Men certainly feel and act as if there were some risk that their wives might deceive them in this domain (Daly et al., 1982). Is their apprehension realistic or a fantastic projection? The answer is that their concern has some foundation. Survey data consistently indicate that although there are sex differences in adulterous inclinations, a substantial minority of women are interested in extramarital sex and turn that interest into action (see, e.g., Johnson, Wadsworth, Wellings, Field, & Bradshaw [1994] and studies reviewed by Buss [1994]).

So the stereotypical characterization of men as polygamous and women as monogamous is at best an exaggeration, and of course this is not exactly news to sensitive observers. There is abundant historical and ethnographic evidence that women are to some degree polyandrously inclined and that even closely guarded women may expend much effort and incur much risk attempting to evade their mates. Moreover, evolutionists have now identified a number of potential benefits that polyandrous females can accrue even in species in which parental investment is predominantly maternal, including both material and genetic benefits, and protection of self and young from future mistreatment by males as a result of having distributed some possibility of paternity (e.g., Hrdy, 1981; Smith, 1984; Wilson & Daly, 1992a).

Undetected cuckoldry and paternal investment pose a major threat to a man's fitness by enhancing the survivorship and reproductive prospects of his rival's offspring. If there is a corresponding threat to a woman's fitness, it is not that she will be analogously cuckolded but rather that her mate will channel resources to other women and their children to the detriment of her own children. It follows that men's and women's proprietary feelings toward their mates are likely to have evolved to be qualitatively different, men being more intensely concerned with sexual infidelity per se and women more intensely concerned with the allocation of their mate's resources and attentions (Daly et al., 1982).

Research indicates that men are indeed more distressed by sexual infidelity of their partners than by affectional infidelity, whereas women are more distressed by affectional infidelity. Buss, Larsen, Westen, and Semmelroth (1992) had undergraduates imagine the following scenario:

> Please think of a serious committed romantic relationship that you have had in the past, that you currently have, or that you would like to have. Imagine that you discover that the person with whom you've been seriously involved became interested in someone else. What would distress or upset you more?
>
> A. Imagining your partner forming a deep emotional attachment to that person.
>
> B. Imagining your partner enjoying passionate sexual intercourse with that other person.

Sixty percent of the men reported that the sexual intercourse would be more upsetting, but 83% of the women chose the "deep emotional attachment" instead (p. 253). Buunk, Angleitner, Oubaid, and Buss (1996) replicated this U.S. study in the Netherlands and in Germany, with similar results. Of course, self-report data are vulnerable to the criticism that people may say what is expected of them rather than what they really feel, so Buss et al. (1992) collected physiological measures of autonomic arousal as well. Electrodermal activity (sweaty palms), pulse rate, and electromyographic activity of the corrugator supercilii muscle (furrowed brow) were all higher when men imagined a sexual infidelity by their partners rather than an emotional infidelity, whereas women showed greater autonomic arousal to the latter scenario. Interestingly, the furrowed brow response appears as a conditioned response to cues associated with anger and not to other emotional states like fear, even if the person is unaware of the conditioned association (Dimberg & Öhman, 1996). These experimental methods could be used to explore variations in anger and jealousy in relation to cues indicative of varying risks of infidelity and desertion (see below).

Male Sexual Proprietariness Is an Adaptation That Evolved to Deal With the Problem of Male-Male Reproductive Competition

There is morphological, physiological, developmental, and psychological evidence that human beings evolved under chronic circumstances of somewhat greater variance in fitness in males than in females. In hunter-gatherer societies, which provide our best model of the social circumstances in which the human psyche's characteristics evolved, there is less disparity of wealth than in agricultural societies or nation-states, and marriage is mainly monogamous, but it is still the case that men are both more likely to have more surviving children than women—and more likely to have none (Hewlett, 1988; Hill & Hurtado, 1996; Howell, 1979). When the zero-sum game that partitions paternal ancestry among males is played with different rules or parameters than the corresponding game among females, the selective process favors different attributes in the two sexes. Sex differences in psychological processes underlying competitive violence, reckless life-threatening risk-proneness, and proprietary concern with the sexual alienation of mates (whether temporarily or permanently) follow logically from consideration of the selection pressures associated with sex differences in the intensity of intrasexual competition (Daly & Wilson, 1988b; Rubin & Paul, 1979; Trivers, 1972; Williams, 1966). So in addition to the selection pressures engendered by the specific risk of unwittingly investing in children one did not sire, there has been a more general selection pressure of male-male competition for access to women and reproductive opportunity affecting the evolution of a masculine sexually proprietary mind-set and its links with violence against wives. It follows that sexual proprietariness is likely to be aroused by informational cues of the intensity of local competition and of one's own value in the "marketplace" of rival courtiers and marital negotiations.

Hypotheses About Patterned Variations
in Male Sexual Proprietariness and Violence

Wilson and Daly (1993a) proposed that variations in violence against wives within and between societies are largely attributable to variations in exposure to social circumstances and other factors that cue the arousal of male sexual proprietariness. We predicted that such cross-culturally general factors as age-related changes in female fertility would account for within-society variability in more or less similar ways, whereas other factors, such as the risk imposed by desperate, disenfranchised male rivals, would vary across societies and thus account for some of the between-society variance in proprietary manifestations. Hypotheses were proposed with respect to five thematic issues.

1. Intensity of Intrasexual Competition

If coercive constraint and violence are responses to perceived threats to sexual exclusivity, then we would expect husbands to be sensitive to indicators of the current local intensity of male sexual competition and poaching. These indicators could include his rate of encounter with potential rivals and evidence bearing on how many of those men are "bachelors." Moreover, the arousal of sexual proprietariness is likely to be affected by indicators of the status, attractiveness, and resources of potential male rivals relative to oneself, because the perceived risk of alienation of one's wife presumably rises as the relative appeal of rival suitors rises.

We also suggested that local cues of life trajectory and life expectancy would be relevant, because they are likely to affect men's tactics of social competition. One's rivals are likely to be relatively undeterred by the dangers associated with adulterous overtures, for example, when their own life prospects are poor, so a husband may be more proprietary in times and places of insecurity (e.g., rumors of impending war or economic disaster). Being part of a relatively large age cohort may also be expected to intensify male-male competition, especially when same-age women are unavailable; thus, cohort size effects on intrasexual rivalry and hence on the coercive constraint of women may be especially evident where age disparities at marriage are large.

Parameters like relative cohort size, expected lifespan, local marital stability, local prevalence of adultery, and so forth clearly cannot be "cued" simply by stimuli immediately available at the time of behavioral decisions. They must instead be apprehended cumulatively over large portions of the lifespan. This suggests that people will develop mental models that cannot be quickly modified or discarded, and these considerations may explain some of the "inertial" aspects of individual differences in behavior, as noted above. Many social scientists seem to imagine that if reliable developmental precursors to violent behavior could be identified, other explanations of violence would be superseded. But developmental processes and sensitivities are themselves products of evolution by selection, and sound hypotheses about the functional significance of their time courses and other details are both useful tools for discovering developmental phenomena and explanatory in their own right.

We also predicted that marital coercion and violence would be more extreme in polygynous than in monogamous societies because of the threat posed by disenfranchised men in the former, and we noted that Levinson's (1989) cross-cultural analyses supported this prediction despite his use of a coarse measure of marital polygyny.

2. Factors Affecting the Woman's Attractiveness to Rivals

A man is vulnerable to the fitness cost of misattributed paternity as a result of wifely infidelity only if his wife is fertile. While he may be concerned to protect a pregnant wife from various sorts of harms, he need not protect her from insemination by rivals, and we might therefore expect that mate-guarding inclinations will have evolved to vary in relation to the partner's reproductive condition.

In a rare investigation of human mate-guarding, Flinn (1988) found that men indeed appear to be sensitive to correlates of the wife's fertilizability. He recorded the identity, whereabouts, and activities of everyone he saw during standardized walks through a Caribbean village in which sexual relationships were unstable and often nonexclusive, and men directed paternal investments selectively to children they believed themselves to have sired. What Flinn found was that (a) men spent more time with partners who reported having menstrual cycles than with those who were pregnant or postmenopausal; (b) men displayed more agonism both to their wives and to other men when their wives were cycling than in other reproductive conditions; (c) there was more agonistic interaction between sexual partners whose relationship was nonexclusive than between monogamous pairs; and (d) hostile male-male interactions were especially characteristic of men who were simultaneously sexually involved with a nonmonogamous woman. All of these contrasts seem to bespeak arousal of sexually proprietary motives in response to cues of risk of rival insemination.

The statistically expected future reproduction of an individual, given her age, condition, and circumstances, is her "reproductive value" (RV) (Fisher, 1930/1958). A woman's RV is maximal soon after puberty and begins to decline steeply in her 30s. As one would then expect, if men have evolved to value women largely as reproductive resources, youth is a major determinant of women's sexual (Kenrick & Keefe, 1992) and marital (e.g., Borgerhoff Mulder, 1988; Buss & Barnes, 1986; Glick & Lin, 1987) attractiveness. These considerations (as well as other factors, especially their greater likelihood of still being childless) suggest that young wives may be more likely than older wives to terminate an unsatisfactory marriage, more likely to be courted by rivals of the husband, and more likely to form new sexual relationships. Hence, we have suggested that men with young wives may be especially proprietary. (It is sometimes suggested that sexual jealousy cannot be an evolved adaptation because men remain jealous of postmenopausal women. This argument ignores the fact that adaptations can only have evolved to track ancestrally informative cues of fertility and not fertility itself. In a modern society with contraception, improved health, and diverse cosmetic manipulations, post-menopausal women are likely to exhibit fewer cues of age-related declining RV than still-fertile women in foraging societies. But even in the modern West, women's sexual attractiveness and their partner's jealousy are both maximal in young adulthood and begin to decline long before menopause.)

In Canada, the highest rates of both lethal and nonlethal marital violence indeed befall the youngest wives (Daly & Wilson, 1988b; Figure 8.2). Mercy and Saltzman (1989) replicated this finding with respect to U.S. uxoricides, and it holds in Australia and Great Britain too (Figure 8.3). This pattern may seem to belie the proposition that male minds place high "value" on young wives, but again, as with the estranged husband who pursues and kills a woman he can't abide losing, violent inclinations seem best understood as coercive tools for controlling wives about whom men feel proprietary—and the lethality is a rare and dysfunctional outcome of the most extreme feelings.

Notwithstanding these interpretations, we must concede that these dramatic age patterns do not establish the direct relevance of wives' youth. Many other variables are confounded with wife's age, including parity and childlessness, duration of the union, and the

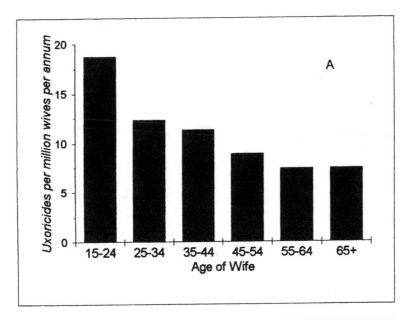

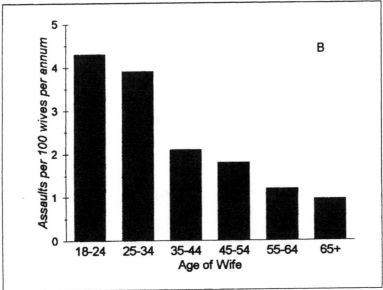

Figure 8.2. Comparison of Age-Specific Rates of Lethal (Upper Panel) and Nonlethal Assaults (Lower Panel) in Registered Marriages
Upper panel: Uxoricides per million wives per annum as a function of wife's age in Canada (1974-1992).
Lower panel: Nonlethal assault rates per hundred wives per annum as a function of wife's age in Canada (1993) (see Wilson, Johnson, & Daly, 1995).

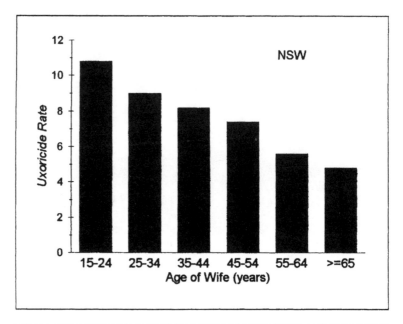

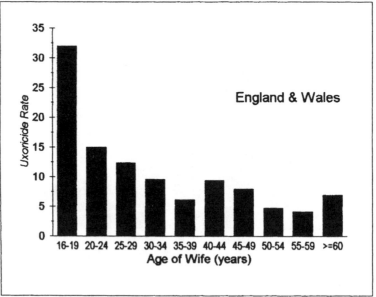

Figure 8.3. Uxoricide Rates by Age of Wife Victims for New South Wales, Australia (1968-1986) and for England and Wales (1977-1990)

NOTE: *Uxoricide rate* is defined as number of wives killed per annum per million wives in the population at large for each age category.

man's own age. Because young men are in general the most violent age-sex class (e.g., Daly & Wilson, 1990; Wilson & Daly, 1985), an obvious hypothesis is that male age is actually the relevant factor. This seems not to be the case, however, or at least not the whole story, because age disparity between husband and wife is a major risk factor for homicide (Daly & Wilson, 1988a, 1988b; Mercy & Saltzman, 1989; Wilson, Daly, & Wright, 1993), such that a young wife is actually more likely to be slain if her husband is much older than she than if he too is in his 20s. (Age disparity had no demonstrable relevance to the risk of nonlethal assaults in the Canadian survey, however; see Wilson, Johnson, & Daly, 1995.)

3. Situational Cues of Possible Infidelity

In addition to those attributes of women that affect their attractiveness to men, husbands may respond to situational information concerning risks of infidelity. A man whose wife has been under continuous surveillance, either by himself or by trusted allies such as close kin, can be relatively confident; conversely, unmonitored absences may be cause for concern (e.g., Fricke, Axinn, & Thornton, 1993). Baker and Bellis (1989) reported a particularly intriguing psychophysiological response to lapses of personal surveillance in the form of increased sperm transfer in sexual intercourse as a function of the proportion of time that one's partner had spent out of sight since the couple's last sexual contact. The utility of increased sperm transfer resides in "sperm competition." It has been shown in other species, although not in humans, that when a female has mated with more than one male in a given fertile period, the relative numbers of sperm transferred are one important determinant of which of the rival males is likely to sire any resultant offspring. We hypothesize that, all else equal, men will also be more sexually demanding, threatening, and coercive when circumstances dictate that their wives are relatively unmonitored.

Where control of women by husbands and husbands' kin is constrained, as, for example, in matrilineal-matrilocal societies in which men may make prolonged excursions fishing at sea or engaging in warfare, men sometimes play little paternal role and direct their "parental" efforts to their sisters' children. Evolution-minded anthropologists have interpreted such "avuncular" investment and inheritance as a response to uncertain paternity (e.g., Flinn & Low, 1986). Because men in these societies incur no risk of misdirected paternal

Table 8.3. Rates of Violence Against Wives by Coresiding Partners According to the Type of Marital Union

	Registered Union	Common-Law Union
Uxoricide	7.2	55.1
Nonlethal assault in past year	2.0	9.0

SOURCE: See Wilson et al. (1993); Wilson et al. (1995).
NOTE: Uxoricide rates are expressed per million couples per annum, and nonfatal assault rates are expressed per hundred couples per annum.

efforts due to cuckoldry, it is sometimes suggested that they should be relatively unconcerned about wifely fidelity. However, sexual proprietariness may still be functional because there is still intense male intrasexual competition (and cues thereof). Male sexual jealousy and violence against wives are not unknown in matrilocal avuncular societies (e.g., Hill & Hurtado, 1996), but whether they are reduced has yet to be adequately explored.

The ease, prevalence, and social acceptability of divorce in the local milieu may also be relevant to risk of violence against wives, because men who perceive marriage as generally unstable may see their own as relatively threatened in otherwise equivalent circumstances. Similar considerations may apply to the contrast between registered and common-law marital unions within a society, as the latter are more easily and in fact more frequently dissolved, hence presumably perceived by the participants as relatively fragile. Furthermore, both men and women report more extramarital sexual partners with common-law than with registered marriages (Forste & Tanfer, 1996; Johnson et al., 1994; Laumann, Gagnon, Micahel, & Michaels, 1994). In Canada, both lethal and nonlethal violence against wives is indeed substantially more prevalent in common-law unions (Table 8.3).

4. Female Choice

To the degree that marriages are politicized transactions between kin groups, women may find themselves married to men they would not otherwise have chosen as husbands. In medieval England, for example, children could be espoused as early as 7 years of age, with the Christian church sanctifying the commitment (Ingram, 1987). Any recalcitrant bride who eloped with the man of her own choice before her espoused marriage was solemnized and consummated could cause severe repercussions for her father who had promised her to another man, and fathers were likely to launch proceedings against their daughters' "abductors" in such circumstances. Legislation reinforced fathers' interests by stripping eloping daughters of claims against their families' property. It would not be surprising to discover that wives in unsatisfactory arranged marriages incurred risk of violence by jealous husbands.

One vivid example of the violence that women will risk to escape from their husbands comes from Chagnon's study of the Yanomamö of Venezuela. Many women are married off by their kinsmen with little regard for their consent, and others are abducted. Violence and threats then deter women from leaving to pursue their own preferences. Chagnon (1992) reports that husbands sometimes mutilate and even kill recaptured wives in front of others. But a woman may take the risk, and "on her own, flees from her village to live in another village and find a new husband there. If the woman's own [husband's] village is stronger than the one she flees to, the men will pursue her and forcibly take her back—and mete out a very severe punishment to her for having run away. Most of the women who have fled have done so to escape particularly savage and cruel treatment, and they try to flee to a more powerful village" (Chagnon, 1992, p. 149).

A paradoxical consequence of living with chronic threats of violence is that women may value men for their violent capabilities. Women often rely on brothers and other male kin to protect them from abusive husbands (Campbell, 1992b); Yanomamö women, for example, "dread the possibility of being married to men in distant villages, because they know that their brothers will not be able to protect them" (Chagnon, 1992, p. 149). Moreover, violent capability may be valued in the husband himself, where women are at risk of being abducted by other men, as among the Yanomamö or even where sexual harassment and assault are chronic risks that a husband with a reputation for vengeful violent action can deter. Thus, we would anticipate that wherever local rates of sexual assault are chronically high or where material and social rewards are gained by the effective use of violence, a reputation for controlled use of violence may be perceived as a valuable trait in a husband, notwithstanding the hazards of affiliating oneself with a violent man.

In a review of mating alliances in the animal kingdom, Mesnick (1997) argues that one benefit to females of forming a bond with a male partner is a reduction in risk of sexual aggression from other males. Several subsidiary hypotheses follow from this "bodyguard" hypothesis, including (a) that females may be most attracted to large and/or dominant males where high risk of sexual aggression prevails and (b) that the cross-species distribution of pair-bonding may be accounted for, in part, by cross-species variation in risks of sexual aggression.

In the case of humans, Mesnick reviews several empirical studies suggesting that being married is associated with significant reductions in risk of sexual assault and harassment. The bodyguard hypothesis suggests that, controlling for the age of the woman, the risk of sexual assault victimization by men other than husbands would be less for "married" women than "unmarried" women. And that is the case in Canada (Figure 8.4).

5. Costs to Husbands of Using Violence

There is no reason to expect an evolved psychology to be insensitive to costs, so we would not expect angry men, however genuine their emotional arousal, to ever be impervious to social controls. Several authors have argued that wife battering is rarer or less severe in societies in which wives retain close contact with their genealogical kin, who deter husbands' violence (e.g., Campbell, 1992b; Chagnon, 1992; Draper, 1992; Smuts, 1992). Variation in the protection provided by male kin is apparently related to variable vulnerability of wives within societies, too, including societies that are relatively matrilocal (H. Kaplan & K. Hill, personal communication, June, 1990).

Oddly, in a cross-cultural analysis, Levinson (1989) could find no support for the hypothesis that access to her kin protects a wife from abuse in nonstate societies; prevalence of wife-beating was apparently unrelated to postmarital residence practices. One problem with this null result is, of course, that estimates from ethnographic materials of wife-beating are noisy. However, Levinson's codings did prove to be significantly related to other variables, including widow remarriage proscriptions and the presence or absence of all-female work groups. A more important problem is that Levinson's test of the hypothesized relationship was a rank-order correlation, even though postmarital residence practices were coded on a five-point scale whose ordering did not correspond to lesser/greater access to genealogical kin. We hypothesize that better cross-cultural methods will overturn Levinson's null result.

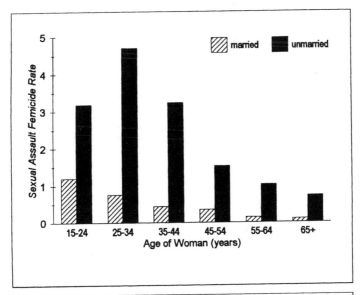

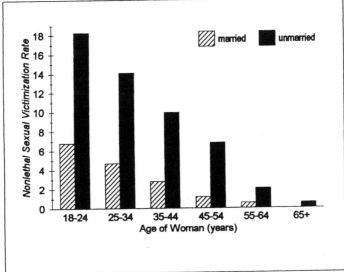

Figure 8.4. Sexual Victimization Rates of Women by Age and Marital Status, Canada

Upper panel: Number of Canadian women (1974-1992) per annum per *million* women in the population at large who were killed by a man other than their husband in the context of a sexual assault.

Lower panel: Number of Canadian women per *hundred* women in the population at large who reported in 1993 either sexual assault or unwanted sexual touching in the past year by men other than husbands or dates or boyfriends (see Wilson & Mesnick, 1997).

Wives themselves can impose retaliatory costs on violent husbands, sometimes even killing them. In most societies, wives vastly
outnumber husbands as homicide victims, but the death toll in spousal
homicide in the United States is almost equal (Wilson & Daly, 1992b).
Ethnocentric U.S. social scientists have cited the near equity in spousal
homicides there as if it were universally true (it is in fact exceptional,
maybe even unique [Wilson & Daly, 1992b]) and as if it constituted
evidence that marital violence is sexually symmetrical (a curiously
fashionable thesis debunked by Dobash, Dobash, Wilson, & Daly
[1992]). Even in the United States, the exceptional similarity in
numbers of female and male spousal homicide victims does not imply
that wives' and husbands' actions or motives are alike. Rather, in
the United States, as elsewhere, men often pursue and kill estranged
wives, whereas women hardly ever behave similarly; men, but not
women, kill spouses as part of planned murder-suicides; men perpetrate familicidal massacres, killing spouse and children together,
whereas women do not; men, but not women, often kill after the
spouse's prolonged subjection to coercive abuse; men kill in response
to revelations of wives' infidelity, whereas women almost never react
similarly; and women, unlike men, kill mainly in circumstances with
strong elements of self-defense or defense of children (references in
Daly & Wilson, 1988b; Dobash et al., 1992; Wilson & Daly, 1992b).

Violence Against Wives and Children

From the perspectives of both evolutionary psychology and cultural anthropology, children (extant or prospective) are central to a
fundamental understanding of marital relationships (see Daly &
Wilson, 1996b; Wilson & Daly, 1992a). Children of the marital union
enhance husband-wife solidarity and reduce the risk of divorce, compared with children of former mates who are often a source of conflict.
How does violence against wives relate to the presence of children?

Certainly, there is some sort of statistical association between
violence against wives and violence directed at the children, too, and
there are probably several reasons for this. One is that men vary in
their individual ("personality") readiness to use violence in general. A
second reason is that threats and assaults against the children can be
another tactic of coercive control of the wife. A third is that a man's

mistreatment of the children, perhaps especially when they are not his own, can be a source of marital strife, as the wife/mother attempts to intervene on their behalf, leading more or less directly to violence against the woman.

Familicidal Massacres

One relatively infrequent but persistent variety of uxoricide is that in which the children are also killed. Wilson, Daly, & Daniele (1995) proposed that there are two rather different types familicide scenario, differing with respect to the killer's emotional state, yet both reflecting an uxorial proprietariness. In the first variety, the killer professes a grievance against his wife, usually with respect to alleged infidelities and/or her intending or acting to terminate the marriage. Overt and even public expressions of his aggrieved hostility are often conspicuous, and a history of violence may be noted. Apparently rather different are cases in which the killer is a depressed and brooding man, who may apprehend impending disaster for himself and his family, and who sees familicide followed by suicide as "the only way out." Expressions of hostility toward the victims are generally absent (or at most ambiguous) in such cases, and the despondent killer may even characterize his deed as an act of mercy or rescue. These despondent men are presumably those who commit suicide at the scene, something that many familicidal men do: About half of Canadian men who killed their wives and children also killed themselves, compared with 25% of other uxoricidal or filicidal men and just 3% of other male killers; similarly, in England and Wales, half the familicide perpetrators committed suicide, compared to 15% of other uxoricides and 11% of other filicidal men (Wilson, Daly, & Daniele, 1995).

This proposed taxonomy of angry versus despondent perpetrators of familicide is founded in the case descriptions, but its validity and usefulness have yet to be established. The distinction is not simply a matter of suicide, because accusatory killers can be suicidal too (and despondent killers' suicide attempts may fail). As different as these two proposed categories of familicides appear, they have this in common: The killer's professed rationale for his actions invokes a proprietary conception of wife and children. The hostile, accusatory familicidal killer is indignant about the alienation of his wife, and may declare "If I can't have her, no one can." The despondent killer bizarrely construes homicide as protection, apparently believing that his victims could not persist or cope in his absence. In both cases, the killer feels entitled to decide his victims' fates.

Violence Against Wives and Stepchildren

There are both theoretical and empirical reasons for suspecting that marital conflict and violence may be elevated in stepfamilies. ("Stepparent" here includes anyone in *loco parentis* to a child by virtue of coresident marital partnership with the child's genetic parent, regardless of whether the marriage is registered or the stepparent has legally adopted the child.) Stepchildren are abused and killed at very much higher rates than genetic offspring (Daly & Wilson, 1988a, 1988b, 1996a, 1996b), so mistreatment of stepchildren is itself a likely source of conflict between the stepparent and the genetic parent.

Daly, Singh, and Wilson (1993) reported that women with children sired by a former partner sought refuge from assaultive husbands in a Canadian women's shelter for battered women at a per capita rate about five times greater than did same-age mothers whose children were all sired by the present husband (Figure 8.5). It was also the case that the stepchildren were more likely to have been assaulted too. In a study of fatal assaults on wives in the same Canadian city, Daly et al. (1997) found that uxoricide rates were also substantially elevated in stepfather families (Figure 8.5). Information was not available on how many children had been assaulted, but in three of the 32 couples, the man killed his wife and child in contexts that were similar to the familicides previously described.

These two studies demonstrate that the presence of children of former unions is a major risk marker for violence against wives. They are the first and only studies to have asked whether that might be so. This discovery is testimony to the value of an evolutionary psychological approach, for no researcher lacking this perspective ever thought to ask. Hotaling and Sugarman (1986) culled a list of 92 proposed "risk markers" for violence against wives from the family violence literature, but paternity of the children was not among them. Similarly, no family violence researcher lacking an evolutionary perspective ever thought to ask whether step-relationship might be associated with assaults against children, and it has turned out to be the most powerful risk factor yet discovered; see Daly and Wilson (1996a, 1996b). Study of how stepparental status may influence the psychology of male sexual proprietariness could be valuable.

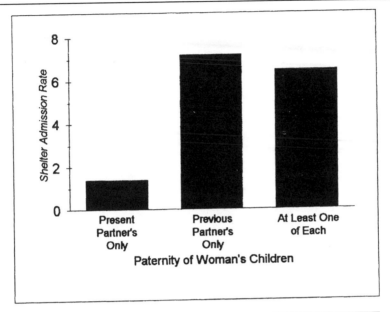

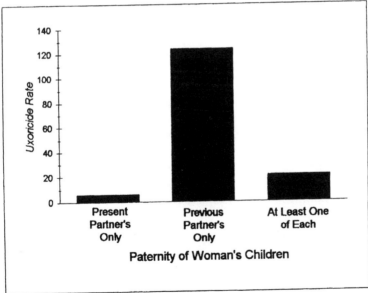

Figure 8.5. Violence Against Wives in Relation to Paternity of Her Children, Hamilton, Ontario, Canada

Upper panel: Comparison of rates of admissions to a shelter for battered women per hundred such women in the population, for women who had children according to whether her children had been sired by the present perpetrator husband or a previous partner (see Daly et al., 1993).

Lower panel: Comparison of uxoricide rates for wives who had children per million such women in the population, according to whether her children had been sired by the killer husband or a previous partner (see Daly et al., 1997).

Concluding Remarks

An evolutionary psychological perspective provided us with the requisite framework to develop several hypotheses about patterns of risk of violence against wives. We used homicide and assault data from Canada and elsewhere to compute rates of violence to assess the merit of our hypotheses. Our findings include the following: (a) much higher rates of uxoricide after estrangement than in coresiding couples, (b) highest rates of uxoricide and nonlethal assaults for the youngest wives and a steady decline with age, (c) higher rates of uxoricide and nonlethal assaults in common-law marital unions than in registered marital unions, and (d) higher rates of violence when the woman has coresident minor children sired by a previous partner. Furthermore, there are empirical regularities in wives' attributions of husbands' efforts to limit their autonomy, indicating that the most violent husbands are the most controlling husbands. These results are consistent with our expectations based on reasoning about the links between sexual proprietariness, coercive control, and assaults against wives. We also have proposed several hypotheses about cross-cultural variations in levels of men's sexual possessiveness and violence against wives, but empirical testing of these hypotheses remains to be done.

Two important assumptions that helped us generate our hypotheses about risk patterns were as follows. First, violence against wives is a product of motives whose adaptive function is coercive control. Uxoricidal husbands have overstepped the bounds of utility, and the fatal outcomes can be considered maladaptive by-products of powerful motives whose utility resides in the effectiveness of sincere, credible threats and nonlethal punishments for defying the assailant's wishes. For every wife who is killed, hundreds or thousands are intimidated, and we simply do not know whether wife assault is often (perhaps even typically) effective in shaping the victim's behavior in ways that suit the perpetrator. It might be worthwhile to try to find out.

Secondly, we have supposed that male sexual proprietariness is modulated by perceptions of cues indicative of a wife's likelihood of sexual infidelity or desertion. The man's perceptions may be veridical or delusional, but in any case, we would anticipate that the perceived "threat" of loss or trespass in this valued relationship will be affected by information or cues pertaining to her apparent attractiveness to other men, her commitment to the marital union, and the sexual rivalry "pressure" indicated by such considerations as local sex ratios and densities of potential competitors and the man's own "mate value" relative to that of rivals. We use the phrase sexual "proprietariness" rather than "jealousy" mainly because the latter implies a sentiment focused on a specific rival, whereas we conceive of proprietariness as a more encompassing mind-set that might be effective in reducing the opportunity for usurpation by any rival.

We expect that sexual proprietariness has a lot in common with the proprietary mind-sets associated with possessing any valued commodity, whether it be food, real estate, money, or people. In all cases, the intensity of guarding may be expected to vary in relation to variations in the attributes for which the commodity is valued and in response to cues of risk of alienation and trespass. There are, however, likely to be some interesting and important differences in such proprietary mind-sets as a function of the particular commodities in question.

This paper offered some suggestions as to the informational cues modulating the perceptions of sexually proprietary men, but there has been a paucity of empirical research delineating the kinds of information affecting perceptions and the effects of such perceptual processing on attention structures, memory, motivational and emotional processing, as well as decision making. Recent research in neuroscience revealing the complex integration of many specific functional domains of neural activity as well as more precisely delineated hypotheses about informational processing for specific tasks and content domains in psychology should facilitate the development of a clearer understanding of the links between male sexual proprietariness and violence.

Such an approach will clarify to what degree individual differences in personality traits associated with using violence against wives represent stable individual differences in information processing and to what degree personality tests have instead indexed relatively short-term states of mind modulated by the current social and material circumstances of the individual. We imagine that personality traits associated with violence against wives do reflect stable individual differences in information processing, at least in part, as a result of considerable inertia in the mental models one builds of one's social universe on the basis of cumulative experience over years.

Research in a diversity of cultural settings is needed in order to determine whether factors such as female youth and children of former unions indeed raise the risk of violence against wives in general, as we have implicitly supposed, or are instead cross-culturally variable in their effects. We also hope to see tests of our several hypotheses about cross-cultural diversity. No one can manipulate life experiences or perceived social costs of using violence against wives or cues of "bachelor pressure" experimentally, but systematic cross-cultural comparisons can test ideas about the factors modulating male sexual proprietariness and violence against wives.

Note

1. "Fitness" refers to the expected value (in the statistical sense and in a natural environment) of a phenotypic design's success in promoting the relative replicative success of its bearer's genes, in competition with their alleles (alternative variants at the same genetic locus). We owe the term *fitness* not to Darwin but to the sociologist Herbert Spencer who epitomized the theory of natural selection as "survival of the fittest." Even Darwin and Wallace adopted Spencer's phrase, but it has produced a lot of misunderstanding, because evolutionists use the term in several slightly different senses, none of which corresponds to its vernacular meaning of physical condition (see Dawkins, 1982).

References

Abdalla, R. H. D. (1982). *Sisters in affliction: Circumcision and infibulation in Africa.* London: Zed.

Abu Lughod, L. (1986). *Veiled sentiments: Honor and poetry in a Bedouin society.* Berkeley: University of California Press.

Abu Lughod, L. (1990). The romance of resistance: Tracing transformations of power through Bedouin women. In P. R. Sanday & R. G. Goodenough (Eds.), *Beyond the second sex* (pp. 313-337). Philadelphia: University of Pennsylvania Press.

Abusharaf, R. M. (1995). Rethinking feminist discourses on female genital mutilation: The case of the Sudan. *Canadian Woman Studies, 15*(2&3), 52-54.

Abusharaf, R. M. (1996, November). Revisiting feminist discourses on female infibulation: Responses from Sudanese indigenous feminists. Paper presented at the annual meeting of the American Anthropological Association, San Francisco, CA.

Adkins, L. (1995). *Gendered work: Sexuality, family and the labour market.* Buckingham, UK: Open University Press.

Al Fanar. (1995). Developments in the struggle against the murder of women against the background of so-called family honour. *Women Against Fundamentalism Journal, 6,* 37-51.

Allen, J. A. (1990). *Sex and secrets: Crimes involving Australian women since 1880.* Melbourne: Oxford University Press.

Al-Sa'dawi, N. (1980). *The hidden face of Eve.* London: Zed.

Ammar, H. (1954). *Growing up in an Egyptian village.* London: Routledge.

Archer, J. (Ed.). (1994). *Male violence.* London: Routledge.

Arensberg, C., & Kimball, S. (1968). *Family and community in Ireland.* Cambridge, MA: Harvard University Press.

Armstrong, L. (1994). *Rocking the cradle of sexual politics: What happened when women said incest.* New York: Addison-Wesley.

Armstrong, S. (1991, February 2). Female circumcision: Fighting a cruel tradition. *New Scientist, 129,* 42-47.

Armstrong, S. (1994). Rape in South Africa: An invisible part of apartheid's legacy. *Focus on Gender, 2*(2), 35-39.

Atkinson, J. (1990). Violence against aboriginal women: Reconstitution of customary law—the way forward. *Aboriginal Law Journal, 46*(2), 6-9.

Aziz, F. A. (1980). Gynecologic and obstetric complications of female circumcision. *International Journal of Gynecology and Obstetrics, 17,* 560-563.

Bachman, R. (1994). *Violence against women: A national crime victimization survey report.* Washington, DC: Bureau of Justice Statistics.

Bachman, R., & Saltzman, L. (1995). *Violence against women: Estimates from the redesigned survey.* Washington, DC: Bureau of Justice Statistics.

Badri, A. E. S. (1984). Female circumcision in the Sudan. *Ahfad Journal, 1*(1), 11-21.

Baker, R. R., & Bellis, M. A. (1989). Number of sperm in human ejaculates varies in accordance with sperm competition theory. *Animal Behaviour, 37,* 867-869.

Barbaree, H., & Marshall, W. (1991). The role of male sexual arousal in rape: Six models. *Journal of Consulting and Clinical Psychology, 59*(5), 621-630.

Barkow, J., Cosmides, L., & Tooby, J. (Eds.). (1992). *The adapted mind.* New York: Oxford University Press.

Barnard, G. W., Vera, H., Vera, M. I., & Newman, G. (1982). Till death do us part: A study of spouse murder. *Bulletin of the American Association of Psychiatry and Law, 10,* 271-280.

Barnes, V. L., & Boddy, J. (1994). *Aman: The story of a Somali girl.* Toronto: Knopf.

Baumgartner, M. P. (1993). Violent networks: The origins and management of domestic conflict. In R. Tedeschi & J. Tedeschi (Eds.), *Aggression and violence: Social interactionist perspectives* (pp. 209-231). Washington, DC.

Bhatia, B., Kawar, M., & Shahin, M. (1992). *Unheard voices: Kagi women on war and sanctions.* London: Change.

Bledsoe, C. (1984). The political use of Sande ideology and symbolism. *American Ethnologist, 11*(3), 455-472.

Bock, G., & Cardew, G. (1997). Characterizing human psychological adaptations. *CIBA Foundation Symposium 208.* Chichester, UK: Wiley.

Boddy, J. (1982). Womb as oasis: The symbolic context of pharaonic circumcision in rural northern Sudan. *American Ethnologist, 9*(4), 682-698.

Boddy, J. (1988). Spirits and selves in northern Sudan: The cultural therapeutics of possession and trance. *American Ethnologist, 15*(1), 4-27.

Boddy, J. (1989). *Wombs and alien spirits: Women, men, and the Zar cult in northern Sudan.* Madison: University of Wisconsin Press.

Boddy, J. (1991a). Anthropology, feminism and the postmodern context. *Culture, 11*(1-2), 125-133.

Boddy, J. (1991b). Body politics: Continuing the anticircumcision crusade. *Medical Anthropology Quarterly, 5*(1), 15-17.

Boddy, J. (1994). Afterword: Some background to *Aman.* In V. L. Barnes & J. Boddy (Comp.), *Aman: The story of a Somali girl* (pp. 289-349). Toronto: Knopf.

Boddy, J. (1998a). Embodying ethnography. In M. Lambek & A. Strathern (Eds.), *Bodies and persons: Comparative perspectives from Africa and Melanesia.* Cambridge: Cambridge University Press.

Boddy, J. (1998b). Remembering Amal: On birth and the British in northern Sudan. In M. Lock & P. Kaufert (Eds.), *Pragmatic women and body politics.* Cambridge: Cambridge University Press.

Bonaparte, M. (1953). *Female sexuality.* New York: International Universities Press.

Bordo, S. (1988). Anorexia nervosa: Psychopathology as the crystallization of culture. In I. Diamond & L. Quinby (Eds.), *Feminism and Foucault* (pp. 87-117). Boston: Northeastern University Press.

Bordo, S. (1989). The body and the reproduction of femininity: A feminist appropriation of Foucault. In A. M. Jaggar & S. R. Bordo (Eds.), *Gender/body/knowledge: Feminist reconstructions of being and knowing* (pp. 13-33). New Brunswick, NJ: Rutgers University Press.

Bordo, S. (1993). *Unbearable weight: Feminism, western culture, and the body*. Berkeley: University of California Press.

Borgerhoff Mulder, M. (1988). Kipsigis bridewealth payments. In L. Betzig, M. Borgerhoff Mulder, & P. Turke (Eds.), *Human reproductive behaviour* (pp. 65-82). Cambridge: Cambridge University Press.

Borst, M. (1992). *Women and domestic violence: An annotated bibliography*. Leiden, Netherlands: VENA.

Boulware-Miller, K. (1985). Female circumcision: Challenges to the practice as a human rights violation. *Harvard Women's Law Journal, 8*, 155-177.

Bourdieu, P. (1977). *Outline of a theory of practice* (R. Nice, Trans.). Cambridge: Cambridge University Press.

Bourdieu, P. (1990). *The logic of practice* (R. Nice, Trans.). Cambridge: Polity.

Bourgois, P. (1996). *In search of respect: Selling crack in El Barrio*. Cambridge: Cambridge University Press.

Breckenridge, J., & Carmody, M. (1992). *Crimes of violence: Australian responses to rape and child sexual assault*. Sydney: Allen and Unwin.

Bresse, S. K. (1989). Crimes of passion: The campaign against wife killing in Brazil (1910-1940). *Journal of Social History, 22*, 653-666.

Briere, J., & Malamuth, N. (1983). Self-reported likelihood of sexually aggressive behaviour: Attitudinal versus sexual explanations. *Journal of Research in Personality, 17*, 315-323.

Briere, J., & Runtz, M. (1989). University males' sexual interest in children: Predicting potential indices of "Paedophilia" in a non-forensic sample. *Child Abuse & Neglect, 13*(1), 65-76.

Brisson, N. J. (1983). Battering husbands: A survey of abusive men. *Victimology, 6*, 338-344.

Browne, A. (1987). *When battered women kill*. New York: Free Press.

Browning, J., & Dutton, D. (1986). Assessment of wife assault with the Conflict Tactics Scale: Using couple data to quantify the differential reporting effect. *Journal of Marriage and the Family, 48*, 375-379.

Bruch, H. (1973). *Eating disorders*. New York: Basic.

Brush, L. (1990). Violent acts and injurious outcomes in married couples: Methodological issues in the National Survey of Families and Households. *Gender & Society, 4*, 56-67.

Bueno, J. (1994). "No one wants machismo anymore": The rise of Bolivian feminism. In G. Kupers (Ed.), *Companeras: Voices from the Latin American women's movement*. London: Latin American Movement.

Bunster-Burotto, X. (1994). Surviving beyond fear: Women and torture in Latin America. In M. Davies (Ed.), *Women and violence* (pp.156-175). London: Zed.

Burgess, A. W., Groth, N., & McCaulsland, M. (1981). Child sex initiation rings. *American Journal of Orthopsychiatry, 51*(1), 110-119.

Buss, D. M. (1991). Evolutionary personality psychology. *Annual Review of Psychology, 42*, 459-491.

Buss, D. M. (1994). *The evolution of desire*. New York: Basic.

Buss, D. M., & Barnes, M. F. (1986). Preferences in human mate selection. *Journal of Personality and Social Psychology, 50*, 559-570.

Buss, D. M., Larsen, R. J., Westen, D., & Semmelroth, J. (1992). Sex differences in jealousy: Evolution, physiology and psychology. *Psychological Science, 3*, 251-255.

Butler, J. (1990). *Gender trouble: Feminism and the subversion of identity*. New York: Routledge.

Buunk, B. P., Angleitner, A., Oubaid, V., & Buss, D. M. (1996). Sex differences in jealousy in evolutionary and cultural perspective: Tests from the Netherlands, Germany and the United States. *Psychological Science, 7*, 359-363.

Campbell, A., & Muncer, S. (1995). Sex differences in aggression: Social representations and social roles. *British Journal of Social Psychology*.

Campbell, B. (1988). *Unofficial secrets*. London: Virago.

Campbell, J. C. (1992a). If I can't have you, no one can: Issues of power and control in homicide of female partners. In J. Radford & D. E. H. Russell (Eds.), *Femicide: The politics of woman killing*. New York: Twayne.

Campbell, J. C. (1992b). Wife battering: Cultural contexts versus western social sciences. In D. C. Counts, J. K. Brown, & J. C. Campbell (Eds.), *Sanctions and sanctuary: Cultural perspectives on the beating of wives* (pp. 229-249). Boulder, CO: Westview.

Canadian Journal of Criminology. (1995). *Focus on the Violence Against Women Survey*, 37(3).

Canadian Panel on Violence Against Women. (1993). *Changing the landscape: Ending violence, achieving equality*. Ottawa: Ministry of Supply and Services.

Chagnon, N. A. (1992). *Yanomamo: The last days of Eden*. New York: Harcourt Brace Jovanovich.

Chesney, J. (1991). U.S. Rapists. *Changes, 9*, 2-9.

Chimbos, P. D. (1993). A study of patterns in criminal homicides in Greece. *International Journal of Comparative Sociology, 34*, 260-271.

Chodorow, N. (1974). Family structure and feminine personality. In M. Z. Rosaldo & L. Lamphere (Eds.), *Woman, culture and society*. Stanford, CA: Stanford University Press.

Chodorow, N. (1978). *The reproduction of mothering. Psychoanalysis and the sociology of gender*. Berkeley, CA: University of California Press.

Clutton-Brock, T. H., & Parker, G. A. (1995a). Punishment in animal societies. *Nature, 373*, 209-216.

Clutton-Brock, T. H., & Parker, G. A. (1995b). Sexual coercion in animal societies. *Animal Behaviour, 49*, 1345-1365.

Cohen, D. (1996). Law, social policy and violence: The impact of regional cultures. *Journal of Personality and Social Psychology, 70*, 961-978.

Collinson, H. (1990). *Women and revolution in Nicaragua*. London: Zed.

Comaroff, J. (1985). *Body of power, spirit of resistance: The culture and history of a South African people*. Chicago: University of Chicago Press.

Comaroff, J. (1993). The diseased heart of Africa: Medicine, colonialism, and the black body. In S. Lindenbaum & M. Lock (Eds.), *Knowledge, power and practice* (pp. 305-329). Berkeley: University of California Press.

Comaroff, J., & Comaroff, J. (1991). *Of revelation and revolution: Christianity, colonialism, and consciousness in South Africa* (Vol. 1). Chicago: University of Chicago Press.

Comaroff, J., & Comaroff, J. (1992). *Ethnography and the historical imagination*. Boulder, CO: Westview.

Conte, J., Wolf, S., & Smith, T. (1989). What sexual offenders tell us about prevention strategies. *Child Abuse & Neglect, 13*(2), 293-301.

Cook, R. (1979). Damage to physical health from pharaonic circumcision (infibulation) of females. In *Traditional practices affecting the health of women and children* (pp. 55-69). Alexandria: WHO/EMRO Technical Publication No. 2.

Counts, D. C. (1990). Beaten wife, suicidal woman: Domestic violence in Kaliai, West New Britain. *Pacific Studies, 13*, 151-169.

Counts, D. C., Brown, J. K., & Campbell, J. C. (Eds.). (1992). *Sanctions and sanctuary: Cultural perspectives on the beating of wives*. Boulder, CO: Westview.

Craig, M. (1990). Coercive sexuality in dating relationships: A situational model. *Clinical Psychology Review, 10*, 395-423.

Crawford, M., & Gartner, R. (1992). *Woman killing: Intimate femicide in Ontario (1974-1990)*. Toronto: The Women We Honour Action Committee.

Cronin, H. (1991). *The ant and the peacock.* Cambridge: Cambridge University Press.

Crosset, T. W., Ptacek, J., McDonald, M. A., & Benedict, J. R. (1996). Male student athletes and violence against women: a survey of campus judicial affairs offices. *Violence Against Women, 2,* 163-179.

Cullen, C. (1994). Experiences of female republican prisoners. In C. Fisher (Ed.), *Policing a divided society* (pp. 14-17). Belfast: Research and Documentation Centre.

Daly, M. (1978). *Gyn/Ecology.* Boston: Beacon.

Daly, M., Singh, L. S., & Wilson, M. I. (1993). Children fathered by previous partners: A risk factor for violence against women. *Canadian Journal of Public Health, 84,* 209-210.

Daly, M., & Wilson, M. I. (1988a). Evolutionary social psychology and homicide. *Science, 242,* 519-524.

Daly, M., & Wilson, M. I. (1988b). *Homicide.* Hawthorne, NY: Aldine de Gruyter.

Daly, M., & Wilson, M. I. (1990). Killing the competition: Male-male and female-female homicide. *Human Nature, 1,* 81-107.

Daly, M., & Wilson, M. I. (1994). Evolutionary psychology of male violence. In J. Archer (Ed.), *Male violence* (pp. 253-288). London: Routledge.

Daly, M., & Wilson, M. I. (1995). Discriminative parental solicitude and the relevance of evolutionary models to the analysis of motivational systems. In M. Gazzaniga (Ed.), *The cognitive neurosciences.* Cambridge, MA: MIT Press.

Daly, M., & Wilson, M. I. (1996a). Evolutionary psychology and marital conflict: The relevance of stepchildren. In D. M. Buss & N. Malamuth (Eds.), *Sex, power, conflict: Feminist and evolutionary perspectives* (pp. 9-28). New York: Oxford University Press.

Daly, M., & Wilson, M. I. (1996b). Violence against stepchildren. *Current Directions in Psychological Science, 5,* 77-81.

Daly, M., & Wilson, M. I. (1997). Crime and conflict: Homicide in evolutionary psychological perspective. *Crime and Justice, 22,* 251-300.

Daly, M., Wilson, M. I., & Weghorst, S. J. (1982). Male sexual jealousy. *Ethology and Sociobiology, 3,* 11-27.

Daly, M., Wiseman, K. A., & Wilson, M. I. (1997). Women with children sired by previous partners incur excess risk of uxoricide. *Homicide Studies, 1,* 61-71.

Dareer, A. E. (1982). *Woman, why do you weep? Circumcision and its consequences.* London: Zed.

Davies, N. B. (1992). *Dunnock behaviour and social evolution.* Oxford: Oxford University Press.

Davis, K. (1991). Remaking the she-devil: A critical look at feminist approaches to beauty. *Hypatia, 6,* 21-43.

Davis, K. (1995). *Reshaping the female body: The dilemma of cosmetic surgery.* New York: Routledge.

Dawkins, R. (1982). *The extended phenotype.* Oxford: Freeman.

DeKeseredy, W. (1989). Woman abuse in dating relationships: An exploratory study. *Atlantis, 14*(2), 55-62.

DeKeseredy, W., & Kelly, K. (1993). The incidence and prevalence of woman abuse in Canadian university and college dating relationships. *Canadian Journal of Sociology, 18*(2), 137-159.

DeKeseredy, W., & MacLean, B. (1990). Research women abuse in Canada: A realist critique of the Conflict Tactics Scale. *Canadian Review of Social Policy, 25,* 19-27.

Dell, S. (1984). *Murder into manslaughter.* Oxford: Oxford University Press.

Department of Health. (1995). *Child protection: Messages from research.* London: HMSO.

Descola, P. (1996). *The spears of twilight: Life and death in the Amazon jungle.* London: HarperCollins.

Dimberg, U., & Öhman, A. (1996). Behold the wrath: Psychophysiological responses to facial stimuli. *Motivation and Emotion, 20,* 149-182.

Ditch, J., & Morrissey, M. (1992). Northern Ireland: Review and prospects for social policy. *Social Policy and Administration, 26*(1), 18-26.

Dobash, R. E., & Dobash, R. P. (1977). Love, honour and obey: Institutional ideologies and the struggle for battered women. *Contemporary Crisis, 1,* 403-415.

Dobash, R. E., & Dobash, R. P. (1977-1978). Wives: The "appropriate" victims of marital violence. *Victimology, 2,* 426-442.

Dobash, R. E., & Dobash, R. P. (1979). *Violence against wives.* New York: Free Press.

Dobash, R. E., & Dobash, R. P. (1981). Community response to violence against wives: Charivari, abstract justice and patriarchy. *Social Problems, 28*(5), 563-581.

Dobash, R. E., & Dobash, R. P. (1983a). The context-specific approach. In D. Finkelhor, R. Gelles, G. Hotaling, & M. Straus (Eds.), *Dark side of families: Current family violence research* (pp. 261-276). Beverly Hills, CA: Sage.

Dobash, R. E., & Dobash, R. P. (1983b). Patterns of violence in Scotland. In R. J. Gelles & C. P. Cornell (Eds.), *International perspectives on family violence* (pp. 147-155). Lexington, MA: D.C. Heath.

Dobash, R. E., & Dobash, R. P. (1984). The nature and antecedents of violent events. *British Journal of Criminology, 24,* 269-288.

Dobash, R. E., & Dobash, R. P. (1988). Research as social action: The struggle for battered women. In K. Yllö & M. Bogard (Eds.), *Feminist perspectives on wife abuse* (pp. 51-74). Newbury Park, CA: Sage.

Dobash, R. E., & Dobash, R. P. (1990a). How research makes a difference to policy and practice. In D. J. Besharov (Ed.), *Family violence: Research and public policy issues* (pp. 185-204). Washington, DC: AEI.

Dobash, R. E., & Dobash, R. P. (1990b). How theory makes a difference to policy and practice. In D. J. Besharov (Ed.), *Family violence: Research and public policy issues.* Washington, DC: AEI.

Dobash, R. E., & Dobash, R. P. (1992). *Women, violence and social change.* London: Routledge.

Dobash, R. E., Dobash, R. P., Cavanagh, K., & Lewis, R. (1995). Evaluating criminal justice programmes for violent men. In R. E. Dobash, R. P. Dobash, & L. Noaks (Eds.), *Gender and crime* (pp. 358-389). Cardiff: University of Wales Press.

Dobash, R. P., Dobash, R. E., Cavanagh, K., & Lewis, R. (1996). *Research evaluation of programmes for violent men.* Edinburgh: Scottish Office Central Research Unit.

Dobash, R. P., Dobash, R. E., Cavanagh, K., & Lewis, R. (1998). Separate and intersecting reality: A comparison of men's and women's accounts of violence against women. *Journal of Violence Against Women, 4*(4), 382-414.

Dobash, R. P., Dobash, R. E., Cavanagh, K., & Lewis, R. (in press). *Changing violent men.* Thousand Oaks, CA: Sage.

Dobash, R. P., Dobash, R. E., Wilson, M., & Daly, M. (1992). The myth of sexual symmetry in marital violence. *Social Problems, 39,* 71-91.

Dorkenoo, E., & Elworthy, S. (1992). *Female genital mutilation: Proposals for change.* London: Minority Rights Group.

Drakulic, S. (1994). The rape of women in Bosnia. In M. Davies (Ed.), *Women and violence* (pp. 176-181). London: Zed.

Draper, P. (1992). Room to maneuver: !Kung women cope with men. In D. C. Counts, J. K. Brown, & J. C. Campbell (Eds.), *Sanctions and sanctuary: Cultural perspectives on the beating of wives* (pp. 43-61). Boulder, CO: Westview.

Driver, E., & Droisen, A. (1989). *Child sexual abuse: Feminist perspectives.* London: MacMillan.

Eckberg, D. (1995, November). *The role of paid employment in battered wives' decisions to leave: Toward a social psychological approach.* Paper presented at the meeting of the American Society of Criminology, Boston, MA.

Edleson, J. L., & Eisikovits, Z. (1985). Men who batter women: A critical review of the evidence. *Journal of Family Issues, 6,* 229-247.

Edwards, J. L. J. (1954). Provocation and the reasonable man: Another view. *Criminal Law Review, 1954,* 898-906.

Ehrenreich, B., & English, D. (1979). *For her own good: 150 years of the experts advice to women.* Garden City, NY: Anchor.

Eisikovits, Z. C., & Edleson, J. L. (1989). Intervening with men who batter: A critical review of the literature. *Social Service Review, 37,* 384-414.

El Bushra, J., & Piza-Lopez, E. (1993). Gender-related violence: Its scope and relevance. *Focus on Gender, 1*(2), 1-11.

El Hassan, A. M. (1990). The influence of education on female circumcision. *Ahfad Journal, 7,* 70-73.

Ellis, D. (1987). Post-separation woman abuse: The contribution of lawyers as "barracudas," "advocates," and "counsellors." *International Journal of Law & Psychiatry, 10,* 401-410.

Ellis, D. (1989). Male abuse of a married or cohabiting female partner: The application of sociological theory to research findings. *Violence and Victims, 4*(4), 235-255.

Ellis, S., Barak, A., & Pinto, A. (1991). Moderating effects of personal cognitions on experienced and perceived sexual harassment of women at the workplace. *Journal of Applied Social Psychology, 21*(16), 1320-1337.

Elman, A., & Eduards, M. (1991). Unprotected by the Swedish welfare state. *Women's Studies International Forum, 14*(5), 413-421.

Elvik, S., et al. (1990). Sexual abuse in the developmentally disabled: Dilemmas of diagnosis. *Child Abuse & Neglect, 14,* 497-502.

Enloe, C. (1994). *The morning after: Sexual politics at the end of the Cold War.* Berkeley: University of California Press.

Estrich, S. (1987). *Real rape.* Cambridge, MA: Harvard University Press.

Evason, E. (1982). *Hidden violence.* Belfast: Farset.

Fagan, J., Stewart, D., & Hansen, K. (1983). Violent men or violent husbands? Background factors and situational correlates. In D. Finkelhor, R. Gelles, G. Hotaling, & M. Straus (Eds.), *In the dark side of families: Current family violence research* (pp. 49-67). Beverly Hills, CA: Sage.

Fagan, J. (1993a). *The criminalization of domestic violence: Promises and limits* (Research Rep.). Washington, DC: National Institute of Justice.

Fagan, J. (1993b). Social structure and spouse assault. In B. Forst (Ed.), *The socioeconomics of crime and justice* (pp. 209-254). Toronto: M. E. Sharpe.

Faller, K. (1987). Women who sexually abuse children. *Violence and Victims, 2,* 4.

Family Violence and Sexual Assault Institute (FVSAI). (1995). *Trauma, amnesia and denial of abuse.* Tyler, TX: Author.

Fanon, F. (1965). *The wretched of the earth.* Harmondsworth: Penguin.

Feldman, A. (1991). *Formations of violence: The narrative of the body and political terror in Northern Ireland.* Chicago: University of Chicago Press.

Female circumcision: Because it's always been done. (1982, September 18). *The Economist, 284,* 42.

Finkelhor, D. (1979). *Sexually victimized children.* New York: Free Press.

Finkelhor, D. (1986). *A sourcebook on child sexual abuse.* Newbury Park, CA: Sage.

Fisher, J. (1994). *Out of the shadows: Women, resistance and politics in South America.* London: Latin America Bureau.

Fisher, R. A. (1958). *The genetical theory of natural selection.* Oxford: Oxford University Press. (Original work published 1930)

Fitzgerald, L., & Hesson-McInnis, M. (1989). The dimensions of sexual harassment: A structural analysis. *Journal of Vocational Behaviour, 35,* 309-326.

Flinn, M. V. (1988). Mate guarding in a Caribbean village. *Ethology and Sociobiology, 9,* 1-28.

Flinn, M. V., & Low, B. S. (1986). Resource distribution, social competition, and mating patterns in human societies. In D. I. Rubenstein & R. W. Wrangham (Eds.), *Ecological aspects of social evolution: Birds and mammals* (pp. 217-243). Princeton, NJ: Princeton University Press.

Foley, M. (1996). Who is in control? Changing responses to women who have been raped and sexually abused. In M. Hester, L. Kelly, & J. Radford (Eds.), *Women, violence and male power* (pp. 66-175). Buckingham, UK: Open University Press.

Forste, R., & Tanfer, K. (1996). Sexual exclusivity among dating, cohabiting, and married women. *Journal of Marriage and the Family, 58*, 33-47.

Foucault, M. (1977). *Language, counter-memory, practice* (D. F. Bouchard, Ed.). Ithaca, NY: Cornell University Press.

Foucault, M. (1979). *Discipline and punish* (A. Sheridan, Trans.). New York: Vintage.

Foucault, M. (1980). *Power/knowledge* (C. Gordon, Ed.). New York: Pantheon.

Foucault, M. (1982). The subject and power. In H. L. Dreyfus & P. Rabinow (Eds.), *M. Foucault: Beyond structuralism and hermeneutics* (pp. 208-226). New York: Harvester Wheatsheaf.

Foucault, M. (1990). *The history of sexuality* (Vol. 1). New York: Vintage.

Frank, R. H. (1988). *Passions within reason: The strategic role of the emotions.* New York: Norton.

Fraser, D. (1995). The first cut is (not) the deepest: Deconstructing "female genital mutilation" and the criminalization of the other. *Dalhousie Law Journal, 18*(2), 310-375.

Fricke, T., Axinn, W. G., & Thornton, A. (1993). Marriage, social inequality, and women's contact with their natal families in alliance societies. *American Anthropologist, 95*, 395-419.

Furby, L., Fischhoff, B., & Morgan, M. (1991). Rape prevention and self defence: At what price? *Women's Studies International Forum, 14*(1/2), 49-62.

Gagné, P. L. (1992). Appalachian women: Violence and social control. *Journal of Contemporary Ethnography, 20*, 387-415.

Gallagher, B., Hughes, B., & Parker, H. (1994). *Organised and ritual abuse research report.* Manchester, UK: Department of Social Policy and Social Work, Manchester University.

Gallagher, C., & Laqueur, T. (Eds.). (1987). *The making of the modern body.* Berkeley: University of California Press.

Gallo, P. G. (1986). Views of future health workers in Somalia on female circumcision. *Medical Anthropology Newsletter, 17*(3), 71-73.

Gavey, N. (1991). Sexual victimization prevalence among New Zealand University students. *Journal of Counselling and Clinical Psychology, 59*(3), 464-466.

Geertz, C. (1973). *The interpretation of cultures.* New York: Basic.

Gelles, R., & Straus, M. (1988). *Intimate violence: The causes and consequences of abuse in the American family.* New York: Simon & Schuster.

Gidycz, C., & Koss, M. (1990). A comparison of group and individual sexual assault victims. *Psychology of Women Quarterly, 14*, 325-342.

Gilliam, A. (1991). Women's equality and national liberation. In C. T. Mohanty, A. Russo, & L. Torres (Eds.), *Third world women and the politics of feminism* (pp. 215-236). Bloomington: University of Indiana Press.

Gilman, C. P. (1973). *The yellow wallpaper.* New York: Feminist Press. (Original work published 1899)

Glick, P., & Lin, S.-L. (1987). Remarriage after divorce: Recent changes and demographic variations. *Sociological Perspectives, 30*, 162-179.

Godenzi, A. (1994). What's the big deal? We are men and they are women. In T. Newburn & E. A. Stanko (Eds.), *Just boys doing business?* (pp. 135-152). London: Routledge.

Gosselin, C. (1996). *The politics of doing feminist ethnography on excision.* Unpublished master's thesis, Department of Anthropology, University of Toronto, Ontario, Canada.

Gould, S. J. (1997). Evolution: The pleasures of pluralism. *The New York review of books, 11,* 26-50 (Vol. XLIV).

Gramsci, A. (1971). *Selections from the prison notebooks* (Q. Hoare & G. N. Smith, Eds. and Trans.). New York: International.

Grant De Pauw, L. (1976). *Remember the ladies: Women in America, 1750-1815.* New York: Viking.

Gray, L. N., & Tallman, I. (1987). Theories of choice: Contingent reward and punishment applications. *Social Psychology Quarterly, 50,* 16-23.

Greer, G. (1971). *The female eunuch.* London: Paladin.

Griaule, M. (1965). *Conversations with Ogotemmêli: An introduction to Dogon religious ideas.* London: Oxford University Press.

Grosz, E. (1987). Notes towards a corporeal feminism. *Australian Feminist Studies, 5*(Summer), 1-16.

Groth, N. (1979). *Men who rape:The psychology of the offender.* New York: Plenum.

Gruber, J. (1992). A typology of per sexual harassment: Research and policy implications for the 1990s. *Sex Roles, 26*(11/12), 447-464.

Grubin, D. (1992). The classification of rapists. *Prison Service Journal, 85,* 45-55.

Gruenbaum, E. (1982). The movement against clitoridectomy and infibulation in Sudan: Public health policy and the women's movement. *Medical Anthropology Newsletter, 13*(2), 4-12.

Gruenbaum, E. (1991). The Islamic movement, development, and health education: Recent changes in the health of rural women in central Sudan. *Social Science and Medicine, 33*(6), 637-645.

Gruenbaum, E. (1996). The cultural debate over female circumcision: The Sudanese are arguing this one out for themselves. *Medical Anthropology Quarterly, 10*(4), 455-475.

Guillaumin, C. (1993). *The constructed body.* (D. G. Crowder, Trans.). In C. Burroughs & J. Ehrenreich (Eds.), *In reading the social body* (pp. 40-60). Iowa City: University of Iowa Press.

Gunning, I. R. (1992). Arrogant perception, world-travelling and multicultural feminism: The case of genital surgeries. *Columbia Human Rights Law Review, 23*(8), 188-248.

Hale, S. (1994). A question of subjects: The "female circumcision" controversy and the politics of knowledge. *Ufahamu, 22*(3), 26-35.

Hale, S. (1996). *Gender politics in Sudan: Islamism, socialism, and the state.* Boulder, CO: Westview.

Hall, M., & Ismail, B. A. (1981). *Sisters under the sun: The story of Sudanese women.* London: Longman.

Hall, R. (1985). *Ask any woman.* Bristol: Falling Wall.

Harding, S. (1986). *The science question in feminism.* New York: Cornell University Press.

Harkin, C., & Kilmurray, A. (1985). Working with women in Derry. In M. Abbott & H. Frazer (Eds.), *Women and community work in Northern Ireland* (pp. 38-45). Belfast: Farset.

Hashi, K. O., & Silver, J. (1994). No words can express: Two voices on female genital mutilation. *Canadian Woman Studies, 14*(3), 62-64.

Hatty, S. (1989). Violence against prostitute women: Social and legal dilemmas. *Australian Journal of Social Work, 24,* 235-248.

Hayes, R. O. (1975). Female genital mutilation, fertility control, women's roles, and the patrilineage in modern Sudan: A functional analysis. *American Ethnologist, 2,* 617-633.

Heise, L. (1994). *Violence against women: The hidden health burden* (Discussion Paper 255). Washington, DC: World Bank.

Heise, L., Moore, K., & Toubia, N. (1995). *Sexual coercion and reproductive health: A focus on research.* New York: The Population Council.

Herman, J. (1992). *Trauma and recovery: From domestic abuse to political terror.* London: Triangle Books.

Hewlett, B. S. (1988). Sexual selection and paternal investment among Aka pygmies. In L. Betzig, M. Borgerhoff Mulder, & P. Turke (Eds.), *Human reproductive behaviour.* Cambridge: Cambridge University Press.

Hilberman, E., & Munson, K. (1978). Sixty battered women. *Victimology, 2,* 460-470.

Hill, K., & Hurtado, A. M. (1996). *Ache life history.* Hawthorne, NY: Aldine de Gruyter.

Hirschi, T. (1969). *Causes of delinquency.* Berkeley: University of California Press.

Hite, S. (1976). *The Hite report.* New York: Dell.

Hoigard, C., & Finstad, L. (1992). *Backstreets: Money, prostitution and love.* Cambridge: Polity.

Holland, M. (1988, February 20). The concepts of mother Ireland. *Irish Times.*

Holtzworth-Munroe, A., & Stuart, G. L. (1994). Typologies of male batterers: Three subsystems and the differences among them. *Psychological Review, 116,* 476-497.

Holy, L. (1991). *Religion and custom in a Muslim society: The Berti of Sudan.* Cambridge: Cambridge University Press.

Hochschild, A. R. (1983). *The managed heart: Commercialization of human feeling.* Berkeley: University of California Press.

Horwitz, A. (1990). *The logic of social control.* New York: Plenum.

Hosken, F. (1982). *The Hosken report: Genital and sexual mutilation of females* (3rd ed.). Lexington, MA: Women's International Network News.

Hotaling, G. T., & Sugarman, D. B. (1986). An analysis of risk markers in husband to wife violence: The current state of knowledge. *Violence and Victims, 1,* 101-124.

Howell, N. (1979). *Demography of the Dobe !Kung.* New York: Academic.

Hrdy, S. B. (1981). *The woman that never evolved.* Cambridge, MA: Harvard University Press.

Huelsman, B. R. (1976). An anthropological view of clitoral and other female genital mutilations. In T. P. Lowry & T. S. Lowry (Eds.), *The clitoris* (pp. 111-161). St. Louis, MO: Warren Green.

Ingram, M. (1987). *Church courts, sex and marriage in England, 1570-1640.* Cambridge: Cambridge University Press.

Innes, C. (1994). Virgin territories and Netherlands: Colonial and nationalist representations of Africa and Ireland. *Feminist Review, 47,* 1-15.

Irigaray, L. (1985). *This sex which is not one* (C. Porter, Trans.). Ithaca, NY: Cornell University Press.

Irwin, A. (1994). Interdisciplinarity or meddling in other people's subjects? *Times Higher Education Supplement, 2*(12), 10.

Jefferson, T. (1994). Theorising masculine subjectivity. In T. Newburn & E. A. Stanko (Eds.), *Just boys doing business? Men, masculinities and crime* (pp. 10-31). London: Routledge.

Johnson, A. G. (1988). On the prevalence of rape in the United States revisited. *Signs: A Journal of Women in Culture and Society, 6*(11), 136-146.

Johnson, A. M., Wadsworth, J., Wellings, K., Field, J., & Bradshaw, S. (1994). *Sexual attitudes and lifestyles.* Oxford: Blackwell.

Johnson, H. (1996). *Dangerous domains: Violence against women in Canada.* Toronto: Nelson.

Johnson, H. (1998). *Social control and the cessation of assaults on wives.* Doctoral dissertation, University of Manchester, Manchester, UK.

Johnson, H., & Sacco, V. (1995). Researching violence against women: Statistics Canada's National Survey. *Canadian Journal of Criminology, 37,* 281-304.

Jones, A. (1980). *Women who kill.* New York: Fawcett Columbine.

Kanner, M. (1993). Drinking themselves to life, or the body in the bottle: Filmic negotiations in the construction of the alcoholic female body. In C. Burroughs & J. Ehrenreich (Eds.), *Reading the social body* (pp. 156-184). Iowa City: University of Iowa Press.

Kapur, R. (1994). The politics of women's rights in India: Report on the women and the law conference in Bangalore. *Rights of Women Bulletin,* Winter, 3-6.

Karim, M., & Ammar, R. (1965). *Female circumcision and sexual desire.* Cairo: Ain Shams University Press.

Kellner, N. I. (1993). Under the knife: Female genital mutilation as child abuse. *Journal of Juvenile Law, 14,* 118-132.

Kelly, L. (1988). *Surviving sexual violence.* Cambridge: Polity.

Kelly, L. (1989). The professionalisation of rape. *Rights of Women Bulletin,* Spring, 8-11.

Kelly, L. (1996). Tensions and possibilities: Community responses to domestic violence. In J. Edelson & Z. Eisikovits (Eds.), *Future interventions with battered women and their families* (pp. 67-86). Thousand Oaks, CA: Sage.

Kelly, L., Burton, S., & Regan, L. (1993). Beyond victim to survivor: The implications of knowledge about children's resistance and avoidance strategies. In H. Ferguson, R. Gilligan, & R. Torode (Eds.), *Surviving childhood adversity: Issues for policy and practice.* Dublin: Social Studies Press.

Kelly, L., Burton, S., & Regan, L. (1996). Beyond victim and survivor: Sexual violence, identity, feminist theory and practice. In L. Adkins & V. Merchant (Eds.), *Sexualizing the social: The social organization of power* (pp. 77-101). London: Macmillan.

Kelly, L., & Radford, J. (1996). "Nothing really happened": The invalidation of women's experiences of sexual violence. In M. Hester, L. Kelly, & J. Radford (Eds.), *Women, violence and male power* (Reprint, pp. 19-33). Buckingham, UK: Open University Press.

Kelly, L., Regan, L., & Burton, S. (1991). *An exploratory study of the prevalence of sexual abuse in a sample of 1244 16-21 year olds* (Final Report to the ESRC: Child Abuse Studies Unit). University of North London.

Kennedy, J. G. (1978). Circumcision and excision ceremonies. In J. Kennedy (Ed.), *Nubian ceremonial life* (pp. 151-170). Berkeley: University of California Press.

Kenrick, D., & Keefe, R. C. (1992). Age preferences in mates reflect sex differences in reproductive strategies. *Behavioral and Brain Sciences, 15,* 75-133.

Kirby, V. (1987). On the cutting edge: Feminism and clitoridectomy. *Australian Feminist Studies, 5* (Summer), 35-55.

Kishwar, M., & Vanita, R. (1984). In search of answers: Indian women's voices from Manushi. In M. Kishwar & R. Vita (Eds.), *Family violence* (pp. 203-242). London: Zed.

Kitzinger, C. (1994). Anti-lesbian harassment. In C. Brant & Y. L. Too (Eds.), *Rethinking sexual harassment* (pp. 125-147). London: Pluto.

Kleck, G., & Sayles, S. (1990). Rape and resistance. *Social Problems, 17*(2), 149-163.

Knight, R., & Prentky, R. (1987). The developmental antecedents and adult adaptions of rapist subtypes. *Criminal Justice and Behaviour, 14*(4), 403-426.

Koso-Thomas, O. (1987). *The circumcision of women: A strategy for eradication.* London: Zed.

Koss, M. (1988). The hidden rape victim: Personality, attitudinal and situational variables. In A. W. Burgess (Ed.), *Rape and sexual assault* (Vol. 2, pp. 3-25). New York: Garland.

Koss, M. (1989). Hidden rape: Sexual aggression and victimization in a national sample of students in higher education. In M. Pirog-Good & J. Stets (Eds.), *Violence in dating relationships: Emerging social issues* (pp. 145-168). New York: Praeger.

Koss, M. (1992). The underdetection of rape: Methodological choices influence incidence estimates. *Journal of Social Issues, 48*(1), 61-75.

Koss, M., & Burkhart, B. (1989). A conceptual analysis of rape victimization: Long-term effects and implications for treatment. *Psychology of Women Quarterly, 13,* 27-40.

Koss, M., & Gidycz, C. (1985). Sexual experiences survey: Reliability and validity. *Journal of Consulting and Clinical Psychology, 53,* 422-423.

Koss, M., & Oros, C. (1982). Sexual experiences survey: A research instrument investigating sexual aggression and victimization. *Journal of Consulting and Clinical Psychology, 50,* 455-457.

Kouba, L. J., & Muasher, J. (1985). Female circumcision in Africa: An overview. *African Studies Review, 28*(1), 95-110.

Kramer, F. (1993). *The red fez: Art and spirit possession in Africa* (M. Green, Trans.). London: Verso.

Kumar, R. (1993). *The history of doing: An illustrated account of movements for women's rights and feminism in India, 1800-1990.* New Delhi: Kali for Women.

Lackey, C., & Williams, K. (1995). Social bonding and the cessation of partner violence across generations. *Journal of Marriage and the Family, 57,* 295-305.

Lancaster, R. N. (1992). *Life is hard: Machismo, danger, and the intimacy of power in Nicaragua.* Berkeley: University of California Press.

Laumann, E. O., Gagnon, J. H., Micahel, R. T., & Michaels, S. (1994). *The social organization of sexuality: Sexual practices in the United States.* Chicago: University of Chicago Press.

Lees, S. (1997). *Ruling passions: Sexual violence, reputation and the law.* Buckingham, UK: Open University Press.

Leidig, M. W. (1992). The continuum of violence against women: Psychological and physical consequences. *Journal of American College Health, 40,* 149-155.

Levinson, D. (1989). *Family violence in cross-cultural perspective.* Newbury Park: Sage.

Lightfoot-Klein, H. (1983). Pharaonic circumcision of females in the Sudan. *Medicine and Law, 2,* 353-360.

Lightfoot-Klein, H. (1989a). *Prisoners of ritual: An odyssey into female genital circumcision in Africa.* New York: Harrington Park.

Lightfoot-Klein, H. (1989b). The sexual experience and marital adjustment of genitally circumcised and infibulated females in the Sudan. *Journal of Sex Research, 26*(3), 375-392.

Lisak, D., & Roth, S. (1990). Motives and psychodynamics of self-reported, unincarcerated rapists. *American Journal of Orthopsychiatry, 60,* 268-280.

Lundgren, E. (1995a). *Feminist theory and violent empiricism* (L. Schenck, Trans.). Aldershot, UK: Avebury.

Lundgren, E. (1995b). Matters of life and death. *Trouble and Strife, 31,* 33-39.

Lyons, H. (1991). Anthropologists, moralities, and relativities: The problem of genital mutilations. *Canadian Review of Sociology and Anthropology, 18,* 499-518.

Mabaso, M. M. (1992). Gang rape in the townships. *Trouble and Strife, 24,* 30-34.

MacCormack, C., & Strathern, M. (Eds.). (1980). *Nature, culture and gender.* Cambridge: Cambridge University Press.

MacKinnon, C. (1979). *Sexual harassment of working women.* New Haven, CT: Yale University Press.

MacKinnon, C. (1989). *Towards a feminist theory of the state.* Cambridge, MA: Harvard University Press.

MacLeod, L. (1992). *Reactions of women's groups to the proposed national survey on violence against women.* Ottawa: Canadian Centre for Justice Statistics.

MacLeod, M., & Saraga, E. (1988). Challenging the orthodoxy: Towards a feminist theory and practice. *Feminist Review (Family Secrets: Child Sexual Abuse), 28,* 16-55.

Mahoney, M. R. (1991). Legal images of battered women: Redefining the issue of separation. *Michigan Law Review, 90,* 1-94.

Makepeace, J. (1986). Gender differences in courtship violence victimization. *Family Relations, 35,* 383-388.

Malamuth, N. (1981). Rape proclivity among males. *Journal of Social Issues, 37,* 138-157.

Malamuth, N., & Check, J. (1983). Sexual arousal to rape depictions: Individual differences. *Journal of Abnormal Psychology, 92,* 55-67.

Marshall, W., & Barbaree, H. (1990). An integrated theory of the etiology of sexual offending. In W. Marshall, D. R. Laws, & H. E. Barbee (Eds.), *Handbook of sexual assault.* London: Plenum.

Martin, E. (1987). *The woman in the body: A cultural analysis of reproduction.* Boston: Beacon.

Martin, E. (1991). The egg and the sperm: How science has constructed a romance based on stereotypical male-female roles. *Signs: Journal of Women in Culture and Society, 16*(3), 485-501.

Mascia-Lees, F. E., & Sharpe, P. (1992a). Introduction: Soft-tissue modification and the horror within. In F. E. Mascia-Lees & P. Sharpe (Eds.), *Tatoo, torture, mutilation, and adornment: The denaturalization of the body in culture and text* (pp. 1-9). Albany: State University of New York Press.

Mascia-Lees, F. E., & Sharpe, P. (1992b). The marked and the un(re)marked: Tattoo and gender in theory and narrative. In F. E. Mascia-Lees & P. Sharpe (Eds.), *Tattoo, torture, mutilation, and adornment: The denaturalization of the body in culture and text* (pp. 145-170). Albany: State University of New York Press.

Mathews, R., & Speltz, K. (1989). *Female sexual offenders: An exploratory study.* Orwell, VT: Safer Society Press.

Mathieu, N.-C. (1989). When yielding is not consenting: Material and psychic determinants of women's dominated consciousness and some of their interpretations in ethnology (Part 1). *Feminist Issues, 9*(2), 3-49.

Mathieu, N.-C. (1990). When yielding is not consenting (Part 2). *Feminist Issues, 10*(1), 51-90.

Matsui, Y. (1989). Dowry and rape: Women against traditional discrimination. In Y. Matsui (Ed.), *Women's Asia* (pp. 75-89). London: Zed.

Matthews, N. (1994). *Confronting rape: The feminist anti-rape movement and the state.* London: Routledge.

McCarthy, M. (1996). Sexual experiences and sexual abuse of women with learning disabilities. In M. Hester, L. Kelly, & J. Radford (Eds.), *Women, violence and male power* (pp. 119-129). Buckingham, UK: Open University Press.

McClintock, A. (1993). Family feuds: Gender, nationalism and the family. *Feminist Review, 44,* 61-81.

McCollum, H., Kelly, L., & Radford, J. (1994). Wars against women. *Trouble and Strife, 28,* 12-18.

McLean, S. (1980). *Female circumcision, excision and infibulation: The facts and proposals for change* (Report No. 47). London: Minority Rights Group.

McMillan, C. (1982). *Women reason and nature: Some philosophical problems with feminism.* Oxford: Basil Blackwell.

McVeigh, R. (1994). *It's part of life here: Security forces and harassment in Northern Ireland.* Belfast: Committee on the Administration of Justice.

McWilliams, M. (1993). The church, the state and the women's movement in Northern Ireland. In A. Smyth (Ed.), *Irish women's studies reader* (pp. 79-99). Dublin: Attic.

McWilliams, M. (1994). The woman other. *Fortnight: An independent review of politics and the arts in Northern Ireland, 328,* 24-25.

McWilliams, M., & McKiernan, J. (1993). *Bringing it out in the open: Domestic violence in Northern Ireland.* Belfast: HMSO.

McWilliams, M., & Spence, L. (1996). *Taking domestic violence seriously: Issues for the criminal and civil justice system.* Belfast: HMSO.

Mehdi, R. (1990). The offence of rape in the Islamic law of Pakistan. *International Sociology of Law, 18,* 19-29.

Mercy, J. A., & Saltzman, L. E. (1989). Fatal violence among spouses in the United States, 1976-1985. *American Journal of Public Health, 79,* 595-599.

Merry, S. E. (1996, March 18). *Global human rights and politics in local places.* Paper presented at Butterworth Lecture, University of London, UK.

Mesnick, S. L. (1997). Sexual alliances: Evidence and evolutionary implications. In P. A. Gowaty (Ed.), *Feminism and evolutionary biology* (pp. 207-257). New York: Chapman & Hall.

Messner, M., & Sabo, D. (Eds.). (1994). *Sex, violence and power in sports: Rethinking masculinity.* California: Crossing.

Mies, M. (1986). *Patriarchy and accumulation on a world scale: Women in the international division of labour.* London: Zed.

Mitchell, T. (1991). *Colinizing Egypt.* Berkeley: University of California Press.

Mohammed, P. (1991). Reflections on the women's movement and Trinidad: Calypsos, changes and sexual violence. *Feminist Review, 38,* 33-47.

Mohamud, O. A. (1991). Female circumcision and child mortality in urban Somalia. *Genus, 67,* 203-223.

Mohanty, C. T. (1991). Under western eyes: Feminist scholarship and colonial discourse. In C. T. Mohanty, A. Russo, & L. Torres (Eds.), *Third world women and the politics of feminism* (pp. 51-80). Bloomington: Indiana University Press.

Moi, T. (1985). *Sexual/textual politics: Feminist literary theory.* London: Routledge.

Møller, A. P. (1988). Paternity and paternal care in the swallow *Hirundo rustica. Animal Behaviour, 36,* 996-1005.

Monahan, J., & Splane, S. (1980). Psychological approaches to criminal behavior. In E. Bittner & S. Messinger (Eds.), *Criminology review yearbook* (Vol. 2). Beverly Hills, CA: Sage.

Montgomery, P., & Bell, V. (1986). *Police response to wife assault.* Belfast: Northern Ireland Women's Aid Federation.

Morgan, K. P. (1991). Women and the knife: Cosmetic surgery and the colonization of women's bodies. *Hypatia, 6*(3), 25-53.

Morrison, T., Erooga, M., & Beckett, R. (1994). *Sexual offending against children: Assessment and treatment of male abusers.* London: Routledge.

Morsy, S. A. (1991). Safeguarding women's bodies: The white man's burden medicalized. *Medical Anthropology Quarterly, 5*(1), 19-23.

Mowat, R. R. (1966). *Morbid jealousy and murder.* London: Tavistock.

Mullen, P. E., & Martin, J. (1994). Jealousy: A community study. *British Journal of Psychiatry, 164,* 35-43.

Mustafa, A. Z. (1966). Female circumcision and infibulation in the Sudan. *Journal of Obstetrics and Gynecology of the British Commonwealth, 73,* 302-306.

Mutilation by any name. (1992, April 25). *The Economist, 323,* 46.

Myers, J. (Ed.). (1994). *The backlash: Child protection under fire.* Thousand Oaks, CA: Sage.

Myers, R. A., Omorodion, F. I., Isenalumhe, A. E., & Akenzua, G. I. (1985). Circumcision: Its nature and practice among some ethnic groups in southern Nigeria. *Social Science and Medicine, 21*(5), 581-588.

Nagel, T. (1986). *The view from nowhere.* New York: Oxford University Press.

National Research Council. (1993). *Understanding and preventing violence.* Washington, DC: Author.

Neibuhr, R., & Boyles, W. (1991). Sexual harassment in the military. *International Journal of Intercultural Relations, 15,* 445-457.

Nevo, J. (1993, February). *Femicide in Israel: The social construction of a problem.* Paper presented at the fifth International Interdisciplinary Congress on Women, San Jose, Costa Rica.

Newburn, T., & Stanko, E. A. (Eds.). (1994). *Just boys doing business? Men, masculinities and crime.* London: Routledge.

Njovana, E. (1994, May). Gender based violence and sexual assault in African women. *Oxfam Report,* 17-20.

Norris, D., & Hatcher, J. (1994). *The impact of interviewer characteristics on response in a national survey of violence against women.* Paper presented at the annual meeting of the American Statistical Association, Toronto.

O'Connell Davidson, J. (1995). British sex tourists in Thailand. In M. Maynard & J. Purvis (Eds.), *(Hetero)sexual politics* (pp. 42-46). London: Taylor and Francis.

Ortner, S. (1974). Is female to male as nature is to culture? In M. Z. Rosaldo & L. Lamphere (Eds.), *Woman, culture and society* (pp. 67-87). Stanford, CA: Stanford University Press.

Oudes, J. (1992). *Broken promises, Sick people: An analysis of the Maori Women's Centre.* Unpublished research paper, cited in M. Borst (1992).

Pedersen, S. (1991, December). National bodies, unspeakable acts: The sexual politics of colonial policy-making. *Journal of Modern History, 63*(December), 647-680.

Petty Jnr, J., McLeod, G., & Dawson, B. (1989). Sexual aggression in normal men: Incidence, beliefs and personality characteristics. *Personality and Individual Differences, 10*(3), 355-362.

Polk, K. (1994a). Masculinity, honour and confrontational homicide. In T. Newburn & E. A. Stanko (Eds.), *Just boys doing business? Men, masculinities and crime* (pp. 166-188). London: Routledge.

Polk, K. (1994b). *When men kill: Scenarios of masculine violence.* Cambridge: Cambridge University Press.

Pugh, D. (1983, November 11). Bringing an end to mutilation. *New Statesman, 106,* pp. 8-9.

Rafino, A. (1994, November). *Violence against women in Brazil.* Paper presented at Fighting Sexism North and South, War on Want Conference, London.

Razack, S. (1994). What is to be gained by looking white people in the eye? Culture, race, and gender in cases of sexual violence. *Signs: Journal of Women in Culture and Society, 19*(4), 24-48.

Rederlechner, M., & Ratz, B. (1993). Giving birth to a new nation: A critique of the programme for the demographic renewal of Croatia. *Rights of Women Bulletin, Spring,* 13-15.

Reeves Sanday, P. (1981). The socio-cultural context of rape: A cross-cultural study. *Journal of Social Issues, 37*(4), 5-27.

Reeves Sanday, P. (1990). *Fraternity gang rape: Sex, brotherhood and privilege in campus.* New York: New York University Press.

Reinharz, S. (1992). *Feminist methods in social research.* Oxford: Oxford University Press.

Rener, T. (1993, January). *Nationalism and gender in postsocialist societies—Is nationalism female?* Paper presented to Women and Politics Workshop, Politics Department, Queen's University, Belfast.

Renteln, A. D. (1988). Relativism and the search for human rights. *American Anthropologist, 90*(1), 56-72.

Reppucci, N. D., & Hauggard, J. (1989). Prevention of child sexual abuse: Myth or reality. *American Psychologist, October,* 1266-1275.

Rich, A. (1980). Compulsory heterosexuality and lesbian existence. *Signs: Journal of Women in Culture and Society, 5*(4), 631-660.

Richters, A. (1994). *Women, culture and violence: A development, health and human rights issue.* Leiden, Netherlands: Women and Autonomy Centre (VENA).

Rounsaville, B. J. (1978). Theories in marital violence: Evidence from a study of battered women. *Victimology, 3,* 11-31.

Royal Ulster Constabulary. (1997). Belfast: Northern Ireland Information Office, Statistics Unit.

Rubin, P. H., & Paul, C. W. (1979). An evolutionary model of taste for risk. *Economic Inquiry, 17,* 585-596.

Russell, D.E.H. (1984). *Sexual exploitation: Rape, child sex abuse, and workplace harassment.* Beverly Hills, CA: Sage.

Sacks, K. (1976). State bias and women's status. *American Anthropologist, 78,* 565-569.

Safilios-Rothschild, C. (1969). 'Honor' crimes in contemporary Greece. *British Journal of Sociology, 20,* 205-218.

Sampson, A. (1994). *Acts of abuse: Sex offenders and the criminal justice system.* London: Routledge.

Sampson, R., & Laub, J. (1990). Crime and deviance over the life course: The salience of adult social bonds. *American Sociological Review, 55,* 609-627.

Saunders, D. (1988). Wife abuse, husband abuse, or mutual combat. In K. Yllö & M. Bograd (Eds.), *Feminist perspectives on wife abuse* (pp. 90-113). Newbury Park, CA: Sage.

Schenck, L. (1986). An investigation into the reasons for dowry murder in India. In M. Borst (Ed.), *Women and domestic violence: An annotated bibliography.* Leiden, Netherlands: Women and Autonomy Centre (VENA).

Scheper-Hughes, N. (1991). Virgin territory: The male discovery of the clitoris. *Medical Anthropology Quarterly, 5*(1), 25-28.

Scheper-Hughes, N., & Lock, M. M. (1987). The mindful body: A prolegomenon to future work in medical anthropology. *Medical Anthropology Quarterly, 1*(1), 6-41.

Schroeder, E. (1985). Female circumcision. *American Journal of Nursing, 85,* 684-687.

Schwartz, M. D., & Nogrady, C. A. (1996). Fraternity membership, rape myths, and sexual aggression on a college campus. *Violence Against Women, 2,* 148-162.

Scully, D. (1991). *Understanding sexual violence: A study of convicted rapists.* Boston: Unwin Hyman.

Shanahan, K. (1994). *Crimes worse than death.* Dublin: Attic.

Shandall, A. A. (1967). Circumcision and infibulation of females. *Sudan Medical Journal, 5,* 178-212.

Sharoni, S. (1992). Every woman is in occupied territory: The politics of militarism and sexism and the Israeli-Palestinian conflict. *Journal of Gender Studies, 1*(4), 447-462.

Sheehan, E. (1985). Victorian clidoridectomy: Isacc Baker Brown and his harmless operative procedure. *Feminist Issues, 5*(1), 39-53.

Shepherd, M. (1961). Morbid jealousy: Some clinical and social aspects of a psychiatric syndrome. *Journal of Mental Science, 107,* 687-753.

Silva, J. A., Leong, G. B., & Weinstock, R. (1992). The dangerousness of persons with misidentification syndromes. *Bulletin of the American Academcy of Psychiatry and Law, 20,* 77-86.

Silva, J. A., Leong, G. B., Weinstock, R., & Wine, D. B. (1993). Delusional misidentification and dangerousness: A neurobiologic hypothesis. *Journal of Forensic Sciences, 38,* 904-913.

Silver, R., Boon, C., & Stones, M. (1983). Searching for meaning in misfortune: Making sense of incest. *Journal of Social Issues, 39,* 2.

Simpson, J. A., & Gangestad, S. W. (1991). Personality and sexuality: Empirical relations and an integrative theoretical model. In K. McKinney & S. Sprecher (Eds.), *Sexuality in close relationships* (pp. 71-92). Hillsdale, NJ: Lawrence Erlbaum.

Slack, A. T. (1984). Female circumcision: A critical appraisal. *Human Rights Quarterly, 10,* 437-486.

Smith, M. (1987). The incidence and prevalence of women abuse in Toronto. *Violence and Victims, 2,* 33-47.

Smith, M. (1990). Sociodemographic risk factors in wife abuse: Results from a survey of Toronto women. *Canadian Journal of Sociology, 15*(1), 39-58.

Smith, M. (1994). Enhancing the quality of survey data on violence against women: A feminist approach. *Gender & Society, 8*(1), 109-127.

Smith, R. L. (1984). Human sperm competition. In R. L. Smith (Ed.), *Sperm competition and the evolution of animal mating systems* (pp. 601-659). Orlando, FL: Academic.

Smithyman, D. (1978). *The undetected rapist.* Unpublished doctoral dissertation, Claremont Graduate School.

Smuts, B. (1992). Male aggression against women: An evolutionary perspective. *Human Nature, 3,* 1-44.

Spelman, E. V. (1990). *Inessential woman: Problems of exclusion in feminist thought.* Boston: Women's Press.

Stanko, E. (1988). Hidden violence against women. In M. Maguire & J. Pointing (Eds.), *Victims of crime: A new deal?* Buckingham, UK: Open University Press.

Stanko, E. (1990). *Everyday violence: How women and men experience sexual and physical danger.* London: Pandora.

Stanko, E. (1996). Police advice to women in Britain. *Violence Against Women, 2*(1), 5-22.

Statistics Canada. (1993). *Violence Against Women Survey questionnaire.*

Statistics Canada. (1994). *Violence Against Women Survey. Public-use microdata file documentation and user's guide.* Ottawa, Ontario: Ministry of Supply and Services.

Steinmetz, S. (1977-1978). The battered husband syndrome. *Victimology, 2*(3-4), 499-509.

Stets, J., & Straus, M. (1990). Gender differences in reporting marital violence and its medical and psychological consequences. In M. Straus & R. Gelles (Eds.), *Physical violence in American families: Risk factors and adaptations to violence in 8,145 families* (pp. 151-165). New Brunswick, NJ: Transaction.

Stoler, A. L. (1995). *Race and the education of desire: Foucault's history of sexuality and the colonial order of things.* Durham, NC: Duke University Press.

Straus, M. (1980). Measuring intrafamily conflict and violence: The Conflict Tactics (C.T.) Scales. *Journal of Marriage and the Family, 41*(1), 75-88.

Straus, M. (1990). Measuring intrafamily conflict and violence: The Conflict Tactics (CTS) Scales. In M. Straus & R. Gelles (Eds.), *Physical violence in American families: Risk factors and adaptions to violence in 8,145 families* (pp. 29-47). New Brunswick, NJ: Transaction.

Straus, M., Hamby, S., Boney-McCoy, S., & Sugarman, D. (1996). The revised conflict tactics scales (CTS): Development and preliminary psychometric data. *Journal of Family Issues, 17*(3), 283-316.

Sturdevant, S., & Stolzfus, B. (1992). *Let the good times roll: The sale of women's sexual labor around U.S. military bases in the Philippines, Okinawa and the southern part of Korea.* New York: Free Press.

Sudan Government. (1982). *The Sudan fertility survey, 1979. Vol. 1: Principal report.* Khartoum: Department of Statistics.

Talle, A. (1993). Transforming women into "pure" agnates: Aspects of female infibulation in Somalia. In V. Broch-Due, I. Rudie, & T. Bleie (Eds.), *Carved flesh, cast selves: Gendered symbols and social practices* (pp. 83-107). Oxford: Berg.

Tang, C., Critelli, J., & Porter, J. (1993). Motives in sexual aggression: The Chinese context. *Journal of Interpersonal Violence, 8*(4), 435-445.

Taussig, M. (1990). *Mimesis and alterity: A particular history of the senses.* New York: Routledge.

Thiam, A. (1983). Women's fight for the abolition of sexual mutilation. *International Social Science Journal, 35*(4), 747-756.

Thornhill, R., & Thornhill, N. W. (1983). Human rape: An evolutionary analysis. *Ethology & Sociobiology, 4,* 137-173.

Thornhill, R., & Thornhill, N. W. (1992). The evolutionary psychology of men's coercive sexuality. *Behavioral and Brain Sciences, 15,* 363-421.

Toch, H. (1992). *Violent men: An inquiry into the psychology of violence* (2nd ed.). Chicago: Aldine.

Toch, H. (1993). Good violence and bad violence: Self-presentations of aggressors through accounts and war stories. In R. B. Felson & J. T. Tedeschi (Eds.), *Aggression and violence: Social interactionist perspectives* (pp. 193-208). Washington, DC: American Psychological Association.

Tooby, J., & Cosmides, L. (1990). On the universality of human nature and the uniqueness of the individual: The role of genetics and adaptation. *Journal of Personality, 58*, 17-67.

Toubia, N. (1985). The social and political implications of female circumcision: The case of the Sudan. In E. W. Fernea (Ed.), *Women and the family in the Middle East* (pp. 148-159). Austin: University of Texas Press.

Toubia, N. (1994). Female circumcision as a public health issue. *New England Journal of Medicine, 331*(1), 712-716.

Toubia, N. (1995). *Female genital mutilation: A call for global action* (2nd ed.). New York: Rainbow/Women Ink.

Trivers, R. L. (1972). Parental investment and sexual selection. In B. Campbell (Ed.), *Sexual selection and the descent of man, 1871-1971*. Chicago: Aldine.

United Nations Draft Declaration. (1992). *Draft declaration on violence against women in all its forms.* (Report of the Secretary-General. Commission on the Status of Women, UNDOC. E/CN. 6/1992/4, Article 2, p. 4).

Van der Kwaak, A. (1992). Female circumcision and gender identity: A questionable alliance? *Social Science and Medicine, 35*(6), 777-787.

Vauhkonen, K. (1968). On the pathogenesis of morbid jealousy. *Acta Psychiatrica Scandinavica, 44*(Suppl.), 202.

Verzin, J. A. (1975). Sequelae of female circumcision. *Tropical Doctor, 5*, 163-169.

Vogelman, L., & Eagle, G. (1991). Overcoming endemic violence against women in South Africa. *Social Justice, 18*(1-2), 209-229.

Von Schulthess, B. (1992). Violence in the streets: Anti-lesbian assault and harassment in San Francisco. In G. Herek & K. Berrill (Eds.), *Hate crimes: Confronting violence against lesbians and gay men* (pp. 65-75). Newbury Park, CA: Sage.

Walker, A. (1992). *Possessing the secrets of joy*. New York: Harcourt Brace Jovanovich.

Wallace, A. (1986). *Homicide: The social reality*. Sydney: New South Wales Bureau of Crime Statistics and Research.

Warner, M. (1994, April). *Ethnicity, nationalism and women*. Paper presented to Centre for Research on Women Workshop, University of Ulster, Coleraine.

Watanabe, K. (1993, February). *Militarism, imperialism, colonialism and the trafficking of women: Military comfort women forced by Japanese soldiers*. Paper presented at the fifth International Interdisciplinary Congress on Women, San Jose, Costa Rica.

Waterhouse, L., Dobash, R., & Carnie, J. (1994). *Child sexual abusers*. Edinburgh: Scottish Office Central Research Unit.

West, D. (1987). *Sexual crimes and confrontation*. London: Gower.

Wild, N. (1989). Prevalence of child sex rings. *Pediatrics, 83*(4), 553-558.

Williams, G. C. (1966). *Adaptation and natural selection*. Princeton, NJ: Princeton University Press.

Williams, K., & Hawkins, R. (1989). Controlling male aggression in intimate relationships. *Law and Society Review, 23*(4), 591-612.

Williams, L. M. (1993, August). *Recall of childhood trauma: A prospective study of women's memories of child sexual abuse*. Paper presented at the annual meeting of the American Society of Criminology, Phoenix.

Williams, R. (1976). *Keywords: A vocabulary of culture and society*. London: Oxford University Press.

Wilson, M. I., & Daly, M. (1985). Competitiveness, risk-taking and violence: The young male syndrome. *Ethology & Sociobiology, 6*, 59-73.

Wilson, M. I., & Daly, M. (1992a). The man who mistook his wife for a chattel. In J. Barkow, L. Cosmides, & J. Tooby (Eds.), *The adapted mind.* New York: Oxford University Press.

Wilson, M. I., & Daly, M. (1992b). Who kills whom in spouse killings? On the exceptional sex ratio of spousal homicides in the United States. *Criminology, 30,* 189-215.

Wilson, M. I., & Daly, M. (1993a). An evolutionary psychological perspective on male sexual proprietariness and violence against wives. *Violence and Victims, 8,* 271-294.

Wilson, M. I., & Daly, M. (1993b). Spousal homicide risk and estrangement. *Violence and Victims, 8,* 3-16.

Wilson, M. I., & Daly, M. (1994). Spousal homicide. *Statistics Canada, 14*(8) 1-15.

Wilson, M. I., Daly, M., & Daniele, A. (1995). Familicide: The killing of spouses and children. *Aggressive Behaviour, 21,* 275-291.

Wilson, M. I., Daly, M., & Wright, C. (1993). Uxoricide in Canada: Demographic risk patterns. *Canadian Journal of Criminology, 35,* 263-291.

Wilson, M. I., Johnson, H., & Daly, M. (1995). Lethal and nonlethal violence against wives. *Canadian Journal of Criminology, 37,* 331-361.

Wilson, M. I., & Mesnick, S. L. (1997). An empirical test of the bodyguard hypothesis. In P. Gowaty (Ed.), *Feminism and evolutionary biology* (pp. 505-511). New York: Chapman & Hall.

Winkel, E. (1995). A Muslim perspective on female circumcision. *Women & Health, 23*(1), 1-7.

Winter, B. (1994). Women, the law, and sexual relativism in France: The case of excision. *Signs: Journal of Women in Culture and Society, 19,* 939-974.

World Health Organization. (1979). *Traditional practices affecting the health of women and children.* (Technical Publication No. 2). Alexandria: WHO/EMRO.

World Health Organization. (1986). A traditional practice that threatens health—Female circumcision. *WHO Chronicle, 40*(1), 31-36.

Wright, R. (1995). *The moral animal.* New York: Pantheon.

Wyatt, G. E., & Powell, G. J. (Eds.). (1988). *Lasting effects of child sexual abuse.* Newbury Park, CA: Sage.

Young, A. W., Reid, I., Wright, S., & Hellawell, D. J. (1993). Face-processing impairments and the capgras delusion. *British Journal of Psychiatry, 162,* 695-698.

Zajovic, S. (1994). Women and ethnic cleansing. *Women Against Fundamentalism Journal, 5*(1), 34-36.

Index

251

About the Editors

Rebecca Emerson Dobash is Professor of Social Research and **Russell P. Dobash** is Professor of Criminology in the Department of Social Policy and Social Work at the University of Manchester, U.K.; they are codirectors of the Violence Research Centre. They have coauthored several books, numerous government reports, and scores of articles in journals and scholarly anthologies. Their books include *Violence Against Wives* (1979); *The Imprisonment of Women* (1986); *Women Viewing Violence* (1992); *Women, Violence and Social Change* (1992); and *Research Evaluation of Programmes for Violent Men* (1997). *Violence Against Wives* won the World Congress of Victimology Award, and *Women, Violence and Social Change* won the American Society of Criminology's Distinguished Book Award for Comparative Research. They have also won the American Criminological Association's August Vollmer Award.

They have twice been scholars in residence at the Rockefeller Foundation Study and Conference Centre in Bellagio, Italy; have held fellowships and/or research grants from the Fulbright Foundation, the Harry Frank Guggenheim Foundation, the Economic and Social Research Council, and several British governmental departments; and have been International Fellows in Criminology at the University of Melbourne.

In over two decades of research on violence, they have collaborated with colleagues in many academic disciplines, worked with women's groups in several countries, and served as research advisors to agencies of the British, U.S., and Australian governments. Their current research includes study of convicted child sex abusers; an evaluation of criminal justice-based treatment programs for violent men; study of bodybuilding, steroids, and violence; a comparison of men's and women's accounts of violent events; and an international comparison of violence and homicide. As committed scholars, they believe that knowledge should play a role in formulating positive responses to important social issues and also in helping advance the process of social change.

About the Contributors

Janice Boddy is Professor of Anthropology at the University of Toronto, Ontario, Canada. She is the author of *Wombs and Alien Spirits: Women, Men, and the Zar Cult in Northern Sudan* (1989) and of numerous articles and reviews, and she is coauthor of *Aman: The Story of a Somali Girl* (1994; translated into 14 languages). She is currently researching attempts by British colonial administrators during the first half of the 20th century to "civilize" Sudanese women's bodies by introducing biomedical and educational reform.

Martin Daly is Professor of Psychology and Biology at McMaster University, Hamilton, Ontario, Canada. He is coauthor with Margo Wilson of the textbook *Sex, Evolution and Behavior* (2nd ed., 1983) and the research monograph *Homicide* (1988). He is coeditor-in-chief of the journals *Behavior* and *Evolution and Human Behavior* and has published the results of his research on nonhuman animal behavior, human behavior, and psychology in more than 100 journal articles and book chapters. He has been elected to the executive committees of the Animal Behavior Society, the International Society for Behavioral Ecology, and the Human Behavior and Evolution Society, of which he is a past president. He is a former J. S. Guggenheim Fellow, Fellow of the Center for Advanced Study in the Behavioral Sciences, and a Fellow of the Royal Society of Canada.

Holly Johnson is a Senior Analyst at Statistics Canada and Project Manager of Statistics Canada's national Violence Against Women Survey. She has been working for the past 10 years on ways to improve statistical methods of measuring women's experiences of violence and fear of victimization and has authored a number of publications on this and other related topics. She is currently completing a doctoral dissertation in the Department of Social Policy and Social Work at the University of Manchester, U.K., on the social control of wife battering.

Liz Kelly is a feminist researcher and activist and Director of the Child and Woman Abuse Studies Unit (CWASU), University of North London, which conducts research, training, and consultancy work in the areas of child sexual abuse and domestic violence. She has worked in the field of violence against women and children for more than 20 years and has been active in establishing and working in local services including refuges and rape crisis centers and in local, regional and national groups. She is the author of *Surviving Sexual Violence,* 12 research reports, and more than 50 book chapters and journal articles. She chaired the Council of Europe Group of Specialists that produced a Plan of Action on violence against women.

Eva Lundgren is Professor of Feminist Studies in Sociology at the University of Uppsala, Sweden. She has carried out analyses of feminist theory, empirical investigations of sexualized violence, exorcism in contemporary Norway, the nature of counseling in the Norwegian State Church, and ritual abuse. She has worked on the dialectical relationship between theoretical development and empirical analyses and on interactions between gendered identity and the gendered body. She established and developed the first Norwegian Centre for Feminist Research in the Humanities in Bergen. She is the author of *The Lost Daughter: Feminist Theology and Women's Liberation* (1982); *In the Grip of the Lord(s)* (1985); *Ministers in Passion and Sin* (1987); *God and All Other Men* (1990); *Violent Empiricism and Feminist Theory* (1993); and *Suffer the Little Children to Come Unto Me: Ritual and Sexual Abuse* (1994).

Monica McWilliams is a Professor of Social Policy and Women's Studies and is course director of the M.A. degree in Women's Studies, University of Ulster, Northern Ireland. Her main areas of study are health and social service responses to domestic violence in Northern

Ireland and the Republic of Ireland. She is the author of *Bring It Out in the Open: Domestic Violence in Northern Ireland* (1993), with J. McKiernan, and *Taking Domestic Violence Seriously: Issues for the Criminal and Civil Justice System* (1996), with L. Spence. Since 1996, she has served as the elected representative for the Northern Ireland Women's Coalition to the Multi-Party Peace Negotiations on the future of Northern Ireland, chaired by Senator George Mitchell, former speaker of the U.S. Senate. The Negotiations include ten political parties, who are considering the issues of future governance, decommissioning of arms; constitutional issues between Northern Ireland, the Republic of Ireland, and Britain; and working toward building new relationships between them. In this capacity, she has been involved in discussions at the presidential level with the United States and South Africa. She also serves on the government working party on domestic violence and has worked to involve more women in decision making about political and social institutions and in challenging politicians to be more inclusive of women's voices in situations of political conflict.

Jill Radford is a Reader in Criminology and Women's Studies at the University of Teesside, U.K. She was with Rights of Women for nine years, at the same time teaching Criminology and Women's Studies at the Open University and the University of Westminster, U.K. She was one of the founding members of the British Sociology Association's Violence Against Women Study Group and has published extensively on this issue. She was a coeditor with Liz Kelly and Marianne Hester of *Women, Violence and Male Power: Feminism, Activism, Research and Practice* (1996) and with Diana E. H. Russell coedited *Femicide: The Politics of Woman Killing* (1992).

Margo Wilson is Professor of Psychology at McMaster University, Hamilton, Ontario, Canada. The results of her research on violence, especially violence against wives, have been published in numerous scientific journals and many edited volumes as well as a monograph (*Homicide*), coauthored with Martin Daly. She has been a Fellow of the Center for Advanced Study in the Behavioural Sciences (1989-90) and was coholder of the PNM endowed chair for visiting scholars at the University of New Mexico, Albuquerque (1996-1997). She is on the editorial boards of *The Gang Journal, Homicide Studies, Human Nature, Theoretical Criminology,* and *Evolution & Human Behavior,* of which she is coeditor-in-chief. She is currently President of the Human Behavior and Evolution Society (1997-1999) and is a Fellow of the Royal Society of Canada.